THE COMEDY OF THE FANTASTIC

Recent Titles in
Contributions to the Study of Science Fiction and Fantasy
Series Editor: Marshall Tymn

The Mechanical God: Machines in Science Fiction
Thomas P. Dunn and Richard D. Erlich, editors

Comic Tones in Science Fiction: The Art of Compromise with Nature
Donald M. Hassler

Formula Fiction? An Anatomy of American Science Fiction, 1930–1940
Frank Cioffi

H. P. Lovecraft: A Critical Study
Donald R. Burleson

A Literary Symbiosis: Science Fiction/Fantasy Mystery
Hazel Beasley Pierce

The Intersection of Science Fiction and Philosophy: Critical Studies
Robert E. Myers, editor

Clockwork Worlds: Mechanized Environments in SF
Richard D. Erlich and Thomas P. Dunn, editors

Apertures: A Study of the Writings of Brian W. Aldiss
Brian Griffin and David Wingrove

The Dark Barbarian: The Writings of Robert E. Howard
A Critical Anthology
Don Herron, editor

The Scope of the Fantastic—Theory, Technique, Major Authors: Selected
Essays from the First International Conference on the Fantastic in Literature
and Film
Robert A. Collins and Howard D. Pearce, editors

Death and the Serpent: Immortality in Science Fiction and Fantasy
Carl B. Yoke and Donald M. Hassler

The Transcendent Adventure: Studies of Religion in Science Fiction/Fantasy
Robert Reilly, editor

The Return from Avalon: A Study of the Arthurian Legend in
Modern Fiction
Raymond H. Thompson

THE COMEDY
OF THE
FANTASTIC

Ecological
Perspectives
on the
Fantasy Novel

Don D. Elgin

CONTRIBUTIONS TO THE STUDY
OF SCIENCE FICTION
AND FANTASY,
NUMBER 15

Greenwood Press
Westport, Connecticut · London, England

Library of Congress Cataloging in Publication Data

Elgin, Don D.
        The comedy of the fantastic.

        (Contributions to the study of science fiction and
fantasy, ISSN 0193-6875; no. 15)
        Bibliography: p.
        Includes index.
        1. Fantastic fiction, English—History and criticism.
2. Fantastic fiction, American—History and criticism.
3. English fiction—20th century—History and criticism.
4. American fiction—20th century—History and criticism.
5. Comic, The, in literature.   6. Ecology in literature.
I. Title.   II. Series.
PR888.F3E4   1985   823'.0876'0936   84-10851

ISBN 0-313-23283-0 (lib. bdg.)

Library of Congress Catalog Card Number: 84-10851
ISBN: 0-313-23283-0
ISSN: 0193-6875

First published in 1985

Greenwood Press
A division of Congressional Information Service, Inc.
88 Post Road West
Westport, Connecticut 06881

Printed in the United States of America

10 9 8 7 6 5 4 3 2 1

Copyright Acknowledgments

        The author and publisher are grateful for permission to reprint from the following
sources.
        Walter Kerr, *Tragedy and Comedy* (New York, N.Y.: Simon & Schuster, 1967).
Copyright © 1967 by Walter Kerr. Reprinted by permission of SIMON & SCHUS-
TER, Inc.
        From *The Lord of the Rings* by J. R. R. Tolkien. Copyright © 1965 by J. R. R. Tol-
kien. Reprinted by permission of Houghton Mifflin Company.
        J. R. R. Tolkien, *The Lord of the Rings* (London: George Allen & Unwin, 1972).
        Gregory Bateson, *Steps to an Ecology of Mind* (New York: Harper & Row, Publishers,
Inc., 1972).
        Joy Chant, *Grey Mane of Morning* (London: George Allen & Unwin, 1977).

Joy Chant, *Red Moon and Black Mountain* (London: George Allen & Unwin, 1970).

A preliminary version of Chapter 3 appeared as Don D. Elgin, "C. S. Lewis and the Romantic Novel," *Bulletin of the New York C. S. Lewis Society* (April 1981).

Don D. Elgin, "Neruda and Mistral: Literary Ecologists of the Third World," *New Mexico Humanities Review* (May 1980).

Permission to include the material from Don D. Elgin, "True and False Myth in C. S. Lewis' *Till We Have Faces*," *South Central MLA Studies*, XLI, 4 (Winter, 1981), 98–101, has been granted by *The South Central Bulletin.*

Frank Herbert, *Dune* (Radnor, Pa.: Chilton Books, 1965).

Frank Herbert, *Dune Messiah* (New York: Berkley Books, 1975).

Frank Herbert, *Children of Dune* (New York: Berkley Books, 1981).

Frank Herbert, *God Emperor of Dune* (New York: G. P. Putnam's Sons, 1981).

C. S. Lewis, *Out of the Silent Planet, Perelandra,* and *That Hideous Strength* (New York: Macmillan, 1965). Reprinted by permission of the Bodley Head Ltd from the *Perelandra* trilogy by C. S. Lewis.

Joseph Meeker, *Comedy of Survival* (New York, N.Y.: Charles Scribner's Sons, 1974).

"On Fairy Stories" and "Tree and Leaf" from *The Tolkien Reader* by J. R. R. Tolkien. Copyright © 1966 by J. R. R. Tolkien. Reprinted by permission of Houghton Mifflin Company.

Charles Williams, *All Hallow's Eve* (New York, N.Y.: Farrar, Straus & Giroux, 1969).

Charles Williams, *Descent into Hell* (Grand Rapids, Mich.: Wm. B. Eerdmans, 1949). Used by permission.

Charles Williams, *The Greater Trumps* (New York, N.Y.: Farrar, Straus & Giroux, 1969).

Charles Williams, *The Place of the Lion* (Grand Rapids, Mich.: Wm. B. Eerdmans, 1969). Used by permission.

Charles Williams, *Shadows of Ecstasy* (Grand Rapids, Mich.: Wm. B. Eerdmans, 1965). Used by permission.

Charles Williams, *War in Heaven* (Grand Rapids, Mich.: Wm. B. Eerdmans, 1968). Used by permission.

For Sean and Shannon,
  whose hearts make the comedy worthwhile,

    and

    for Joe,
      whose head made this comedy possible.

CONTENTS

THE COMEDY
OF THE
FANTASTIC

PROLOGUE

As Frodo Baggins leaves home on that fateful journey to the Mountain of Doom, he remembers and quotes a song which Bilbo had made up many years before, a song about the roads that go ever on until they return at last to the familiar things they have always known. Contained in those simple words is, I think, a truth which applies to far more than a group of hobbits in the Third Age of Middle Earth. It applies to both literature and people's perception of themselves in relation to the world, for humanity, its literature, and its perception of its relationship to the universe have followed a pattern similar to that outlined in the song. The road began with rituals of hunting and gathering, with celebrations of life and rebirth. It proceeded to agricultural society, to civilization, to philosophy and literature, where it promptly took a new turn, at least in western society. That new turn consisted of a rejection of the past and a division of philosophy and literature into two broad categories, the comic and the tragic, with the tragic quickly being elevated to a superior position because of its basic presuppositions about the nature of the human being who created it and because of its effect on the physical world which it in turn created. Throughout the journey literature has continued to predict and to create as well as to catalogue what people have been about. But in the last one hundred years, writers have begun to turn, often feebly and unwillingly, back to what they knew originally. That is— in short—what this book is all about. It is about one phase of that turning, the development of the fantasy novel as a major alternative to the forms and philosophies of the novel which had developed to that point. It is about the development of the idea of ecology and the implications of that idea for the future development of western culture. It is about the role the comic and tragic have played in providing both a mirror image and crystal ball for humanity's perception of itself. It is, finally, an affirmation of hope, hope that the road has returned in time for people to do something more than preside over their own demise.

What I hope to do, in more concrete terms, is to apply the concepts of literary ecology to the twentieth-century fantasy novel in an attempt to establish that it is the comic, ecological perspective that principally distinguishes the fantasy novel from the tragic, formally realistic, and/or existential approaches of the traditional novel. Then I will suggest reasons for my belief in the current popularity of the fantasy novel as both a prelude to a different kind of future for the genre of the novel and as a philosophical model for the reintegration of people into a physical universe from which they have been too long estranged. Chapter 1 will examine the basic ideas of literary ecology, the major ideas and assumptions of the tragic and comic forms, and the relationship that twentieth-century fantasy novels bear to these traditions. Subsequent chapters will apply these observations to the works of five major fantasy writers in an attempt to understand both the possibilities and limitations of fantasy as an artistic and philosophic alternative to the more traditional forms of the novel and the tragic concept of humanity which those forms uphold.

1

LITERARY FANTASY AND ECOLOGICAL COMEDY

LITERARY ECOLOGY

That the twentieth century is in the midst of an ecological crisis of monumental proportions is an accepted fact. What are not accepted, however, are the reasons why that crisis has arisen or how it may be solved. The usual answer to the question of why the crisis has arisen is that humans have been greedy and unreasonable in their use of natural resources, with practices such as single-crop farming, failure to limit and/or control birth rates, and strip mining being singled out for criticism. The usual answer to the question of how the crisis may be solved is to suggest that new technology will increase the food and energy supplies, thereby accommodating both the present and future needs of people by making them the greater masters over their environment. The problem with both answers, of course, is that they miss the point. Strip mining and single-crop farming are not the causes of the crisis; they are logical end results of the central attitudes western humanity has developed and propagated about the relationship between itself and its environment. And technology, far from providing the ultimate solution, is itself a part of the problem.

But what has literature to do with any of this? And what is the significance of the term "literary ecology"? The answers to both questions were first suggested by Joseph Meeker in *The Comedy of Survival: Studies in Literary Ecology*, published in 1974. Taking as a basis of his work the idea that literature both reflects and creates attitudes about the relationship between human beings and nature, Meeker posed a question which all who write, read, defend, or teach the validity of literature must face: "Is it an activity which adapts us better to the world or one which estranges us from it? From the unforgiving perspective of evolution and natural selection, does literature contribute more to our survival than it does to our extinction?"[1] Inherent in this question is the implication that literature contains ecological perspectives, that indeed it may create such perspectives, and the majority of Meeker's book, dealing with works from *Hamlet* and *Lysistrata* to *Catch-22* and *The Divine Comedy*, is a brilliant illustration of exactly what kinds of perspectives exist and how literature has participated in propagating them. Meeker's conclusion is one thoroughly in the context of an ecological perspective: "The way out of the environmental crisis does not lead back to the supposed simplicity of the cave or the farm, but toward a more intricate form of living guided by a complex human mind seeking to find its appropriate place upon a complex earth." (pp. xx–xxi)

Though the reasons for the current ecological crisis are usually attributed to our ideas of land use, resource management, and energy availability, in fact they have much deeper roots, roots that emerge inevitably from the basic philosophic and religious attitudes which it has been the central province of literature to examine, present, and often to create. And, although the possible number of such roots is indeed large, it is convenient to group them into three major attitudes: those attitudes growing out of religion, particularly western Christianity; those attitudes growing out of the movement from a hunter-gatherer to an agricultural civilization; and those attitudes growing out of the French and Industrial Revolutions.

Although it was not the first such treatment, certainly the most widely known analysis of the effect religion has had upon our ecological attitudes was that set forth by Lynn White in his 1967 article. His central thesis was that western Christianity, in its emphasis upon humanity as the center of creation and its insistence upon humanity's dominance over all creation, laid the groundwork for most of our attitudes toward nature. Pointing out that by A.D. 1000 at the latest the West had become the leader in science and technology, White went on to demonstrate how, along with that leadership, western Christianity had diverged dramatically from earlier religions: "Christianity, in absolute contrast to ancient paganism and Asia's religions (except, perhaps, Zoroastrianism), not only established a dualism of man and nature but also insisted that it is God's will that man exploit nature for his proper ends."[2] He went on to point out that, in spite of Darwin, western humanity has never considered itself a part of the natural process, but rather superior to it. He concluded that the solutions to the crisis lay in the substitution of the beliefs of St. Francis for the beliefs of the majority of western Christianity, for only in his beliefs was there the humility toward the natural environment that was necessary if either it or humankind was to be preserved:

The greatest spiritual revolutionary in Western history, St. Francis, proposed what he thought was an alternative Christian view of nature and man's relation to it. He tried to substitute the idea of the equality of all creatures, including man, for the idea of man's limitless rule of creation. He failed. Both our present science and our present technology are so tinctured with orthodox Christian arrogance toward nature that nó solution for our ecologic crisis can be expected from them alone. Since the roots of our trouble are so largely religious, the remedy must be essentially religious whether we call it that or not. We must rethink and reflect our nature and destiny. The profoundly religious, but heretical, sense of the primitive Franciscans for the spiritual autonomy of all parts of nature may point a direction.[3]

White's argument has been the center of controversy since it appeared, and there is no doubt that there are valid objections to some of the details of his argument, but there is also little doubt that his central thesis has merit. Whether we draw the examples from the story in the Garden of Eden of Adam's being granted dominion over the earth and all its creatures or whether we note the Psalmist's amazed but ultimately affirming question concerning humanity's being raised above the earth and all its creatures, the position of humankind in regard to nature has been very clear in orthodox Christian thought. Equally clear, of course, has been the effect of that thought upon the environment. Gregory Bateson notes this clearly in *Steps to an Ecology of Mind*:

If you put God outside and set him vis-à-vis his creation and if you have the idea that you are created in his image, you will logically and naturally see yourself as outside and against the things around you. . . . The environment will seem to be yours to exploit. Your survival unit will be you and your folks or conspecifics against the environment of other social units, other races and the brutes and vegetables.

If this is your estimate of your relation to nature *and you have an advanced technology*, your likelihood of survival will be that of a snowball in hell.[4]

Rene Dubos, Paul Shepard, and Bateson, among others, argue that the movement from a hunter-gatherer culture to an agricultural one has had more effect on the ecological crisis than any other single historical or cultural event. Dubos's point is a fairly traditional albeit important one: "The primitive hunter necessarily saw himself as part of his natural surroundings and usually placed the community decision above his own self-interest. In contrast, the primitive farmer functioned in an environment which he manipulated; his lifestyle put a premium on competition, savings, and ownership, class structures and hierarchies."[5] It is important to note here, however, that Dubos is questioning the very idea of agriculture which has dominated almost every strain of western civilization. Shepard takes this question and turns it into the central thesis of *The Tender Carnivore and the Sacred Game.* Beginning with the notion that most accept the idea that the change from hunting to subsisting on field crops was a positive evolutionary adaptation since it enabled many more people than previously to support themselves in each square mile, Shepard immediately points out a too often ignored assumption of that notion: "This is true only if it is assumed that it is better to have more people per square mile, and there is no evidence that the evolution of any species is favored by its increasing density."[6] Shepard goes on to suggest that as armed cities and mercantile civilizations began to emerge, humanity began to justify its "genocide" of the hunter-gatherers on the excuse of furthering civilization and to extend its "biocide" of selected wild plants and animals on the basis of politically structured values. He concludes that the myth of agriculture's improving our civilization is central to the ecological crisis which followed:

Because a fortunate few controlled the recording of history, civilized culture became a propaganda machine for itself, which easily manipulated the resentments of peasants and, by redirecting their distorted lives, helped rationalize the genocide of the hunter-gatherers on agriculture's enlarging frontier. It is a tragedy euphemistically called historical destiny, economic progress, or the inexorable surge of the political state. Yet, from the beginning, agriculture failed our species, and now, after fifty centuries with scarcely a word raised against its mythology of virtue and security, it is failing the modern world, failing to nourish it both physically and spiritually.[7]

The way out of the crisis, then, for Shepard and others, is a rejection of the false myths of agriculture, particularly of pastoralism, and a return to the ideas of the "integrity of solitude" and "human sparseness" which characterized the hunter-gatherers. Most surprising of all, though, is Shepard's insistence that such a return is perhaps more realistically attuned to the life of modern humankind than to the life of earlier men and women:

There are many striking parallels between post-industrial men and hunter-gathering men. They are both highly mobile, non-territorial, non-soil-working, nature-interested, much leisured, function-oriented, small-familied, and altruistic. The most modern men are ready to abandon, if they only knew how, civilization based on war and competition and on an industry so heavy that human personality as well as the surface of the earth is stamped by its obscenity. Most important of all, the urban man today is less deformed, in spite of his lack of nature contact, than the peasants, farmers, and their small-town collaborators who have predominated in the agricultural era. The modern city man was not born on a farm, and his world was not perverted by the spectacles of the barnyard. New shifts in social thought bring urban man and hunting man closer in their mutual belief in tradition as opposed to existential behavior, in permanence instead of progress, in small-group democracy rather than mass society.[8]

Bateson, approaching the matter from a biologist and scientist's point of view, comes to startlingly similar conclusions. Noting that hunter-gatherers took clues from nature and applied them in a metaphoric way to their own society—an application usually referred to as totemism—Bateson concludes that such applications were more sensible ecologically than any other approach used since:

In a way it was all nonsense, but it made more sense than most of what we do today, because the natural world around us has this general systemic structure and is therefore an appropriate metaphor to enable man to understand himself in his social organization.

    . . . But when you separate mind from the structure in which it is immanent, such as human relationship, the human society, or the ecosystem, you thereby embark, I believe, on fundamental error, which in the end will surely hurt you.[9]

What seem most interesting about this argument for the hunter-gatherer lifestyle are not its differences with the argument advanced by White and other "religionists," but rather its similarities. In both there is a rejection of the idea of humanity's dominance over nature; in both there is a rejection of the idea of humanity's moral and intellectual superiority and separateness from the natural world; in both there is a rejection of the primacy of the individual over the system of which he or she is a part. Since these are, as we shall see later, the same kinds of rejections that literary comedy makes of the ideas of literary tragedy, it should be no surprise to see how the growth of the tragic view of life has reflected and in turn helped to create the current ecological crisis.

A third group sees the crisis as having been caused more directly by the ideas of the French and Industrial Revolutions. Those who argue this point focus on the emphasis on romantic individualism sparked by the French Revolution and on the rise of the middle class, the capitalist ethos, and the goals of economic productivity and efficiency emphasized by the Industrial Revolution. Harold Schilling, in attempting to find an ethic that would lead humanity out of the crisis, focuses rather sharply on how the notions of romantic individualism have caused it:

> Such an ethic would accept the inevitability of tension between individual and group, between what is best for the individual and what is best for the common good, and would seek a balance between the two by emphasizing the needs, not of the individual in and of himself, but of the *individual in community*. This would be recognizing the supremacy of relatedness, interdependence, and wholeness rather than of rugged individualism. Also it would be taking cognizance of the great fact of natural existence that the individual— human and non-human—derives existence, character, and meaning from the relationships that make up the community.[10]

Lewis Moncrief, in an article written largely to refute White's claim that religious attitudes lay at the base of the ecological crisis, insists that the French and Industrial Revolutions precipitated it and that America's close adherence to the ideas of these two revolutions, coupled with the perception of the American frontier as an infinite resource to be conquered and managed, has presented us with an apparently insoluble dilemma:

> America is the archetype of what happens when democracy, technology, urbanization, capitalistic mission, and antagonism (or apathy) toward environment are blended together. The present situation is characterized by three dominant features that mediate against quick solution to this impending crisis: (i) an absence of personal moral direction concerning our treatment of our natural resources, (ii) an inability on the part of our social institutions to make adjustments to this stress, and (iii) an abiding faith in technology.[11]

Ian Barbour and Bateson follow a similar line of reasoning, but they emphasize the effects of the Industrial Revolution more than those of the French Revolution. Barbour particularly insists that it is the growth of technology that, more than any other single facet, has brought about the crisis:

But with the growth of technology—whose goal is to control nature rather than to understand it—more exploitative and utilitarian motives predominated. The economic interests of the rising middle class, the competitiveness and rugged individualism of the capitalist ethos, the goals of economic productivity and efficiency—aided, no doubt, by the "Protestant ethic" of frugality, hard work and dominion over the earth—all these encouraged a ruthlessness and arrogance toward nature unknown in earlier centuries.[12]

Bateson focuses more sharply on the scientific advances of the Industrial Revolution, pointing out that those advances were accompanied by a corresponding advance in scientific arrogance:

. . . and Occidental man saw himself as an autocrat with complete power over a universe which was made of physics and chemistry. And the biological phenomena were in the end to be controlled like processes in a test tube. Evolution was the history of how organisms learned more tricks for controlling the environment; and how man had better tricks than any other creature. But that arrogant scientific discovery is now obsolete, and in its place there is the discovery that man is only a part of larger systems and that the part can never control the whole.[13]

From this brief survey of the possible causes of the ecological crisis, three things should become immediately apparent. First, in spite of the differences in approach, all of the approaches agree that the dominant idea in establishing humanity's relationship toward nature has been its insistence upon their separateness from it. Whether that separateness comes from a belief in a special creation, in the development of an agriculturally based civilization, or in a determination to manipulate the environment through advanced technology, the fact is that humanity does not see itself as a part of the natural environment. Following closely upon this fact is the assumption of humanity's superiority to nature. Such superiority carries with it the obligation to manage, to rule, or to manipulate that environment for personal benefit, and, since humanity is not a part of the system but rather its ruler, it has neither need nor obligation to seek anything beyond that which is of immediate benefit. Finally, humanity's separateness and superiority lead it to the inevitable conclusion that ethical and moral structures must be drawn, not from the natural world, but from the supranatural sphere, and humanity's greatest achievements may, then, lie not in the physical world but in the realm of the moral, the mental, and the abstract. The consequences of these beliefs are staggering, but it is precisely these staggering consequences that are the province of literary tragedy.

TRAGEDY

Ever since tragedy was first recognized in the Greek world in 486 B.C., it has been seen by western humanity as embodying the highest ideals possible to western civilization. Its writers have been the most glorified, and its traditions and philosophical premises have been those that have dominated religious, ethical, and social values. What so few have seemed to realize, however, is the effect which that glorification has had upon western humanity's attitudes toward nature, land use, resource management, and basic social doctrines.

Evidence of the paramount place tragedy has held in the western world since its first inception is abundant, but it is perhaps nowhere more apparent than in these words of Walter Kerr:

We rise in the morning to look for the transformation that will cleanse us and marry us to gods. We are not confused. The path is as deeply marked in our brains as the footprints that still climb the Acropolis, with such effort and so much promise of pain, toward Athena. Agony, death, transfiguration make up the compulsive rhythm of the only universe we know.

It is small wonder that with so powerful an instinct prodding us to repeat eternally these three simple but difficult gestures we should have given our first energies, and our deepest protective loyalties, to what we call tragedy. Tragedy must stand in the way. It *is* the way.[14]

Now it is not surprising that this almost religious coupling with tragedy has taken place, for nowhere else can such an incredibly flattering portrait of humanity be found. It establishes humankind as clearly superior to all other creatures and, in fact, clearly asserts that the world revolves around humanity. Such a position, of course, could never hold sway by itself, for that would glorify pride and egotism. So what tragedy does, as indicated by Kerr, is to make of humanity a sacrifice, whether to the good of its people, its gods, or its ideals. Further, it asserts that suffering is both necessary and good, for in suffering humanity transcends its natural being and ascends into moral and/or spiritual rebirth which reaffirms its ties to the gods and emphatically denies a relationship to the physical universe. Whether that transcendence is called knowledge, goodness, or progress matters little. What does matter is that it is accomplished. Karl Jaspers phrases it this way:

Looking back, we can see how history was rent asunder by the birth of Tragic Man. His tragic insight need not be the product of a flowering civilization, but may be quite primitive. But, primitive or not, man seems truly awake only when he has such knowledge. For now he will face each realization of his ultimate limits with a new restlessness that drives him beyond them. Nothing that is stable will endure, for nothing that is stable will satisfy him. Tragic knowledge is the first phase of that historical movement which takes place not only in external events but in the depths of man himself.[15]

Thus the tragic looking glass may show humanity "darkly," but even that darkness is preferable to the alternatives posed by comedy, science, or anything else, for ultimately what humans are seeking in tragedy is the avoidance of death in an individual and particular way. Gilbert Murray notes this facet of tragedy well as he comments upon the reasons for its centrality in western humanity's conception of itself: "Tragedy in the same way, facing a still more pressing need, hides or adorns the coming bulk of death, magnifies the glory of courage, the power of endurance, the splendour of self-sacrifice and self-forgetfulness, so as to make us feel, at least for the fleeting moment, that nothing is here for tears, and that death is conquered."[16]

From what has been said about the position tragedy holds for western humanity, it is clear that there are three basic assumptions indissolubly wed to the tragic belief or ideal: that nature is made for humankind; that human morality transcends natural limits; and that the individual human personality is supremely important. The simple statement of these beliefs may, however, not indicate clearly enough their importance, for they have determined to a great extent the relationships that humans have established between themselves and their environment, their fellow creatures, and their gods.

The belief that nature was made for humanity at once establishes the relationship between the two. Humanity is the master of all natural things, but it is not a part of them at all. It is not only its right but its duty and obligation to rule nature for its own benefit. Thus, in any question involving the survival of humanity or of one's fellow human creatures or even their comfort or convenience, it is clear that all else must give way or be sacrificed. Grasslands are turned to irrigated farms, species of insects are eradicated, and wars are carried on because an obligation to advance must be fulfilled. Moreover, it is evident that, since nature is made for humanity, it is humanity's ethic, derived from its own need, to which nature must conform. Without this rule, there would be only purposelessness and senselessness; nature could be trusted to run amuck and morality would vanish because there would be no one to impose it. The natural world is thus a tool which humanity uses to advance the higher goals which only it can know. Oedipus must drive Thebes into famine and plague so that he can gain knowledge; Lear must bring his kingdom into civil strife and his family into destruction so that they all can learn of their responsibilities; Milton's Adam must bring sin and death into the world so that the world can know the redemptive power of Christ and the love of God. The list of examples is endless, but all make clear the fact that humans must rule the natural environment if there is to be morality, goodness, or knowledge in the world.

That human morality transcends natural limits is equally important, for it clearly establishes the superiority of humans to nature in every way. It means, of course, that their moral and ethical codes will be drawn from supranatural rather than natural phenomena, but it also means that their position in relation to the natural world is never in doubt. Joseph Wood Krutch, in one of the most brilliant modern essays on the tragic spirit, comments on this relationship particularly well:

Man as it sees him lives in a world which he may not dominate but which is always aware of him. Occupying the exact center of a universe which would have no meaning except for him and being so little below the angels that, if he believes in God, he has no hesitation in imagining Him formed as he is formed and crowned with a crown like that which he or one of his fellows wears, he assumes that each of his acts reverberates through the universe. His passions are important to him because he believes them important throughout all time and all space; the very fact that he can sin (no modern can) means that his universe is watching his acts; and though he may perish, a God leans out from infinity to strike him down.[17]

Jaspers also affirms this point when he says, "*There is no tragedy without transcendence*. Even defiance unto death in a hopeless battle against gods and fate is an act of transcending: it is a movement toward man's proper essence, which he comes to know as his own in the presence of his doom."[18] Thus the knowledge that is sought is not of this world;

rather it is beyond it. After all, remember what Marlowe's Faust gave up his soul for—knowledge, and not knowledge of this world but universal knowledge of the soul of the universe. Ibsen's Master Builder did not seek to build for the people of the earth; he sought a temple for the soul and spirit of aspiring human beings. Williams's Laura did not seek physical love and human sexuality; she sought the mystical, transcendent love of the unicorn. The list goes on and on of the catalogue of characters who sought above all else to overcome their animal instincts. Even when the romantics turned to nature, they didn't turn to actual nature; they turned to idealized, pastoral nature, on the one hand, or to the equally idealized, turbulent nature of Byron's *Manfred* or Coleridge's "Rime of the Ancient Mariner" on the other. In all cases, as Kerr comments, "We may hold, on considerable evidence, that whenever the tragic action is disclosed to us in its fullness, we are likely to share the experience Nietzsche envisioned for the spectator: 'he will have shuddered at the sufferings about to befall the hero and yet divined in them a higher, overmastering joy.' "[19] So a morality remains which, in every case, serves to reaffirm humanity's separation from that same natural world. Dorothea Krook summarizes it particularly well:

In the greatest tragedy, I suggest, what is in the end affirmed is something more than the dignity of man and the value of human life. We are made to feel that, through the affirmation of man and the life of man, there is at the same time being affirmed an order of values transcending the values of human order. This order of values is not, or is not felt to be, a mere projection of the human mind: it is felt to have a real, objective existence—an existence independent of, other than, and antecedent to man and the life of man. . . . An objective moral order which at once incorporates the human and transcends it: this, I am suggesting, is what is finally affirmed in great tragedy.[20]

The last of the basic assumptions of tragedy, that the individual human personality is supremely important, is perhaps the most peculiar feature of all, at least as it stands in relation to ecology. It is also part of the fabric upon which the myths of western culture have been based. The supremacy of the individual as opposed to the supremacy of the group, whatever that group may be, is the most immediately apparent characteristic of any tragedy. Aristotle centered his discussion of tragedy around the tragic hero, and Shakespeare's great tragedies are all named after the central character, who in every case exists as a unique individual whose personal seeking and suffering is the very reason for the play's being. Lear's actions may plunge his kingdom into chaos; Hamlet's failure to act may lead directly to the deaths of innocent people; Othello's jealousy may feed Iago's malevolence; Macbeth's ambition may destroy his wife as well as his king. The point is that none of these things matter; at least when compared to the spectacle of each character's agony, learning, and death. It is Oedipus about whom we care, not Thebes; Medea, not her children. And if tragedy does not end in the physical salvation of the individual being, it does most certainly end in the spiritual regeneration or the moral learning of the consequences of individual action. Milton claimed that he wrote *Paradise Lost* to justify the ways of God to man, but it was not man in general but each individual man and woman in particular that he was trying to convince of God's justice. Western religion insists upon individual salvation, and the entire tradition of western art focuses upon the individual, not the group. It is, after all, the individual who suffers and thereby affirms his or her own importance in the universe: "Man is ennobled by the vengeful spite or injustice of the gods. It does not make him innocent, but it hallows him as if he had passed through flame. Hence there is in the final moments of a great tragedy, whether Greek or Shakespearean or neo-classic, a fusion of grief and joy, of lament over the fall of man and of rejoicing in the resurrection of his spirit."[21] Individuals suffer and are justified. Individuals seek knowledge and are saved. Individuals define morality, challenge fate, and ultimately insist that the world and all those in it must accommodate themselves to the highly personal knowledge to which the tragic hero's individual seeking has led. If they do not so accommodate themselves, then the hero is sacrificed, but through that sacrifice is gained the personal moral stature which the group could never attain. Even in the eighteenth century when poets talked about the importance of types rather than individuals, it was the individual who was ultimately glorified by the most eighteenth-century of all poets, Alexander Pope:

> Placed on this isthmus of a middle state,
> A being darkly wise and rudely great:
> With too much knowledge for the Sceptic side,
> With too much weakness for the Stoic's pride,
> He hangs between; in doubt to act, or rest,
> In doubt to deem himself a God, a Beast;

Born but to die, and reas'ning but to err . . .
Created half to rise, and half to fall:
Great lord of all things, yet a prey to all;
Sole judge of Truth, in endless Error hurl'd:
The glory, jest, and riddle of the world.[22]

What is most interesting of all about the assumptions of tragedy is that they are reflected in each of the "causes" of the ecological crisis of the twentieth century which were discussed earlier. The idea that humanity rules nature is implicit in the religious thesis outlined by White; the idea that human morality transcends natural limits is the same justification offered for the elimination of the hunter-gatherers and the ravaging of nature in order to achieve a greater good defined by humans outside of nature and imposed by them on the environment; the idea of the supreme importance of the individual is closely tied to the birth of romanticism as well as to the capitalistic ethic upon which the industrial state is largely based. So it is not simply a case of tragedy's reflecting social values which have led to environmental catastrophe. It is a case in which the adoption of the tragic mode and its promulgation through literature as the highest, noblest, and most worthwhile of human activities actually reduces all other events or ideas to a secondary role. Thus it becomes clear that literature, as Meeker points out, can provide us with either adaptive or maladaptive models to follow within our own ecological communities. The study of literature from an ecological perspective ultimately becomes an attempt to determine, not whether a particular genre or even literature itself will continue to exist, but what the possibilities are for humanity to continue to exist and, if so, the conditions under which that existence may be maintained. The approach is a frightening one, for it means dealing with infinitely more complex systems than simply philosophies and/or theories of art and literature. It means investigating the manner in which politics, economics, science, religion, language, medicine, and countless other matters go into the making of a piece of literature. It means trying to see the whole, and the whole is so enormous and complex that the temptation is to retreat to the comfort of specialized knowledge, information that is reassuring precisely because it has simplified the world to the point at which it can be understood. Such simplification is at best tenuous, in the same way that simple ecosystems are ultimately less stable and less continuous than the more complex ones. Thus, if the task is a seemingly difficult or impossible one, it is nevertheless eminently more worthwhile than the alternatives, or, as Meeker puts it: "A hopeless attempt to see things whole is at least as worthy as the equally hopeless task of isolating fragments for intensive study, and much more interesting." (p. 12)

COMEDY

Having explored the maladaptive posture presented by tragedy, it becomes necessary to look briefly at an adaptive posture, that given by the comic view and approach, for if tragedy has long been dominant in western culture, it has never been able to rid itself of its often embarrassingly crude and overwhelmingly physical alter ego, comedy.

Like the philosophy of the tragic, three basic assumptions govern the philosophy of the comic: that its primary virtue or goal is the affirmation of life; that comic humanity sees itself as but one part of a system to which it must accommodate itself and whose survival must be a primary concern if it hopes to continue to exist; and that comic humanity puts aside all abstractions, for adherence is likely to cost its freedom, if not its life, and comic humanity is most unwilling to give up either.

The center of comedy has always been the celebration of life. Suzanne Langer says that "the pure sense of life is the underlying feeling of comedy, developed in countless different ways."[23] Wylie Sypher, in an analysis of the origins of comedy, makes the point in an even more dramatic way: "If the authentic comic action is a sacrifice and a feast, debate and passion, it is by the same token a Saturnalia, an assertion of the unruliness of the flesh and its vitality. Comedy is essentially a Carrying Away of Death, a triumph over mortality by some absurd faith in rebirth, restoration, and salvation."[24] Finally, Meeker illustrates the idea most clearly and simply of all when he says: "Its (comedy) only concern is to affirm man's capacity for survival and to celebrate the continuity of life itself, despite all moralities. Comedy is a celebration, a ritual renewal of biological warfare as it persists in spite of any reasons there may be for feeling metaphysical despair." (p. 24) The significance of this conception is immediately apparent. Comedy does not care about love, honor, glory, heroism, courage, justice, or any other virtue which occupies the center of tragedy's attention. It cares only about life itself, not the eternal spiritual life, but the physical life of the individual human animal. That is why sex and sexuality are the central themes of virtually all comedy. In *Lysistrata*, for example, the women seek to re-establish peace in their world, not because peace is an abstract good to which they aspire, but because war takes the men away from home and thereby prevents women's receiving the sexual affection they desire. The conclusion of that play, with the success of the women in achieving their goal, leaves no doubt that it is achieved to gratify the lust of the man as well. Nor has the emphasis on sexuality changed throughout the years. Henry Burlingame, the many-faced tutor in Barth's *The Sot-Weed Factor*, while extolling the sexual attractiveness of Portia, the large hog over whom he stands as he speaks, tells Ebenezer that he has sown his seed in every part of creation, in the bodies of men and women and the boles of trees and in virtually everything else, and he has found it all to be good. Comedy is full of lovers and lusters, and, while it usually has little to say about the salvation of souls, it has a great deal to say about sexuality and the likelihood that the species will continue as a result.

All this means, of course, is that the image of humanity in comedy is vastly different from that in tragedy. Kerr, although he finds this to be a severe limitation of comedy, points out the nature of this difference in image when he says, "The crust, the vulnerable and demanding and embarrassing casing of the body, is the first comic fact because it is the improbability that is closest to man: it is *he*."[25] Because humans are seeking survival rather than any abstraction, comedy portrays them as often foolish, irrational, bumbling, greedy, lustful, and overwhelmingly real. After all, it is the tragic hero Hamlet who speaks of what a piece of work man is; it is the comic hero Jacques who speaks of the parts a man plays in his lifetime, including the mewling and puking infant, whining schoolboy, woeful lover, quarrelsome soldier, fat-bellied justice, and piping ancient with shrunk shanks. And therein lies the rub. Comedy provides a mirror in which humans see themselves as they are, not as they would like themselves to be. They may be fat, skinny, slightly misshapen, smelly, stupid, and weak, but regardless of what they are, they are human, and a part of the animal kingdom. And they seek life within that kingdom, according to its laws and the needs of their own physical beings. Comedy points out the limitations of humans, *and it accepts those limitations*, as Cyrus Hoy notes so pointedly:

Comedy imposes, then, an acceptance of life, which implies as well an acceptance of man. And to accept man, one must be prepared to forgive the weakness, the treachery, the downright depravity which, in spite of man's best intentions, are inherent in his behavior. To accept and to forgive, one must be, above everything else, clearsighted about what man is, and what can properly be expected of him. Only then will one refrain from asking the impossible, of himself and of others, and escape being plunged into the depths of tragic despair when the impossible is not achieved. Comedy is nothing if not hardheadedly realistic about the nature of man and the nature of forgiveness and its acceptance of human failings, because it recognizes the existence of these. That is why comedy, again and again, emphasizes the need for man to undeceive himself about the limitations of humanity, to see life for what it is, and to make the best of it.[26]

The second major idea inherent in the comic tradition is that humans are part of a natural environment and must seek to accommodate themselves to it rather than expecting or demanding that it accommodate itself to humanity. Virtually every writer about comedy has noted its close ties to social organization, and the generally static pattern of comedy has been the subject of equal attention. Kerr analyzes it well even as he finds it to be unsatisfactory, at least as compared to what tragedy does:

Another design finds the clown willing to engage in the struggle. But he does not engage in it as a tragic hero does. To begin with, he *assumes* that matter cannot be altered to suit him and he wastes no time trying to dominate it by spiritual force. He knows that *he*, being so limited, cannot hope to change the greater limitations that press in upon him. But, in the course of his generally frustrating experiences, he has noticed something. He has noticed that while he can never defeat matter, matter can be made to defeat matter. Matter can be used against itself to further, however temporarily, the clown's own ends.

And so he tricks the universe by obeying its laws.[27]

Comic humanity is never superior to the natural environment, and it never seeks to rule over it. Humanity can and will seek to use its laws for its own benefit, but only to such an extent that the system remains stable, for humanity knows that its continued existence depends on the continued existence of the system. As a result, humanity strives to maintain the greatest degree of personal freedom possible within a given system and, if the system is disturbed, to return the system to its original form, which is perhaps the greatest single pattern common to biological life:

But living things strive to persist in a particular chemical balance, to maintain a particular temperature, to repeat particular functions, and to develop along particular lines, achieving a growth that seems to be performed in their earliest, rudimentary, protoplasmic structure.

That is the basic biological pattern which all living things share: the round of conditioned and conditioning organic processes that produces the life rhythm. When this rhythm is disturbed, all activities in the total complex are modified by the break; the organism as a whole is out of balance. But, within a wide range of conditions, it struggles to retrieve its original dynamic form by overcoming and removing the obstacle, or if this proves impossible, it develops a slight variation of its typical form and activity and carries on life with a new balance of functions—in other words, it adapts itself to the situation.[28]

Comic humanity is not free to manipulate or change its environment for its own benefit; what it is free to do is to use the laws of that environment to its own best advantage, knowing that in so doing the chance for survival is increased. Falstaff follows this rule to the letter in *Henry IV*, part I, when he insists that the tavern mistress owes him money rather than vice versa, and the old Italian whoremaster in *Catch–22* illustrates the importance of the rule when he tells Nately that he was pro-German when the Germans ruled, pro-Italian when the Italians ruled, and will now be pro-American when the Americans rule.

What this means is that the structure of the comedy and the nature of its characters will be vastly different from those of tragedy. Comedy will not show a progression from good fortune to bad, or from bad fortune to worse, nor will it turn on the ironies inherent in *De Casibus* or Italianate tragedy. Instead, it will turn on clever plot lines manipulated by one or more of the characters for his or her own advantage, and at the end there will have been no appreciable change in the circumstances of either the characters or their environment. Comedy is not a fairy tale; it does not deal with those who "live happily ever after." Rather it affirms the return of the system to a state of stability by its enhancement of their own chances for success. Neither do the characters change or develop appreciably. They do not learn a moral law of the universe, nor do they understand their own superiority to natural law and the sacrifice they must render for that knowledge. They are not destroyed, and rarely are their antagonists destroyed. Theirs is simply not a world of complete victory or utter defeat:

The real antagonist is the World. Since the personal antagonist in the play is really that great challenger, he is rarely a complete villain; he is interesting, entertaining, his defeat is a hilarious success but not his destruction. There is no permanent defeat and permanent human triumph except in tragedy; for nature must go on if life goes on, and the world that presents all obstacles also supplies the zest of life.[29]

So comic humanity accepts the world, not, perhaps, as a matter of principle, but as a matter of practical necessity, and it would much rather feign death in Falstaff's style while giving up total victory than it would feign life and adopt death as Lear does to gain moral and intellectual knowledge and victory.

The third major idea inherent in the comic tradition, that humanity eschews abstractions entirely, follows logically from the first two. If humans seek to survive, and if they are aware that their survival is likely to be enhanced by the survival of the system, then abstractions will be avoided for one simple reason: they are likely to get people dead. Bergson's criticism of comedy suggests that comedy was a game that imitated life with types, while tragedy was a heightened vision of life that represented the full life-history of a soul. The soul doesn't eat, breathe, or drink, but the body does, and it is the body in which comedy is interested. It is precisely for this reason that western humanity has insisted that comedy is a lower form than tragedy, and the doctrine of tragedy became the central philosophical and ethical position of the western world. Kerr puts it well:

Compromise, resignation, doubt, frank disbelief on all sides, the denial of dignity, the reminder that victory changes nothing and that the bumbler will go on bumbling—these are the indispensable ingredients of a comic "happy" ending. Without at least one of them, the ending will not be comic. To be comic, the ending must forcefully call into question the issues of "happiness" and "forever after." Comedy is not lyric, not rhapsodic, not reassuring; putting its last and best foot forward, it puts it squarely down in the dung.[30]

Kerr doesn't like this image of humanity; neither does western civilization in general. It prefers Othello and his plumed troops, Faust and his quest for godhood, Stephen Dedalus and his attempts to fly by the nets of language, religion, and nationality to a drunken Sancho Panza, a lecherous Moll Flanders, or a cowardly Yossarian. And yet the interesting thing is that these latter three survive for a relatively long period of time with a relatively high degree of satisfaction. But mere survival has never been enough for tragedy, just as it has never been enough for western humanity. "Mere" survival has always been acceptable for the animals, but for humanity, that higher and more spiritual entity, moral justification has to come from spiritual knowledge and from accordance with the laws of the universe, not the natural laws springing from the environment but those being drawn from the laws of the gods.

The comic character, then, acts from completely different reasons than does the tragic character. The comic character is kind, not because of a creed or dogma that dictates it, but because it has been experienced and it felt good. The comic character knows that food and drink and sex are good, not because someone says so or because a philosophical position justifies them, but because the character has experienced them. In short, the comic character acts on the basis of experience rather than abstraction, and in so doing, the character sets up a view of humanity and its future that emphasizes the limited nature of its powers and the likelihood of the system's long-range existence instead of its own:

As long as human existence is a limited and finite affair, as long as actuality pursues a dialectic course, as often as organizations are set up or discovered and customs and institutions taken as final entities, there will echo the sound of laughter, a sound reminiscent of an indefinitely repeated round of humour and improvement stretching on into the boundless future of an unlimited community.[31]

This comedic thrusting aside of abstractions puts humanity in a tradition that is clearly not so "noble" as that of tragedy, but it is one that is more realistic and more human. It may see humans as often foolish, bungling, lecherous, smelly, and pretentious, but it also sees them as compassionate, not in obedience to a dogma or creed, but in response to the accumulation of experience. Comedy pictures abstractions and absolutes as nonsensical and/or unknowable, but it also reaffirms the ancient ties to the physical world and all its processes in a manner that is precisely opposite the divorce which tragedy demands between humanity and the environment.

THE FANTASY TRADITION

Because the authors of fantasy novels explicitly or implicitly recognized the flaw in the presentation of the tragic as the ideal for western humanity, the fantasy novel arose and gained a major place in western literature. Drawing upon an aesthetic which was largely romantic, they created a new form for the novel, the romantic novel, peopling it with a comic conception that is ultimately ecological. Important differences exist, however, between the major traditions of the novel and that romantic strain developed by the fantasy novelists.

The basis for growth of the novel in English was what Ian Watt has called "formal realism." The term essentially describes a new perception of reality which arose in the works of Richardson and Fielding and which, not surprisingly, is linked closely to the rise of the Industrial Revolution and the growth of the middle class discussed earlier. Watt says that the novel "surely attempts to portray all the variety of human experience, and not merely those suited to one particular literary perspective: the novel's realism does not reside in the kind of life it presents, but in the way it presents it."[32] The emphasis of those words on the idea of a more formal, scientific approach to the presentation of *external* reality, then, was what the novel was all about. As Watt says:

the premise or primary convention, that the novel is a full and authentic report of human experience, and is therefore under an obligation to satisfy its reader with such details of the story as the individuality of the actors concerned, the particulars of the times and places of their actions, details which are presented through a more largely referential use of language than is common in other literary forms.[33]

Since it is precisely this kind of "realism" that Watt saw as the "lowest common denominator of the novel," it is no surprise to note that the terms "romantic" and "novel" seem to be contradictory. Austin Warren calls the novel realistic and the romance poetic or epic.[34] Northrop Frye insists that the romance is that form in which the hero is a man who is superior in degree to other men as well as to the environment and whose actions are marvelous.[35] Wilbur L. Cross makes the distinction clearer when he insists that romance is prose fiction that deals with life in a false or fantastic manner,[36] and Arnold Kettle amplifies the idea still more when he says that "romance was the nonrealistic literature of feudalism."[37] Finally, Francis Stoddard speaks most clearly when he insists that "there came a day when the tale of all these external, far-off, glorious unrealities passed away . . . and when that day came, it was the birthday of the English novel."[38]

It would, of course, be a serious mistake to confuse the term "romantic novel," which I am using here, with what Hawthorne and James referred to as "romances." They were referring to forms which did not claim any kinship to the novel other than having been written in prose; they did not pretend to portray reality in the vein of the novel, but rather in the vein of medieval romances. Moreover, I am using the term "romantic" specifically to refer to the philosophic cast of mind and the basic aesthetic ideas of the English and German romantics, particularly Coleridge and Kant, whose romantic concepts and whose axiology and epistemology of the imagination formed the foundation for the development of the fantasy novel in the late nineteenth and twentieth centuries. An enormous gulf existed between the romantic imagination and the novel until the fantasy novel began to develop, and even the beginnings of the fantasy novel in William Morris and Lord Dunsany owed at least as much to the medieval romance tradition as to the novel itself. The romantic imagination insisted upon seeing the world and art in a sense that was bounded only by such ideas as beauty and love, as a sense in which external reality was but the key by which humanity associated itself with eternity in some form. The novel, however, insisted on formal realism, for what truth it found lay in the external world, in the interaction of men and women in a society, in a rationality which, objectively applied, could discern and define a clear moral and a sense of being in the present, with the future a thing directly dependent on that knowable present. It was not until the fantasy novel began to develop—something which occurred only when the extremes of romanticism and realism began to fail in both form and content—that the romantic novel, of which such novels as J. R. R. Tolkien's, Frank Herbert's, C. S. Lewis's, Joy Chant's, and others are examples, could develop.

I am suggesting that the fantasy novel is unique in at least two ways. First, it has adopted a comic conception of humanity, placing its emphasis upon humanity as part of a total environment or system and acknowledging the absolute dependence of humanity upon that system. Second, the fantasy novel began to move away both from the tradition of medieval romance and from the tradition of formal realism which had become the province of the novel. What it did instead was to create a hybrid form, one that recognized the wonder, mystery, and magic inherent in the medieval romance and the possibilities for the writer to become the kind of subcreator Coleridge had described in *Biographia Literaria*. At the same time, however, it acknowledged and put to use the dependence of the novel on character presentations and sequences of events that were logically inevitable results of the natural environment in which they occurred. The end result was a new kind of realism, one that depended upon the truth of experience rather than the confusion of abstractions, and one that created characters true to the social situation of the created environment rather than to the external environment which was the traditional subject of the novelist. This tradition, which may be said to have begun as well with William Morris as with any other, grew slowly throughout the late nineteenth and early twentieth centuries largely because the traditions of formal realism and empirical science seemed to offer all the philosophical and aesthetic answers necessary. However, when science began to acknowledge its inability to provide absolutes and when formal realism turned futilely to stream of consciousness and to the existential novel in an attempt to justify its own existence as well as the continued existence of humanity, its subject, then the fantasy novel began to take on greater prominence. And, in the last forty years, it seems that the fantasy novel has become one of two ways out for modern humanity. That is why I think that Tolkien, Lewis, Herbert, and others have become so popular and important. They have offered an alternative to the tragic conception which has brought humanity and its environment to the point of imminent destruction; they have offered an alternative to the effete exhaustion of the experimental novel, an exhaustion that has brought into question both the possibility and the desirability of the novel's continued existence as a literary genre.

It is J. R. R. Tolkien who is most responsible for the critical attention which has been given to the fantasy tradition within the last thirty years. *The Hobbit* and *Lord of the Rings* stand out as the prime examples of fantasy with which most twentieth-century readers are familiar. That being so, it is fortunate that his work is a masterpiece by any standard. Bearing strains of those fantasy writers who came before him, both the modern fantasy novelists and the ancient writers of Eddas, epics, and sagas, Tolkien creates a world whose panoramic sweep and comprehensiveness may be favorably compared with that of any historical novelist. The sense of mystery, awe, magic, heroism, and allegory are combined with some of the most realistic monsters and characters imaginable to create a world appallingly and appealingly like our own. Using his essay, "Beowulf: The Monsters and the Critics" and "On Fairy Stories" as a basis for establishing his clear theoretical adherence to the doctrine of the "romantic novel" as I have defined it, we can see easily how *The Hobbit* and *Lord of the Rings* encompass virtually all the traditions of the comic and ecological traditions. Using a physical environment shaped by humanity's own actions, characters who affirm the imperative of survival while recognizing that the system must survive if they are to survive with any degree of freedom, and a general tone that suggests the importance of experience over abstraction, Tolkien portrays a world so incredibly complex and interrelated that comparisons to the diversity and complexity of the climax ecosystem are unavoidable. At the same time, however, he points out the sense of loss which he must feel at the demise of the tragic conception. It was, he seems to say, attractive and for a time even possible, so long as resources seemed to be unlimited. But now that resources have become limited, the tragic era must pass from the earth, just as the Third Age of Middle Earth had to pass. Moreover, the work and its reception seem to affirm that the older forms of the novel seem to be passing away as well while new forms—such as the fantasy and the picaresque—gain the strength and stature necessary to ensure the endurance of the novel as an art form.

For any fantasy novelist to move into the world of allegory, and particularly of intentional allegory, is to invite immediate disaster, and more particularly so if, as I am suggesting, fantasy is concerned with reality and comedy and experience. Yet C. S. Lewis makes this move brilliantly. In the Space Trilogy, *Till We Have Faces*, and *The Chronicles of Narnia*, Lewis meets allegory on its own ground and transforms it into some of the most enchanting and powerfully real and comic fantasy ever written. Borrowing with both hands from all elements of the Christian, Greek and classical traditions, Lewis's allegorical representations of unfallen humanity, of unfallen humanity after Christ, and of fallen humanity's resurrection and/or salvation are far more "realistic" than the works of such writers as Sartre, Joyce, Robbe-Grillet, or Hemingway. They are also more clearly within the comic, ecological tradition than any of the fantasy works preceding them. This observation is all the more strange when we consider White's argument that Christianity is the major cause of the current ecological crisis. Be that as it may, Lewis creates a series of creatures who do participate in a climax ecosystem on Malacandra and on Perelandra, and those systems are infinitely more complex than any on Earth where humanity, whether in Greek myth or in modern times, is still evolving. Moreover, the Great Dance in which all creatures participate is perhaps the clearest statement in all fantasy literature of an ecological ethic and perspective.

The fantasy novels of Charles Williams take off in still another direction. Different from the other fantasy novelists considered in this study, Williams is the only one to at least begin with the trappings of the present place and time rather than imaginatively created ones. This does not mean that the best of Williams's work partakes any less of the sense of strangeness and wonder which invests all the superior works in the fantasy tradition. Instead, the nature of that strangeness and wonder changes. Another major difference seen in Williams's work is that he writes in the vein of the realistic or detective novel, not in the vein of the romance or epic or quest tale. Thus it is no surprise that Williams's participation in the comic and ecological tradition is quite different from that of other fantasy novelists. His focus is clearly upon the system and upon humanity's obligation to find itself in it.

Frank Herbert's *Dune* tetralogy is often called science fiction, but it is far more accurate to see it as part of the fantasy tradition than as part of anything else. Moreover, from a strictly ecological point of view, it is perhaps the clearest overview of ecological ethics and practices at work present in any fictional work of any kind. Most important, it blends science, religion, and art in an integral system of thought and feeling by the conclusion of Book 4. That the work is not science fiction is clear: it presents an entirely created world in which the primary interest lies, not in technology or its manifestations, but in the relationship of its people to the physical environment and geography of Arrakis. Like Tolkien, Herbert has created a world in which the elements of the tragic conception are presented as enormously appealing; unlike Tolkien, however, he is ultimately not able to accept that the time for the concept has passed and that a new comic ethic based on the humility and the complex interrelationship of all things must develop. Herbert attempts an almost impossible task—the merging of the prophet/priest and the fool, of the tragic hero and the comic animal to produce a new kind of protagonist, one who could be a new kind of parent to a new kind of world. His ultimate lack of success is the result of his inability to resolve the conflict between the ecological and tragic themes of the series.

Finally, Joy Chant, whose writing is of as high a quality and worth as can currently be found either within or outside the fantasy tradition, uses a variety of approaches in her two very different books, indicating the almost limitless range of the fantasy novel. *Red Moon and Black Mountain*, the first of her fantasy novels, is much in the tradition of Tolkien. The idea of the quest, the implicit blending of religion and ecological ethics, and the somewhat sorrowful farewell accorded the tragic and/or heroic tradition are present in her magically evocative descriptions. *Grey Mane of Morning*, however, is a different type, even though it uses one of the same groups of people that appear in *Red Moon and Black Mountain*. It is as if, in this second work, she sets out to demonstrate artistically the thesis Shepard advances critically in *The Tender Carnivore and the Sacred Game*—that the ethic of the hunter-gatherers offers ultimately the best chance humanity has of presiding over something other than its own demise. Additionally and perhaps inevitably, she follows clearly in the line of the fantasy tradition in establishing the impossibility of the romantically pastoral ideal as even a symbolically or mythically desirable alternative.

CONCLUSIONS

To summarize, ecology itself underscores three features of natural life: interdependence, diversity, and vulnerability. These features are enormously important in evaluating the role literature plays in creating attitudes toward nature since they are a direct contradiction of the tragic idea and a direct affirmation of the comic. The interdependence of all things, particularly apparent in the climax ecosystem, suggests incredible complexity, complexity as absent from the tragic musings of a strictly "chain of being" universe as it is in the ideals of romantic pastoralism. At the same time, however, such complexity is in harmony with the seemingly confusing and chaotic combination of social, economic, religious, ethical, and physical demands placed upon the comic character. Likewise, the diversity of natural life is a condition which leads to a more stable system. Since ecologists state that complex ecological communities are vastly more stable and enduring than simple ones, it follows that anything encouraging that diversity is likely to help humans adapt more readily to the exigencies of the natural selection process. The vulnerability of life lends poignance to the present moment, suggests that death and decay are as much a part of the system as life and growth, and gives good cause to reject abstractions, which only heighten the likelihood of death while at the same time they remove the opportunity of experiencing the present.

Given these conditions of natural life, ecologists have reached four conclusions. The first is that the populations of most species have negative feedback processes which keep their numbers within relatively narrow limits. As applied to human beings, this suggests that ignoring or pushing aside those feedback processes without replacing them with other equally effective ones can have but one result: the extermination of a species so successful that it destroyed its own ecosystem and, in the process, destroyed itself as well. The second conclusion is that two basic laws of physics hold and are particularly important to ecology: the law of the conservation of matter, and the law which states that there is less energy and more biomass in higher food levels than in lower ones. These laws suggest that the reason more complex systems are more stable than less complex ones is that the energy transformation is less dependent upon a single source and is, therefore, less likely to be destroyed by a change in a single element. It also re-emphasizes the idea of the interrelationship of all things as well as the knowledge that energy use is more efficient at higher and more complex levels of the food chain. The third conclusion is that on any given piece of earth with a stable climate, a climax ecosystem will develop. Merely a restatement of the principles inherent in the notion of evolution, this idea illustrates the importance of adaptability and the necessity for a continuous process of change, even within a system that has already reached stability. The final conclusion is one that has already been discussed, the fact that complex ecological communities are more stable than simple ones.

The similarities between the biological and literary communities have already been outlined, yet a return to the most salient features is warranted. As Langer, Bateson, and Paul Weiss point out, the apprehension of beauty in art is built on the same principles as apply to nature. As snail shells, fiddler crabs, wave fronts, sand dunes, brain and sea-fan coral, nerve cells of the cerebellum, and the venation of leaves clearly illustrate, beauty is the apprehension of order, not a fixed and exact pattern but one that is unique within a general pattern of conformity to norms and laws of structure. Moreover, human beings perceive that beauty because the human mind itself is part and parcel of that order. The same is true of the apprehension of beauty in literature and art. The mind perceives uniqueness over a layer of pattern and acknowledges the infinite diversity of elements, both beautiful and ugly, which together make up that pattern. Weiss phrases it well when he says:

Yet man, whatever else he be, is a part of nature. So his artistic world cannot be one of sharply demarcated opposition to his natural world, but rather must be viewed as a fluid and continuous extension of his domain as ordinary member of animate nature—subject to all the limitations of biological reality, into a realm of unreality of his own making, stripped of those limitations. And since artistic endeavor is thus a direct organic outgrowth of nature, its elements are, of necessity, the same as those of primitive biological experience.[39]

And so art and nature are more than just mirrors of each other; they are parts of the same biological impulse to life. That is why it is important to examine how humanity is using that impulse to better adapt itself to or to divorce itself from those conditions that determine whether the species survives or becomes extinct.

All these points lead to the conclusion that to look at humanity and literature from an ecological perspective is to take up a viewpoint that is scientifically sound, aesthetically sensible, and practically necessary. Shepard and McKinley indicate this in the introduction to their ecology reader:

We brought this collection of papers together because we think it embodies the universality of ecology. Romanticism and primitive mythology which united men with the natural world in the past no longer teach us the unity of life. Scientific conservation, as a benign resource, is too narrowly and economically centered.

A truly human ecology must be consistent with the broad trans-organic scope of ecology, not merely in an analogical way but as a real extension.

. . . To a world which gives grudging admission of the "nature" in human nature, we say that the framework of human life is all life and that anything adding to its understanding may be ecological. . . . Beyond the essential biological framework, the arts and social studies give human ecology its distinctive quality—its heart.[40]

Humanity at large has not accepted this view. Whether from religious, historical, or philosophical reasons, humanity prefers to believe and to act upon the following beliefs:

(a) It's us *against* the environment.

(b) It's us *against* other men.

(c) It's the individual (or the individual company, or the individual nation) that matters.

(d) We *can* have unilateral control over the environment and must strive for that control.

(e) We live within an infinitely expanding "frontier."

(f) Economic determinism is common sense.

(g) Technology will do it for us.[41]

But to say that humanity at large has accepted this view is not to say that all prefer the tragic ideal with its many consequences. Comedy has been the somewhat embarrassingly omnipresent, somewhat disreputable black sheep of the literary family. And within the comic tradition lie the basic traditions of sound ecological practices. When combined with ideas inherent in the romantic tradition of the late eighteenth and early nineteenth centuries, the result has been the production of a new kind of novel, the fantasy novel. And, because of this merging of form and theme, the fantasy novel has become one of the two major strains that the novel as a genre will be taking in the coming years. This does not guarantee the continued existence of the novel or of humanity, but it does offer to both the promise and opportunity to take the wandering, unknown road of which Bilbo sings. And it offers to both the opportunity to go beyond the tragic ideal, with all the horrors which its abstractions have brought to western humanity. In Chant's *Red Moon and Black Mountain* one of the Iranani puts it this way just before a battle against an evil which may engulf the whole world: "We of Iranani, we have no magic and no strength of arms to offer, but we are *his* enemies. And if it comforts you I think he may find our power, the power of life and laughter, the hardest in the end to overthrow; too quick to catch, too frail to bind. We cannot destroy him, if you fail; but we can outlive him."[42] That too is the premise of this book: that literature, particularly the fantasy novel, offers humanity a way to reintegrate itself into the natural world and, in so doing, invites a new relationship between itself, its fellow creatures, and the science and literature that create and mirror that world.

2

J. R. R. TOLKIEN

When J. R. R. Tolkien's *Lord of the Rings* first appeared in 1954 and 1955, it set the stage for the phenomenal growth of interest in the fantasy tradition. There had been interest previously, of course. Followers of epic and heroic fantasy had read the works of William Morris, Lord Dunsany, and E. R. Eddison, and many Christian readers had been charmed by the supernatural thrillers of Charles Williams and the religious allegories of C. S. Lewis, but fantasy had never commanded the attention of a truly broad public. *Lord of the Rings* changed that. With critical reactions ranging from Edmund Wilson's description of the work as "juvenile trash" to C. S. Lewis's contention that it was a book "good beyond hope" and with the kind of popularity indicated by the fact that the Ballantine edition went through twenty-three printings between October 1965 and March 1970, *Lord of the Rings* introduced fantasy to the general public in unmistakable fashion. Tolkien calendars, shirts, posters, and clubs appeared, but along with these fads were also growing numbers of critical studies which began to make clearer the undeniably rich fabric from which the novels were woven. Thus, while it would be a mistake to claim that the fantasy tradition began with Tolkien, it would be accurate to say that Tolkien's was the first fantasy work to become so popular that it could spark a growth of interest in the history of the fantasy tradition as well as serve as a springboard and model for the large numbers of fantasy writers which were to follow.

The reasons for this sudden surge of interest in fantasy were numerous. First, the ground had been prepared by the works of Morris, Dunsany, Eddison, Williams, Lewis, and others. Second, Tolkien's work, growing naturally out of his scholarly fascination with Anglo-Saxon, Norse, and Germanic literature and tradition, presented a world of arresting strangeness with parallels to but no definite points of reference in contemporary history and events. Third, the world of Middle Earth was complete, consistent, and infinitely complex, and the range of experiences and characters it presented was consistent with humanity's growing perception of the increasingly complex society with which it had to deal following World War II. Fourth, the work exhibited a unity of theme and form which arose from a consistent critical theory and philosophical belief which Tolkien had outlined earlier in his essays, "Beowulf: The Monsters and the Critics" and "On Fairy Stories." Such consistency stood in marked contrast to the kind of pessimism and self-mockery characteristic of the experimental and/or existential novels which had been predominant to that time. Finally, Tolkien's work, affirming as it certainly does the comic and ecological traditions while acknowledging sadness at the passing of the heroic, tragic conception, appeared at the same time that awareness of the ecological crisis was beginning to grow.

Any examination of Tolkien should include, in addition to *Lord of the Rings*, a look at *The Hobbit*, *The Silmarillion*, *Unfinished Tales*, and such incidental works as "Leaf by Niggle" and "Farmer Giles of Ham." However, such complete examination must be reserved for another time. Here I am concerned principally with establishing the basically romantic critical approach that forms the foundation for the fantasy tradition, and the relationship of that approach to the traditional concerns of comedy and ecology.

Tolkien's basic critical approach is romantic, though it is a romanticism which goes significantly beyond traditional romantic theory. Like Coleridge, he sees the writer of fantasy in the role of subcreator, a maker and creator whose secondary world of art may be as real as the primary world, though there may be few discernible points of reference between the two. Like Kant, he sees the imagination functioning to create a set of images by which the writer can "strip away the veil of familiarity" and to make more accessible the world which holds a kind of unchanging truth seldom perceived save through the magic of the faerie.[1] Tolkien indicates these ideas clearly in "Beowulf: The Monsters and the Critics" and "On Fairy Stories."

In "Beowulf: The Monsters and the Critics" Tolkien sets out to defend the Beowulf poet against charges of telling a wild folk tale that is weak in structure due to its inclusion of the monsters and its relegation of major historical episodes to digressions. In a brilliant analysis which has become the single most influential article on *Beowulf* written in the twentieth century, Tolkien defends the poem as a poem rather than as a historical piece. At the same time, he finds that critics of the poem have operated in such a way as to destroy the integrity of the poem because they could not accept the very central elements which provide that integrity.

In short, what critics have done, Tolkien believes, is to ignore the monsters at the heart of the poem in favor of the less significant historical/sociological materials at its periphery. As he notes, "Correct and sober taste may refuse to admit that there can be an interest for *us*—the proud *we* that includes all intelligent living people—in ogres and dragons; we then perceive its puzzlement in face of the odd fact that it has derived a great pleasure from a poem that is actually about these unfashionable creatures."[2] Grendel and the dragon are certainly symbols, adversaries of God, but they are also real inhabitants of a world which the poet makes complete and consistent. Part of that reality is that the monsters are ultimately victorious, *in time*, that humans cannot win a final victory over them. But another part is at least the possibility, the hope that the temporal defeat may be set aside by the eternal victory which Beowulf himself pursues. The poem "glimpses the cosmic and moves with the thought of all men concerning the fate of human life and efforts; it stands amid but above the petty wars of princes, and surpasses the dates and limits of historical periods, however important." (p. 277) It is precisely because of the poet's creation of a world amazingly like and unlike our primary world that the readers have been moved by that world: "Yet it is in fact written in a language that after many centuries has still essential kinship with our own, it was made in this land, and moves in our northern world beneath our northern sky, and for those who are native to that tongue and land, it must ever call with a profound appeal—until the dragon comes." (p. 278)

The ties to romantic critical theory are immediately apparent here. Tolkien sees the poet as a subcreator, one whose responsibility is to create a convincingly believable world that is consistent with its own laws and is yet true to the experience with which humanity is familiar. Thus reality transcends physical reality, for it insists upon emotional reality as well. The monsters are emotionally real, perhaps even spiritually so, though the poet does not rely upon their spirituality. Instead the poet uses them to make concrete the fear, pain, and death which are so much a part of the physical world, and, if humanity is unable to defeat them in time, then perhaps it may be able to do so outside of time.

However, clear differences exist between Tolkien's romanticism and that of Keats, Byron, Shelley, and Wordsworth. Tolkien's does not insist that the world be uniformly evil, nor uniformly pleasant. Neither does he see it in terms of black and white. After all, Beowulf died, and the poet has let us know throughout of the sufferings that will fall on the Geats after Beowulf's death. So, instead of the Pellagian reliance upon the physical and spiritual victory that springs inevitably from the innate goodness of humanity, there is a definite Augustinian acceptance of the evil and unhappiness that spring from humanity's own place and behavior in the world, and it is not likely that either of those will be changed.

"On Fairy Stories," an essay originally prepared as an Andrew Lang Lecture in 1938 and published in a collection entitled *Essays Presented to Charles Williams* in 1947, is the richest single source of information concerning Tolkien's critical ties to and differences from traditional romantic beliefs. Tolkien's world of the faerie is, to begin with, a conventionally romantic one: "It cannot be caught in a net of words: for it is one of its qualities to be indescribable, though not imperceptible."[3] Faerie is a "realization, independent of the conceiving mind, of imagined wonder" (p. 14) and is thus a vastly different and richer world than that of allegory or its relatives, since the writers of fairy tales put what they do not know rationally as well as what they do know into their stories.

The link between this concept of humanity as subcreator and Coleridge's idea of the poet as subcreator is obvious. Art, according to Tolkien, is "the operative link between Imagination and the final result, Sub-creation." (p. 47) Fantasy, or the fairy story, then, simply combines that idea with the idea of arresting strangeness to provide "freedom from the domination of observed 'fact,' " (p. 47) thereby producing an "inner consistency of reality" that is difficult to maintain but which engenders a secondary belief that defines more clearly the world of the fact itself. And here is one major point at which Tolkien differs from the traditional romantic viewpoint. He sees fantasy as a natural activity not inimical to reason: "It certainly does not destroy or even insult Reason; and it does not either blunt the appetite for, nor obscure the perception of, scientific verity. On the contrary. The keener and clearer is the reason, the better fantasy will it make." (p. 54) Thus, in Tolkien's view, a sharp distinction exists between knowing fact and being enslaved by it. In the traditional comic vein, fact becomes that which is manipulated by the fantasy writer to produce a keener perception of the primary world and a greater ability to survive in it. As Tolkien concludes, "For creative Fantasy is founded upon the hard recognition that things are so in the world as it appears under the sun; on a recognition of fact, but not a slavery to it." (p. 55)

However, it is when describing the virtues of the fairy story that Tolkien reveals the most about his own critical perception. Fairy stories bring about recovery, escape, and consolation. Recovery is simply the traditional romantic idea of stripping away the veil of familiarity. It brings a new vision with which to see the world, helping humanity to regain a clear view, to see things apart from and in relation to itself. Fantasy takes the world of nature and often places it in a setting touched by a different light, with predictably expansive results: "For the story-maker who allows himself to be free with Nature can be her lover not her slave. It was in fairy-stories that I first divined the potency of the words, and the wonder of the things, such as stone, and wood, and iron; tree and grass; house and fire; bread and wine." (p. 59)

Escape also begins for Tolkien as a traditionally romantic value, but it soon goes beyond that role. Explaining that the escape is from things of an ephemeral nature to those of a more permanent nature, Tolkien emphasizes the difference between the "Escape of the Prisoner" and the "Flight of the Deserter." The former recognizes the intolerableness of a situation or circumstance and determines to change it or his or her perception of it so as to make it acceptable. The latter refuses to recognize what exists, the flight thereby absolving the necessity of dealing with it at all. To this extent, the view is traditionally romantic. But Tolkien adds something more to his explanation when he points out that fairy stories deal with the greatest escape of all, the escape from death. They do so in a curious manner, however, for they almost always point out the futility of "serializing" life in the manner of Swift's Struldbruggs. At the same time, they establish a *possibility* of a happy ending which Tolkien calls eucatastrophe and which he explains in these terms:

The consolation of fairy-stories, the joy of the happy ending: or more correctly of the good catastrophe, the sudden joyous "turn" (for there is not true end to any fairy-tale):[36] this joy, which is one of the things which fairy-stories can produce supremely well, is not essentially "escapist," nor "fugitive." In its fairy-role—or otherworld—setting, it is a sudden and miraculous grace: never to be counted on to recur. It does not deny the existence of *dyscatastrophe*, of sorrow and failure; the possibility of these is necessary to the joy of deliverance; it denies (in the face of much evidence, if you will) universal final defeat and in so far is *evangelium*, giving a fleeting glimpse of Joy, Joy beyond the walls of the world, poignant as grief. (p. 68)

In this fashion, Tolkien ties escape directly to consolation, the consolation of the happy ending that denies one defeat while affirming the likelihood of another. *Beowulf* is a good case in point. Beowulf defeated Grendel, but the dragon defeated Beowulf. We might draw from this the notion that humanity's defeat in time is assured, for as humanity ages, its strength and ultimately its life wanes. It also suggests the notion that at least a possibility exists that the tribe or species of humans will continue, for even though Beowulf dies, his people live on and carry with them the memory of his deeds. Now that may be a small consolation, but it indicates that humanity may endure in one form or another as a species if not as an individual. If it does not offer an escape from death completely, it does offer the possibility of the continuance of life and its pleasures. In this possibility lies the essence of the comic. As seen from his discussion of Beowulf, his examples in "On Fairy-Stories," and from *Lord of the Rings* itself, Tolkien would like to affirm the heroic code and the tragic tradition, but he cannot, for he sees too clearly the disasters those once proud ideas have wrought. Neither is he able to counsel despair, for he sees that life continues, though its form changes from one age to another. Instead he sends his characters on a quest, a traditionally romantic quest drawing upon all elements of the medieval quest and upon the ritual and pageantry of the grail quest itself. He does not give his characters an ultimate victory that will preserve them or the particular order they represent. In this fashion, he transforms the quest tale into a sad farewell for the enormously attractive tragic and heroic code and a poignantly happy realization of the possibilities inherent in the coming of the new age, a comic one.

Lord of the Rings has been called by a variety of names. It has been called a novel, an epic, a saga, a quest tale, and a romance. Those who have chosen one of these terms have usually specifically rejected the possibility of the others. Reasons for this confusion are many. First, Tolkien includes elements of all these genres in *Lord of the Rings*. Second, the voluminous detail and the enormous scope of the work present a complexity so vast that it threatens to overwhelm the critic, thereby inviting the adoption of any theory or approach that will simplify the task and categorize the critic's response. Finally, the ultimate rejection of the tragic, heroic, quest motifs for the comic, ecological ones is done with such evident regret that many critics fail to notice who endures and why. Perhaps the easiest way to approach the work, then, is to examine the various attitudes toward nature contained in the work, to look at the effect human action has on nature, and finally to indicate the necessity of seeing Middle Earth and its inhabitants as a system in which life, or at least the possibility of life, is reaffirmed. It will then be possible to understand more clearly why Tolkien rejects so unwillingly the heroic, tragic code and why he must ultimately affirm the comic, ecological tradition which is at the heart of this novel as much as it is at the heart of virtually every successful fantasy novel.

At least four distinctly different attitudes toward nature are outlined in *Lord of the Rings*. One is that represented by Sam Gamgee and the farmers of the Shire; another is that represented by Tom Bombadil; a closely related one is that represented by Treebeard and the Ents; a final one is that attributed to Sauron and his minions.

The most prevalent and obvious of the attitudes toward nature is that often misleadingly pastoral one represented by Sam Gamgee and the farmers of the Shire. This attitude, often seen by critics as Tolkien's own attempt to idealize certain aspects of English country life, is outlined briefly in Book I as Frodo and his companions make plans to leave the Shire, but even further description appears in the Prologue: "Hobbits are an unobtrusive but very ancient people, more numerous formerly than they are today; for they love peace and quiet and good tilled earth: a well-ordered and well-farmed countryside was their favorite haunt. They do not and did not understand or like machines more complicated than a forge-bellows, a water-mill, or a hand-loom, though they were skillful with tools."[4] While this is not entirely a pastoral description, it has within it several of the elements of the pastoral. There is, for example, the clear preference for simplicity and order which seems to be found in a relatively idealized nature. As Meeker puts it:

Rural life seems rational at such times because it is thought to be governed by natural rather than man-made laws. Crops sprout, mature, and are harvested for human sustenance in dependable cycles. Animals graze placidly in their pastures without all the jostling and conflicts generated among civilized men who crowd the marketplaces. And the rustic farmer who supervises nature's nourishing processes appears to be a contributing part of the sensible system around him, unlike his socially alienated urban brother. To a tired and frustrated aristocrat, agriculture is a symbol of tranquillity and order, God's image of what life should be like everywhere.[5]

Along with this preference is a definite rejection of technology as well as of the crowds and confusion that constitute the various cities of Middle Earth. And this idealization of ritual life by the Shire continues at the conclusion of the novel. Once they have been scoured of the Chief and his Shirriffs, Sam plants the seed given him by Galadriel and spreads the magic dust over the entire kingdom, with results which create a pastoral Eden beyond almost any in western literature:

Altogether 1420 in the Shire was a marvellous year. Not only was there wonderful sunshine and delicious rain, in due times and perfect measure, but there seemed something more: an air of richness and growth, a gleam of a beauty beyond that of mortal summers that flicker and pass upon this Middle-earth. All the children born or begotten in that year, and there were many, were fair to see and strong, and most of them had rich golden hair that had before been rare among hobbits. The fruit was so plentiful that young hobbits very nearly bathed in strawberries and cream; and later they sat on the lawns under the plum-trees and ate, until they had made piles of stones like small pyramids or the heaped skulls of a conqueror, and then they moved on. And no one was ill, and everyone was pleased, except those who had to mow the grass. (III, p. 375)

However, three important elements must be noted about Tolkien's pastoral Eden that mark it as strikingly different from the usual ones. First, it is clear that the Shire does not exist alone. It is equally clear that its peace is a temporary one at the beginning of the novel, as Gildor, one of the High Elves, points out: " 'But it is not your own Shire,' said Gildor. 'Others dwelt here before hobbits were; and others will dwell here again when hobbits are no more. The wide world is all about you: you can fence yourselves in, but you cannot for ever fence it out.' " (I, p. 123) The pastoral Eden, then, is a kind of false peace, as the subsequent savaging of the region by Saruman and his followers demonstrates. Moreover, it is equally clear that even the beauty that Sam creates with the magic of Galadriel cannot last. Galadriel passes away; eventually so will the King. There is no doubt, then, that the Shire will pass away also. The second point to note about this pastoral Eden, even in the lyrical description cited from Book III, is that the references throughout are to the continuation of life and the giving of birth. This is a comic tradition as well as a pastoral one, and that sense of the comic is further heightened by the conclusion of the lyric description, which reminds us gently but unmistakably that the real world of mowing grass, with all its attendanct irritations, is always present. So, even as Tolkien creates his pastoral setting, he takes pains to modify it in ways that remove it from the traditional pastoral ideals so aptly criticized by Meeker and in ways that place it much closer to the comic tradition which ultimately characterizes the entire novel.

The second attitude toward nature presented in the novel is that represented by Tom Bombadil, one of the novel's most enigmatic characters. One of only two figures over whom the Ring has no power, Tom seems to be a kind of elemental life force, older and more powerful than the abstractions of time and power that surround him. When Frodo asks if all of the land belongs to Tom, Goldberry's answer is remarkable: "No indeed! . . . That would indeed be a burden, . . . The trees and the grasses and all things growing or living in the land belong each to themselves. Tom Bombadil is the Master. No one has ever caught old Tom walking in the forest, wading in the water, leaping on the hill-tops under light and shadow. He has no fear. Tom Bombadil is the Master." (I, p. 174) The answer is remarkable for its apparent contradiction. Tom is master, but the land does not belong to him. Thus Tom is not the ruler of nature, nor does he use and direct it to his own wishes. Rather, Tom is a part of nature, one who participates in its laws and operates in accord with its system. For that reason, the Ring has no power over him. Tom does not disappear when he puts it on, and he does not want it. Neither, however, can he break or destroy it. He would eventually fall, not to the power of the Ring, but to the power of Sauron and the dark forces he represents. Glorfindel points this out when he says, "I think that in the end, if all else is conquered, Bombadil will fall, Last as he was First; and then Night will come." (I, p. 348) It is Galdor, however, who effectively summarizes what Tom represents: "Power to defy our Enemy is not in him, unless such power is in the earth itself. And yet we see that Sauron can torture and destroy the very hills." (I, p. 348) Thus Tom represents not so much an attitude toward nature as a symbol of nature itself, and nature alone cannot defeat the abstractions of evil and the technology of progress. Rather, ultimately nature will fall, will be destroyed by a power that can shape and direct the very evolutionary capacity of the earth itself. If the reader, then, were deceived by the apparently pastoral Eden of the Shire into thinking that such was the answer that Tolkien ultimately suggested for the continuation of life, Tom serves as a clear corrective. Moreover, since Tom's world contains Old Man Willow and the Barrow-wights as well as Goldberry and the lovely waters of the Withywhindle, there can be no mistake about the complexity or the diversity of the created universe. Nature is not enough; it can be destroyed by those who through carelessness or actual intent try to bend it to their own will. Finally, it should be noted that nature, in the person of Tom, is in fact amoral. Tom simply does not care about the Ring. Gandalf points out that, if given the ring, Tom would accept it into his care but that he would subsequently forget about it or lose it because it is unimportant to him. The Ring is an abstraction, one which does not and cannot ultimately matter to Tom. Sauron and all he represents may eventually destroy Tom, but in so doing they will have destroyed themselves as well, for then, as Glorfindel notes, "Night will come."

The third attitude toward nature, that illustrated by Treebeard and the Ents, is closely associated with the attitude represented by Tom. Like Tom, Treebeard is relatively untouched by the Ring and its power. Like Tom, Treebeard is old, associated with the beginning and, we expect, with the ending of nature itself. Like Tom, Treebeard is unbothered by the abstractions of power. However, unlike Tom, whose lands remain untouched by Sauron, Treebeard's own fold is hurt and destroyed by the effects of the war, and Treebeard is forced to go to war himself, not in order to fight for justice or right, but simply to ensure the survival of himself and the trees of which he is shepherd. When asked by Merry what his real name is, Treebeard responds with a poem that begins with the line, "*Learn now the lore of Living Creatures!*" (II, p. 84) In so doing, Treebeard does precisely what anthropomorphic creations in tragic literature almost never do: he ties himself to all of creation in a logical sequence rather than placing himself outside or above it. Later, when he describes himself in greater detail, he places himself somewhere between other living creatures, and in so doing, he attributes his age and the ability of the Ents to endure to the most important of all evolutionary principles, the ability to adapt:

We are tree-herds, we old Ents. Few enough of us are left now. Sheep get like shepherds, and shepherds like sheep, it is said; but slowly, and neither have long in the world. It is quicker and closer with trees and Ents, and they walk down the ages together. For Ents are more like Elves: less interested in themselves than Men are, and better at getting inside other things. And yet again Ents are more like Men, more changeable than Elves are, and quicker at taking the colour of the outside, you might say. Or better than both: for they are steadier and keep their minds on things longer. (II, p. 89)

Treebeard can no more defeat Sauron than can Tom. As he says, "There is naught that an old Ent can do to hold back that storm: he must weather it or crack." (II, p. 95) However, unlike Tom, Treebeard must go to battle because his world is immediately threatened, not by an abstraction, but by a neighbor: "But Saruman now! Saruman is a neighbor: I cannot overlook him. I must do something, I suppose. I have often wondered lately what I should do about Saruman." (II, p. 95) Treebeard must go to battle because he and the Ents are immediately threatened, not by power, but by death: "We Ents do not like being roused; and we never are roused unless it is clear to us that our trees and our lives are in great danger." (II, p. 113) Thus it is clear that Treebeard, as a part of nature, is concerned with precisely what any ecological system is concerned with, survival. He will not take action until threatened; he knows that any action he takes will not, in the end, be able to defeat those who can manipulate his environment more successfully; and he knows that "weathering the storm" is preferable to dying. So the role of Treebeard and the Ents is a precisely limited one, just as was Tom's earlier in the novel. Treebeard goes to battle against the immediately present danger, Saruman, because Saruman has destroyed the trees and threatens the search for the Ent-wives, their principal objective. That is, I suppose, the most convincing illustration of the view of nature which the Ents represent, for without their mates they are doomed. There are no Entlings, and so the search for the Ent-wives is by far more important than all the Rings of Power ever created. Like Tom, then, they are basically amoral, reacting to the nature of changing circumstances by adapting themselves. Nonetheless they maintain a level of compassion, evidenced in their release of Saruman from Orthanc. He could do no lasting harm, at least to them, and as a part of nature itself, the Ents consider the freedom of another creature of greater importance than any abstraction, such as keeping promises: "Now do not tell, Gandalf, that I promised to keep him safe; for I know it. But things have changed since then. And I kept him until he was safe, safe from doing any more harm. You should know that above all I hate the caging of live things, and that I will not keep even such creatures as these caged beyond great need." (III, p. 319)

The last of the clearly expressed attitudes toward nature is that attributed to Sauron and his minions. What is perhaps most remarkable about this attitude is how closely associated it is with the attitudes of Gandalf and the Captains of the West. This similarity should not be surprising, though, if we remember that both Sauron and the Captains of the West are cut from the tragic mold and that the ideas they express are simply two sides of the same coin. Sauron sees nature as that which can, should, and must be manipulated for his own purposes. Witness, for example, the shroud of darkness and fog that surrounds Gondor immediately prior to and during the great battle surrounding that city. The mornings came like a "brown dusk," (III, p. 108) and "the darkness weighed heavier on men's hearts, and a great dread was on them." The darkness is both a physical condition and an emanation from Sauron. It is nature responding to his will and being manipulated to serve his ends. Since those ends are evil, then the results are unpleasant for all those who are good. Likewise, the lands under Sauron's sway reflect his will. The Dead Marshes are his creation, and they serve his purposes—to repel intruders and to safeguard Mordor from its enemies. They are monstrously unpleasant largely because they are shifting tombs of the dead whom Sauron has enslaved:

It was dreary and wearisome. Cold clammy winter still held sway in this forsaken country. The only green was the scum of livid weed on the dark greasy surfaces of the sullen waters. Dead grasses and rotting reeds loomed up in the mists like ragged shadows of long-forgotten summers. (II, p. 195)

. . . I saw them: grim faces and evil, and weeds in their silver hair. But all foul, all rotting, all dead. A fell light is in them. (II, p. 297)

More important for our consideration, however, is the fact that Sauron has, thus, taken an elemental fact of nature and, by his will and his power, changed its very face and laws. Thus has the tragic hero ever sought to make the world conform to his view of it and to reflect his will.

But the Captains of the West are no different in attitude, though the effects of their attitude are generally intended as good, at least for a time. The caverns of Moria, those deep delvings of the dwarves, were intended as things of beauty, but it was precisely those intentions of good, those aspirations for forcing nature to produce things of beauty and desirability to humans, that awoke Durin's Bane, the flame of Udun which brought Gandalf the Grey to ruin. Saruman and Denethor both sought to use the palantir to see the present and the future and thereby to gain power over nature and events, and it was this same palantir that brought one to flaming death and one to ignominious slaughter by an angry Grima Wormtongue. Even the Lady Galadriel, wielder of one of the Three, hidden from the eyes of Sauron, cannot help but manipulate nature to the ends that best serve her and her people, and yet the end is ultimately the destruction of that land when she must leave. Lothlorien must fade away, for its power has been based on the power of the Rings, and the Rings made their possessors rulers over all things which came under their spell. Gandalf and the Captains of the West do not desire the destruction of nature and nature's creatures, but because they must seek to bend all things to their will, just as Sauron must seek to bend all things to his, they do in fact bring destruction on a scale more enormous than has previously been seen in all of Middle Earth.

So both Sauron and the Captains of the West must ultimately pass away. The Captains of the West are successful in their quest to defeat Sauron, and Aragorn will rule as King for a time, but ultimately the Third Age of Middle Earth will pass away. And, interestingly enough, those characters will survive who regard themselves as something other than rulers. Tom will remain, the Ents will remain, and the hobbits will remain. It is not coincidence that all of these characters see themselves as an integral part of nature and as being parts of a whole, the existence of which is more important than is its mastery.

Much of what has been said about the various attitudes toward nature has a direct bearing on the effect human action has on nature. However, two different kinds of examples should make these effects much clearer; they will also illustrate the differences between the ecological and the tragic perspectives.

Many unattractive landscapes appear in *Lord of the Rings*. The land outside of Bree, the land between Rivendell and Moria, and all the land surrounding Isengard exhibit similar qualities of barrenness, desolation, and harshness. However, it is in the land immediately surrounding and inside the walls of Mordor where these qualities are best exhibited.

Dreadful as the Dead Marshes had been, and the arid moors of the Nomanlands, more loathsome far was the country that the crawling day now slowly unveiled to his shrinking eyes. Even to the Mere of Dead Faces some haggard phantom of green spring would come; but here neither spring nor summer would ever come again. Here nothing lived, not even the leprous growths that feed on rottenness. The gasping pools were choked with ash and crawling muds, sickly white and grey, as if the mountains had vomited the filth of their entrails upon the lands about. High mounds of crushed and powdered rock, great cones of earth fire-blasted and poisoned-stained, stood like an obscene graveyard in endless rows, slowly revealed in the reluctant light.

They had come to the desolation that lay before Mordor: the lasting monument to the dark labour of its slaves that should endure when all their purposes were made void; a land defiled, diseased beyond all healing—unless the Great Sea should enter in and wash it with oblivion. (II, p. 302)

The remarkable similarity of this description to those of the slag heaps, garbage dumps, and ghettos of modern cities should be immediately apparent. Of perhaps greater significance, however, is the fact that this is seen as the conscious creation of Sauron. There is no purpose to its creation, save that it reflects the will of its creator, and the effects of that will cannot be erased by the Captains of the West no matter how complete their victory. Moreover, it is clear that this savagery, this ugliness and desolation, is a direct reflection of choices which have been made, for as Frodo, Sam, and Gollum travel away from the entrances to Mordor, the land improves. As Tolkien puts it, "The growing light revealed to them a land already less barren and ruinous. . . . It seemed good to be reprieved, to walk in a land that had only been for a few years under the dominion of the Dark Lord and was not yet fallen wholly into decay." (II, p. 325) By this means, Tolkien makes it apparent that the amount of desolation increases according to the number of years spent under the dominion of the Dark Lord and the proximity of the land to the center of the Dark Lord's power and purpose.

The land within Mordor moves beyond a merely physical description, for it more clearly than anything else within the novel becomes symbolic. With its sharp, jagged crags, its twisted, dragon-shaped stones that had been "vomited from the tormented earth," and the swirling smoke and fire, the land within Mordor represents hell itself. Reminiscent of Milton's hell, it is a place of fire without light and of torment without hope. The land is also described in terms reminiscent of the plain of fire in the sixth circle of Dante's hell: "Between them and the smoking mountain, and about it north and south, all seemed ruinous and dead, a desert burned and choked." (III, p. 245) Perhaps most significant about this dead land is that it robs those who inhabit it of even the knowledge of other conditions. When Sam tries to lighten Frodo's heart by reminding him of earlier good times they had experienced (Sam can do so because he is not tied to Mordor by the weight of the Ring), Frodo's reply is remarkable in what it reveals about the relationship between creatures and an environment to which they are inextricably tied: " 'No, I am afraid not, Sam,' said Frodo. 'At least, I know that such things happened, but I cannot see them. No taste of food, no feel of water, no sound of wind, no memory of trees or grass or flower, no image of moon or star are left to me. I am naked in the dark, Sam, and there is no veil between me and the wheel of fire. I begin to see it even with my waking eyes, and all else fades.' " (III, p. 264)

The effects of human action on the environment, then, are simple. It creates a living hell, not because the environment is a reflection of humanity's moral or spiritual evil, but because it reflects humanity's own absolute will. In the tragic tradition, Sauron assumes that his will is all that is needed. Just as orcs, balrogs, demons, and trolls are made to serve him, so too is nature designed to serve him and his needs. Just as his arrogance in asserting his rule over all living creatures is the direct cause of the deformation and death of so many, so too his arrogance in controlling the weather and his "re-modeling" the entire land of Mordor and its surroundings are the direct causes of the barrenness and desolation which effectively deny the possibility of the continued existence of any successful ecological model.

A second example which illustrates this point is somewhat easier to understand because it is less dramatic and less obviously symbolic. That example is found in what happens to the Shire while Frodo, Merry, Pippin, and Sam are making their slow way home after the successful conclusion of their quest. Though often seen by critics as simply Tolkien's revulsion at the changes that the war had wrought in the English country scene, the "Scouring of the Shire" is in fact a necessary conclusion to the comic and ecological themes which have moved throughout the entire work. The description of what had happened to the landscape is well illustrated by two examples. The first occurs when Farmer Cotton describes what happened to Sandyman's mill: "But since Sharkey came they don't grind no more corn at all. They're always a-hammering and a-letting out a smoke and a stench, and there isn't no peace even at night in Hobbiton. And they pour out filth a purpose; they've fouled all the lower Water, and it's getting down into Brandywine. If they want to make the Shire a desert, they're going the right way about it." (III, p. 361) Present are all the elements of a modern industrial pollution, but also present is the knowledge that this occurs because of Sandyman's greed for more than the old mill could grind or the countryside round about it produce; because of the malice of Sharkey; because of the apathy and/or fear of the hobbit population. It is worth noting that even though the hobbits recognize what is happening, they do not take action of any kind to stop it. Failing to recognize the importance of the survival of the ecological system of which they are a part, they would allow themselves to be hustled off into a quiet and deserted grave, not because of an active and overwhelming evil like that which ruled Mordor, but because of their own unwillingness to recognize the difference between tragic revolt and comic survival.

The second example is similar to the first, but it adds two elements, the destruction of the trees and other elements specific to the environment, and the actual physical ugliness of that destruction:

It was one of the saddest hours in their lives. The great chimney rose up before them; and as they drew near the old village across the Water, through rows of new mean houses along each side of the road, they saw the new mill in all its frowning and dirty ugliness: a great brick building straddling the stream, which it fouled with a steaming and stinking outflow. All along the Bywater Road every tree had been felled.

As they crossed the bridge and looked up the Hill they gasped. Even Sam's vision in the Mirror had not prepared him for what they saw. The Old Grange on the west side had been knocked down, and its place taken by rows of tarred sheds. All the chestnuts were gone. The banks and hedgerows were broken. Great waggons were standing in disorder in a field beaten bare of grass. Bagshot Row was a yawning sand and gravel quarry. Bag End up beyond could not be seen for a clutter of large huts. (III, pp. 365–366)

Sam's reaction here is even sharper than it had been when he saw parts of this same scene in the Mirror of Galadriel much earlier. What was merely an abstraction of a possibility to him before is now presented in all its incredible ugliness and unattractiveness. It is in these last two words that we understand the difference between the ruined landscapes of Mordor and the Shire, and in that difference lies the reason why the "Scouring of the Shire" is necessary to complete the theme of the novel. It is similar to what must happen to Satan in Milton's *Paradise Lost*. In the first two books of the poem, he achieves a nobility of stature that makes him almost a tragically romantic figure, but by the time he has finished the temptation of Adam and Eve in Book IX, that stature has been reduced to its proper perspective: that of stupidity and ugliness. The same thing must happen to the romantically attractive figure of Sauron in *Lord of the Rings*, but it cannot happen directly; it happens through the agency of Saruman instead. What we see in the Shire is the evil of Sauron reduced to its essentials and stripped of a false glory and magnificence. There are no tragically evil figures in the Shire; there are only stupid and greedy ones, for that is the true nature of evil. Petty malice like that of Saruman, petty jealousy like that of Sandyman, and the petty desire to establish oneself and one's wishes as pre-eminent to those of all other creatures as well as to the environment itself are what produce the ugliness of the Shire. Those same things were, of course, what produced Sauron, but that factor is obscured by the romanticizing that surrounds him.

This tendency to romanticize evil is nothing but an attempt to romanticize good as well and, in the process, to give humanity that special place which the tragic view has always proclaimed for it. Medea was tragically evil for Euripides, Macbeth was tragically evil for Shakespeare, and Faust was tragically evil for Goethe. On the other hand, Calonice is simply lustful for Aristophanes, Volpone is stupidly greedy for Jonson, and Tartuffe is hypocritically devious for Molière. What Tolkien did in *Lord of the Rings*, then, was to present both elements. Sauron is the romantically evil figure who is battled by the romantically good Captains of the West to achieve an ultimate victory. But the victory is not ultimate, and in a sense it is not even a victory, since Gandalf and his companions must pass away as surely as must Sauron. Moreover, much as he may regret it, Tolkien acknowledges in the "Scouring of the Shire" that the war was really about preserving the system, protecting the ordinary pleasures of eating, drinking, and making love, for it is these things that are necessary if life is to continue. All the Rings of Power pass away shortly after Sauron; Aragorn and the men of Gondor will last for a longer period of time, but they too must pass away eventually. The Shire, or at least its kind of people, will remain. They will endure precisely because they are comic rather than tragic figures and precisely because they understand implicitly, if not explicitly, their own role in an overall system. The Shire recovers in part from Saruman's malice because of Galadriel's magic gift to Sam, but its survival is ensured because of the nature of its people and their understanding of their role in and relationship to the system of which they are a part.

That brings us, then, to the point of departure at which so many critics lose their way. Seeing the glory and splendor of the Captains of the West and noting Tolkien's obvious admiration and love for the kind of heroic reward presented at the Field of Cormallen, they assume that the work is a tragic, allegorical, or romantic quest tale, and they dismiss the sequence of events at the novel's conclusion as being out of place or out of tone. What they are missing is the fact of the comic tradition. It is not, I think, that Tolkien preferred or even rationally set out to construct a work which would bring home so powerfully the disastrous consequences of the tragic and the inherent possibilities of the comic. Clearly he loved the tragic for the nobility it gave to humanity; he also presented the tragic, however, as something that was no longer possible for the world if it wished to endure.

That Tolkien loved the tragic, heroic mold cannot be denied, for he writes of it with a majesty and movement which characterizes the very best of his prose. For example, he describes the last charge of Theoden in these words:

Fey he seemed, or the battle-fury of his fathers ran like new fire in his veins, and he was borne up on Snowmane like a god of old, even as Orome the Great in the battle of the Balar when the world was young. His golden shield was uncovered, and lo! it shone like an image of the Sun, and the grass flamed into green about the white feet of his steed. For morning came, morning and a wind from the sea; and darkness was removed, and the hosts of Mordor wailed, and terror took them, and they fled, and died, and the hoofs of wrath rode over them. And then all the host of Rohan burst into song, and they sang as they slew, for the joy of battle was on them, and the sound of their singing that was fair and terrible came even to the City. (III, p. 138)

Reminiscent of descriptions in *Beowulf, The Nibelungenlied,* and other of the early epic poems which Tolkien devoted so much of his life to studying, the last charge of Theoden becomes a glorious paean to humanity's worth, dignity, and importance. Theoden's joy in battle wiped out the baseness to which he had sunk under the influence of Grima Wormtongue, and it was a tragic loss when he fell. It was also a statement of the superiority of Theoden to the physical world of which he was a part and a justification of all his efforts to regain moral superiority to nature itself. He would not live, but his glory would be remembered, for he would have transcended life by his death. Now this is a magnificent picture, one immensely flattering to the human spirit. The problem is that Theoden's death solved nothing; it did not guarantee the continuance of his people and did not even guarantee the safety of those who most loved and depended on him. All it did was to affirm Theoden, to establish beyond question the tragic emphasis on the superiority of the individual to all systems. A supremely egotistical statement, Theoden's last battle lies directly in the traditions of the tragic and the heroic. It is a little like Beowulf's battle with the dragon, for there too an aged warrior fought bravely to bring greater glory to his name and, perhaps, greater safety to his world. However, it is also like Beowulf's battle in its ineffectuality. Neither Beowulf nor Theoden could defeat his enemy, and neither could, by his action, ensure anything more than the remembrance of his own name.

Perhaps the best single example of Tolkien's fondness for the tragic, heroic concept can be seen in his description of the welcome of Frodo and Sam on the Field of Cormallen. In a setting of extraordinary pageantry, richness, and regal splendor, Tolkien's prose effectively joins honor and glory with pity and joy:

"Praise them with great praise!"
And when the glad shout had swelled up and died away again, to Sam's final and complete satisfaction and pure joy, a minstrel of Gondor stood forth, and knelt, and begged leave to sing.

. . . And when Sam heard that he laughed aloud for sheer delight, and he stood up and cried: "O great glory and splendour! And all my wishes have come true!" And then he wept.

And all the host laughed and wept, and in the midst of their merriment and tears the clear voice of the minstrel rose like silver and gold, and all men were hushed. And he sang to them, now in the Elven-tongue, now in the speech of the West, until their hearts, wounded with sweet words, overflowed, and their joy was like swords, and they passed in thought out to regions where pain and delight flow together and tears are the very wine of blessedness. (III, p. 286)

Frodo and Sam have been victorious. The Captains of the West have been victorious. Wickedness and evil have been defeated, and now all are free to establish and acknowledge the reign of the King.

The problem with all of this, of course, is that the book does not end here, though many critics have suggested that it should have. Those critics would be right, if this were a heroic lay or an epic poem with a tragically triumphant hero, but *Lord of the Rings* is neither. It is a fantasy novel with an ultimately comic perspective, and for such a work the last chapters are essential. As they point out, Frodo at least has not been victorious in an ultimate sense; neither has the returned Gandalf. Neither they nor Aragorn nor any of the other tragic and heroic characters stop Saruman's brutalizing of the Shire, and none of them can stop the passing of the Third Age of Middle Earth. Sauron passes, just as Beowulf's dragon had done; but, like Beowulf, so Frodo and all those associated with the Third Age of Middle Earth had to pass. Of all the Captains of the West, only Aragorn is left, and, we are told, eventually even his line will fail. The only one who we know will survive is Sam, for in Sam and Sam's children and the life of the Shire itself there are sufficient adaptability, sufficient desire to live, and sufficient humility to make survival possible.

That is perhaps the key to understanding Tolkien's intentions in the novel. When examined carefully, it reveals that what is important is not the individual, glorious or heroic though he or she may be. What is important is the system, the continuance of the system, for only if the system continues can life continue. What is accomplished is not an ultimate victory, but a temporary respite, one which illustrates clearly that only those with the ability to adapt will continue to exist. Frodo and Gandalf and Galadriel and Elrond cannot do so, and they must pass away. Sam and Merry and Pippin can, for, as they have known all along, it is survival that is most important.

Hobbits know from the start of the novel about the relationship between themselves and nature, and they understand that they cannot rule over, dominate, or change it. When, for example, Bilbo enjoyed "(apparently) perpetual youth as well as (reputedly) inexhaustible wealth," the hobbits knew that there would be trouble: " 'It will have to paid for,' they said. 'It isn't natural, and trouble will come of it!' " (I, p. 43) Moreover, these same hobbits are interested in eating and drinking and raising children. They welcome birthday parties as a chance to feed their children at someone else's expense: "For hobbits were easy-going with their children in the matter of sitting up late, especially when there was a chance of getting them a free meal. Bringing up young hobbits took a lot of provender." (I, p. 52) Nor do these practical interests diminish during the course of the novel. When Merry and Pippin have been captured by the Orcs, for example, and the battle between the Orcs and the Riders of Rohan is raging, Pippin's comment is perfectly in line with his practical interests in surviving: "I suppose I ought to be glad that the beastly Orcs look like being destroyed, but I would rather be saved myself." (II, p. 70) Then again later as they join the Ents in the destruction of Isengard, their principal concerns are not the imprisonment of Saruman nor the defeat of his minions. Their concerns are instead the matters of finding enough food, drink, and tobacco to make themselves comfortable while waiting for their comrades. Gandalf identifies well their practical interests when he remarks: "These hobbits will sit on the edge of ruin and discuss the pleasures of the table, or the small doings of their fathers, grandfathers, and great-grandfathers, and remoter cousins to the ninth degree, if you encourage them with undue patience. Some other time would be more fitting for the history of smoking." (III, p. 208) It is noteworthy that, for Gandalf, "some other time would be more fitting," while for the hobbits it is always fitting to take the pleasures available at a given moment.

What is true of hobbits in general is even more true of Sam in particular. From the very beginning, Sam's interest in the quest differs sharply from that of the "noble" characters. He wants to go to "see the elves," to accompany Frodo, and to discover whether oliphaunts really exist. His concern for the quest is founded on his concern for Frodo, and when he has the chance to become the Ringbearer himself he quickly rejects it because he knows his own nature so well: "Of course not, for the Ring'll be found, and there'll be no more songs. I can't help it. My place is by Mr. Frodo. They must understand that—

Elrond and the Council, and the great Lords and Ladies with all their wisdom. Their plans have gone wrong. I can't be their Ring-bearer. Not without Mr. Frodo." (II, p. 438) He cannot commit himself to the abstraction of the quest at this point any more than he could have at the beginning of the journey. He can only commit himself to a person out of love and friendship. Thus it is reality, not the abstraction to which he is committed, as he indicates when he understands that Frodo is not actually dead: "You fool, he isn't dead, and your heart knew it. Don't trust your head, Samwise, it is not the best part of you." (II, p. 444)

This sudden insight on Sam's part is not news to any reader who has followed Sam's activities carefully throughout the novel. It was Sam, after all, who was interested in the practical matters of the quest from the beginning. Whether the company had a rope when they left Rivendell, whether Bill the pony would survive outside the gates of Moria, whether he and Frodo had enough food to make it both to *and* from the Mount of Doom!—these were Sam's concerns rather than anyone else's. And the difference between Sam's and Frodo's views was even more clearly revealed early in the novel when the two of them looked into the Mirror of Galadriel. Frodo's vision included the risen Gandalf, various scenes of the upcoming war, and finally the eye of Sauron himself. Though tied to the reality of the quest, each of these items involved more nearly than anything else an abstraction or a symbol that threatened to engulf Frodo. Sam's visions, however, were limited to the Shire being defaced and to Frodo lying on the stairs of Cirith Ungol, neither of them even remotely connected with an abstraction. The defacement of the Shire appealed to Sam's love for the land and his sense of being a part of it; Frodo lying on the stairs appealed to his love for and loyalty to another of his own kind. And Sam's response to the vision in the mirror is perfectly in tune with his character as was demonstrated in all other examples which were shown. He first decides he must immediately go back to the Shire, then reluctantly agrees to continue the quest for reasons that are abundantly clear: " 'I wish I had never come here, and I don't want to see no more magic,' he said and fell silent. After a moment he spoke again thickly, as if struggling with tears. 'No, I'll go home by the long road with Mr. Frodo, or not at all,' he said. 'But I hope I do get back some day. If what I've seen turns out true, somebody's going to catch it hot!' " (I, p. 470) It is this desire to return that moves Sam to insist that, after the destruction of the Ring in the heart of Mount Doom, he and Frodo move down its slopes so that they can endure a little while longer, so that they can have a better chance of rescue. Frodo considers his task complete with the destruction of the Ring; Sam wants to live, not because good has been ultimately triumphant, but because living is itself a good thing.

So it is Sam who finally ends the novel, Sam surrounded by his wife Rose and his daughter Elanor. It is worthwhile to note that no other major character in the novel is even remotely associated with children and family and the continuance of life. There are other marriages, those of Aragorn with Arwen and Faramir with Eowyn, but in both cases Tolkien describes the marriages in terms of the courtly, chivalric love that is far from the kind of comfortably realistic setting of Sam and Rose. Moreover, it is appropriate that Sam end the novel on the same kind of instinctual plane with which the entire affair of the Ring had begun with Bilbo. Bilbo had refused to kill Gollum when he had the opportunity to do so. Sam had done the same thing on Mount Doom when Gollum so richly deserved death:

It would be just to slay this treacherous, murderous creature, just and many times deserved; and also it seemed the only safe thing to do. But deep in his heart there was something that restrained him: he could not strike this thing lying in the dust, forlorn, ruinous, utterly wretched. He himself, though only for a little while, had borne the Ring, and now dimly he guessed the agony of Gollum's shrivelled mind and body, enslaved to that Ring, unable to find peace or relief ever in life again. (III, p. 173)

Sam's refusal to kill Gollum comes not from a creed or a dogma, but from an unwillingness to kill a fellow creature and a sympathy for Gollum which arose from their sharing of a common experience. Thus, at the conclusion of the novel, when Frodo leaves on his final journey, there is no question about Sam's coming. As Frodo says to Sam: "But you will be healed. You were meant to be whole, and you will be." (III, p. 379) Sam is whole at the end of the novel just as he was at its beginning. He has not changed, though he has proved that he can adapt to changing situations. From this perspective, then, the conclusion of the novel makes ultimate sense. The noble characters pass away; Sam and the other hobbits continue, and it is this continuance around which *Lord of the Rings* centers, though I am not at all sure that Tolkien was happy with that continuance. Sam was, in some ways, his Sancho Panza, and try as he might and lament it as he clearly did, Tolkien clearly recognizes by that characterization the necessity of the passage of the heroic, tragic age and the emergence of the comic and ecological perspective.

One idea remains to be examined before concluding this look at Tolkien's relation to the ecological perspectives discussed earlier in this book. That idea is Tolkien's insistence that the survival of the system is of ultimate importance.

One of the first and earliest examples of this acknowledgment of a system which encompasses everything and which surpasses individual existences occurs as Frodo cites Bilbo's old poem and then explains what Bilbo meant by it:

> The Road goes ever on and on
>> Down from the door where it began.
> Now far ahead the Road has gone
>> And I must follow, if I can,
> Pursuing it with weary feet
>> Until it joins some larger way,
> Where many paths and errands meet.
>> And whither then? I cannot say.

. . . He used often to say there was only one Road; that it was like a great river: its springs were at every doorstep, and every path was its tributary. "It's a dangerous business, Frodo, going out of your door," he used to say. "You step into the Road, and if you don't keep your feet, there is no knowing where you might be swept off to." (I, p. 110)

Bilbo was, of course, generalizing from his own experience, and Frodo, at the time he repeats the poem and explanation, does not understand what they mean. But, in terms of the complete novel, their meaning is perfectly clear. All things are interrelated; all things are dependent upon each other, and to attempt either to withdraw from or to rule over the world is likely to bring destruction of self as it brings destruction of the system. There is no implication of a destiny which shapes all ends, but there is a clear implication of an overall system of which all things are a part, to which all things must contribute, and for which all things are responsible. Frodo had commented earlier in the novel that he wanted to save the Shire because "I feel that as long as the Shire lies behind, safe and comfortable, I shall find wandering more bearable: I shall know that somewhere there is a firm foothold, even if my feet cannot stand there again." (I, p. 96) These are not the words of a hero of either a tragedy or a chivalric quest; they are the words of a figure who undertakes a task for the practical reason that he knows that unless the system survives he cannot survive, and because he has perhaps a better chance of accomplishing the task than anyone else. Gandalf, Aragorn, Galadriel, Elrond, and all the other noble characters refuse even to take the Ring because of their fear of being corrupted by it, just as Saruman, Boromir, and Denethor are destroyed by it or the desire for it. Frodo the hobbit, however, can take it because he holds a humility which none of the others possess, because like other hobbits he understands that he is only a small part of a great whole over which he cannot and does not want to reign. Tolkien sums this up nicely when he has Sam reject the Ring for reasons closely aligned to what Frodo has explained so much earlier in the novel: ". . . but also deep down in him lived still unconquered his plain hobbit-sense: he knew in the core of his heart that he was not large enough to bear such a burden, even if such visions were not a mere cheat to betray him. The one small garden of a free gardener was all his need and due, not a garden swollen to a realm; his own hands to use, not the hands of others to command." (III, p. 216) Common sense, humility, and acknowledgment that one belongs to a larger system whose survival is essential to the survival of individual members—these are the qualities, combined with the insistence on experience and the heart rather than on abstractions, which move Frodo and Sam initially; and it is Frodo's ultimate rejection of these qualities and Sam's adherence to them which makes inevitable Frodo's passing away and Sam's remaining at the end of the novel.

The second example occurs just after Gandalf has explained to Theoden about Ents. Theoden, in his response, outlines clearly the falsity of the views which humans have held and, by implication, sets the stage for the departure of himself and all other characters whose philosophy has been that they must rule the world which they inhabit:

The king was silent. "Ents!" he said at length. "Out of the shadows of legend I begin to understand the marvel of the trees, I think. I have lived to see strange days. Long we have tended our beasts and our fields, built houses, wrought our tools, or ridden away to help in the wars of Minas Tirith. And that we called the life of Men, the way of the world. We cared little for what lay beyond the borders of our land. Songs we have that tell of these things,

but we are forgetting them, teaching them only to children, as a careless cus-
tom. And now the songs have come down among us out of strange places,
and walk visible under the sun." (II, p. 197)

What Theoden says is what each of the noble characters in the novel
has believed and acted upon at one time or another. Now there has
been a difference in the extent of the rule they have practiced. Gandalf and Elrond, for example, have sought to rule much as Shakespeare's Prospero sought to rule his desert island, with only that degree of firmness necessary to bring about the order which they saw as
desirable. Sauron, on the other hand, sought to rule absolutely and to
impose without exception his own rigid controls over all creatures, to
transform them and their world in their own image, and it is for that
reason that both groups must pass; it is perhaps for that reason that
the two groups are so inextricably wed, a wedding which is acknowledged explicitly many times in the novel. What Theoden has recognized is that humanity is but one part of an incredibly complex system
that humanity has effectively ignored due to its own egotistical assumption that only its own perception of the world is real and its life
and kind the only life and kind that matters. The Ents have proved
to Theoden the wrongness of that view, just as the Fellowship's earlier
experiences on Caradhras and in Lothlorien had proved to them the
folly of assuming the superiority of humanity and its views to all other
parts of the system. Ents, dwarves, hobbits, elves, orcs, men, eagles,
horses, balrogs, weather, mountains, and rivers are all a part of the
system, and each occupies a place that must be acknowledged and dealt
with. To fail to do so is to doom oneself and possibly the creatures for
whom one may have direct responsibility to isolation and ultimately
to extinction.

The final example occurs during the bitter exchange between Denethor and Gandalf just after Gandalf has come to Minas Tirith. When
Denethor remarks that Minas Tirith is his alone to rule unless the king
comes again, Gandalf pointedly reminds him of the fact that they are
all stewards:

Well, my lord Steward, it is your task to keep some kingdom still against that
event, which few now look to see. In that task you shall have all the aid that
you are pleased to ask for. But I will say this: the rule of no realm is mine,
neither of Gondor nor any other, great or small. But all worthy things are in
peril as the world now stands, those are my care. And for my part, I shall not

wholly fail of my task, though Gondor should perish, if anything passes through this night that can still grow fair or bear fruit and flower again in days to come. For I am also a steward. (III, p. 33)

This remarkable exchange occurs after Gandalf the Grey has passed and Gandalf the White has returned, as it were, from the dead. What is perhaps even more significant, however, is what it reveals about the ultimate importance of Gandalf and, by implication, about all the other noble characters who pass away: their existence is less important than the continued existence of the system. Galadriel acknowledges this fact when she refuses the Ring which Frodo offered to her freely: " 'I pass the test,' she said. 'I will diminish, and go into the West, and remain Galadriel.' " (I, p. 474) Even Frodo ultimately acknowledges this fact when, at the conclusion of the novel, he tells Sam, "I tried to save the Shire, and it has been saved, but not for me. It must often be so, Sam, when things are in danger: some one has to give them up, lose them, so that others may keep them." (p. 382) Ultimately, then, that is Tolkien's justification for all the noble characters. They act, he implies, to save the Shire for Sam and Barliman Butterbur, and then they pass away when their task is fulfilled. Thus their heroism, their tragic loss is in some measure justified, and the exalted status given them is clearly merited. Gandalf puts it best when he describes the war the Captains of the West carry to the very gates of Barad-dur:

We must walk open-eyed into that trap, with courage, but small hope for ourselves. For, my lords, it may well prove that we ourselves shall perish utterly in a black battle far from the living lands; so that even if Barad-dur be thrown down, we shall not live to see a new age. But this, I deem, is our duty. And better so than to perish nonetheless—as we surely shall if we sit here—and know as we die that no new age shall be. (III, pp. 191–192)

These are brave words, and they are matched by noble actions which are ultimately rewarded when Frodo and Sam complete the quest, when Gollum destroys the Ring and himself at the same time. But the victory means nothing insofar as the survival of the noble characters is concerned. Yes, Aragorn will reign, and Eomer along with Faramir and Eowyn will hold sway in Rohan, but eventually even their lines will pass, just as the line of Gandalf, Elrond, Galadriel, and that of the Ring-bearer himself has passed. There is no place, no time left for them in the new world that is to be inhabited by Sam and the rich fruitfulness of the Shire.

And that is, I think, the conclusion to which Tolkien ultimately leads his readers in what is perhaps the greatest work of fantasy ever written. The noble, heroic, tragic age has passed, and in that passing is a great sadness, for there was beauty, charm, and an incredible appeal in the portraits of humanity which it painted and the positions in which humanity was placed in relation to the rest of the created universe. In spite of all those things, it is clear that the passage had to come. It was simply not possible to continue in that vein, for to do so would be to predict, nay to demand, the destruction of the species as well as the system. Sauron was possible because Gandalf was possible, and Frodo, when he adopted the perspective of one, embraced the destruction which was an inevitable result of either point of view. Thus I think that Hugh Keenan was ultimately correct when he insisted that "the major appeal of *The Lord of the Rings* grows from its underlying and pervasive presentation of the struggle of Life against Death."[6]

Life is affirmed in *Lord of the Rings*. The survival of the system is clearly more important than the survival of one individual; as a matter of fact, the survival of the individual is made possible only through the survival of the system. The survivors, Sam and the other hobbits, reject abstractions in favor of food, drink, comfort, and generation, and their role throughout is to remind us that those who dedicate themselves to abstractions of whatever kind are finally doomed to fail and to die. Nature in *Lord of the Rings* is seen from two perspectives: the perspective of the noble characters breeds destruction of the physical landscape as well as destruction of the life forms which inhabit it, and the perspective of the hobbits breeds gardens and forests and complex partnerships which result in a new richness for all engaged in such partnerships. These are the things that *Lord of the Rings* does directly. Indirectly it reaffirms the purpose and potential of its own form, the novel, for a novel it most certainly is. Like Lewis's novels, it is a new kind of novel, a "romantic" novel in precisely the same sense in which the term will be defined in the next chapter.

Toward the conclusion of *Steps to an Ecology of Mind*, Bateson makes a comment about the relationship between nature, art, philosophy, and survival which applies directly to what *Lord of the Rings* accomplishes and why it stands as the pivotal point for the development and tradition of the genre of the fantasy novel:

> Anthropologically, it would seem from what we know of the early material, that man in society took clues from the natural world around him and applied those clues in a sort of metaphoric way to the society in which he lived. That is, he identified with or empathized with the natural world around him and took that empathy as a guide for his own social organization and his own theories of his own psychology. This was what is called "totemism."
> In a way it was all nonsense, but it made more sense than most of what we do today, because the natural world around us has this general systemic structure and is therefore an appropriate metaphor to enable man to understand himself in his social organization.
> . . . But when you separate mind from the structure in which it is immanent, such as human relationship, the human society, or the ecosystem, you thereby embark, I believe, on fundamental error, which in the end will surely hurt you.[7]

Lord of the Rings concludes that humanity's behavior and social structure must be based on the natural laws of the universe in which it finds itself, on the fact that it is a part of a larger system upon whose survival its own depends. It also concludes that literature grows out of that relationship and that it takes its metaphors from those same natural laws. When all of these conclusions are taken together, their sum is a richness of art, a renewal of faith in the possibilities of life, and an enhanced understanding of the relationship—not only between art and life—but between ourselves as individual creatures and ourselves as parts of an incredibly more complex whole than the old tragic philosophy could ever imagine.

3

C. S. LEWIS

In a very real sense, C. S. Lewis is the most problematic of all the fantasy writers considered in this book. First, Lewis is writing directly out of the Christian tradition in each of his four novels. Second, Lewis's novels are constructed on the basis of a critical doctrine that is avowedly romantic and platonic, with many of the characters being obvious allegorical or symbolic representations of Christian dogma and tradition. Third, Lewis's novels, with the exception of *Till We Have Faces*, are set in present times and make use of current technological systems and theories. Finally, Lewis's ideas concerning the system of order which governs a properly functioning universe insist upon the spiritual as well as the physical, something that is usually in direct conflict with either ecological ideas or the comic tradition.

In spite of these apparent contradictions, however, Lewis stands as one of the clearest examples of how fantasy integrates the comic and ecological traditions into a romantic fabric to create a new novel and a new critical perspective for the philosophical and ethical traditions which that new kind of novel requires. In order to understand how these apparent contradictions are resolved, it is useful to begin by looking briefly at Lewis's concept of myth, his ties to the romantic tradition, and the new kind of novelistic form that he created.

LEWIS AND MYTH

To arrive at an understanding of what Lewis means by myth and the effect of that myth on his own theories of literature, we may begin with his description of himself as a literary dinosaur. What he meant by such a statement was that he was a survivor of a much older time and system of values, and more particularly that he was a survivor of a myth quite different from that under which the modern world operates. Helen Fowler says that Lewis describes himself as a "survivor from the old Western culture, which had one of its peaks in the Age of Romance, and as one of the few people alive today to whom its language is native."[1]

Lewis's idea arises from a particular set of conditions under which he sees history operating. In "De Descriptione Temporum" he outlines those conditions with a definition of three historic periods: Pre-Christian, Christian, and Post-Christian. This view becomes particularly important because of Lewis's insistence that a much greater difference lies between the latter two than between the first two: "I am not here considering either the christening or the un-christening from a theological point of view. I am considering them simply as cultural changes. When I do that, it appears to me that the second change is even more radical than the first. Christians and Pagans had much more in common with each other than either has with a Post-Christian."[2] This cultural change, then, is for Lewis an integral part of a change in philosophy or in myth, at least myth as the basic assumptions by which a society guides itself.

It is important to realize that Lewis is not simply bemoaning the loss of a particular myth in the Post-Christian era. He is rather insisting that every historical era has operated under some concept of myth that has been embodied in either written or oral literature. The modern myth, however, is significantly different in that its base is not in any kind of organic metaphor, but in an inorganic, lifeless, and mechanistic one which is divorced completely from its original source. It is the myth of the machine, the myth which inherently defines the newer and more progressive as better and more true than that which has come before; and, since Lewis finds order and truth to have always existed in the world, he sees this idea as false both logically and theologically. Thus his distinction is essentially between true and false myth.

True myth for Lewis relates to that element of being that contains universal truth caused by an unconditioned reality at the heart of things. Myth aids reality by picture-making, and it is thus by nature both a literary and an extraliterary quality. Dabney Adams Hart, in what is perhaps the best study of Lewis's poetics, insists that Lewis's claim for the instinctive imagination as the criterion of reality depends on his conviction that myth is the embodiment of universal truth, a belief which depends on the validity of the imagination.[3] Hart goes on to define the effect of this belief on Lewis's literary theories in these terms:

Lewis conceives of myth in much wider perspective. He feels that the same power of human imagination which created the old myths and which responds to them in new forms can also create new myths just as valid as the old ones. This creation of a story or an image which expresses and haunts the imagination with an inexplicable significance is what Lewis means by myth-making. He affirms that its myth-making power makes poetry more meaningful than rational exposition.[4]

The qualities and operative powers of myth Lewis outlines clearly in *An Experiment in Criticism*. First, the myth is extraliterary. It springs from a source that is intuitive and is too clear for words to be able to capture it. Second, it is felt to be inevitable and is chiefly valuable in introducing humanity to a permanent object of contemplation. Third, human sympathy is held to a minimum in it. We may feel that the pattern of the character's movements has profound relevance to our own life, but we do not imaginatively transport ourselves into the character's world. Fourth, myth is always fantastic, involving the supernatural or the unfamiliar in order to strip the veil of familiarity from humanity's eyes. Fifth, the myth itself may be sad or joyful, but it is ever grave, for it deals with that which goes even beyond the tragic. Sixth and last, the experience of myth is always awe-inspiring and numinous. It moves individuals through a sense of wonder, and its effect is to make them desire to join themselves to that which they may apprehend intuitively. Lewis clarifies this last point in a letter written in September of 1956: "My view wd. be that a good myth (i.e. a story out of which ever varying meanings will grow for different readers and in different ages) is a higher thing than an allegory (into which *one* meaning has been put). Into an allegory a man can put only what he already knows; in a myth he puts what he does not yet know and cd. not come by in any other way."[5] Thus, in Lewis's concept of myth there is ever an element of conflict, the conflict arising from the difference between those faculties which demand to know and apprehend rationally and those faculties which claim to know and represent truths intuitively.

LEWIS AND THE ROMANTIC TRADITION

The theory of literature that evolves from Lewis's idea of myth is significantly different from either the tradition of formal realism that was the basis for the original growth of the novel or the "new" realism that led to the experimental and/or existential novel in the twentieth century. That is, Lewis's ideas are Platonic rather than Aristotelian, drawing far more from the medieval other-worldliness and romantic idealism than from the ideas of Cartesian or scientific reality. Furthermore, his theories of reality undercut formal realism by suggesting that the distinction between myth and history is an arbitrary one based on the premise of evil and the fall of humanity, a result of separations in the universe never meant to exist. Thus, Lewis's theory of literature is basically romantic. Like the basic romantic ideas, Lewis's own theory suggests a universe which is both eternal and ineffably good. The result is that he chooses a fictional form for these ideas which is unique in that it takes the prose narrative form of the novel, but embodies the basic doctrines of romanticism and the creative imagination. Lewis is interested in humanity and things, not only as he can see them, but also as they become a part of a rich, full, and complex picture in which they are transformed to their true shape and purpose.

The basis for Lewis's affiliation with the romantic tradition comes from his quarrel with the modern age. The modern age, as Lewis understands it, operates under two assumptions, one of realism and one of science as the myth that embodies that realism, and both of these assumptions are false, for they are ridiculously self-contradictory:

The Myth asks me to believe that reason is simply the unforeseen and unintended by-product of a mindless process at one stage of its endless and aimless becoming. The content of the Myth thus knocks out from under me the only ground on which I could possibly believe the Myth to be true. If my own mind is a product of the irrational—if what seem my clearest reasonings are only the way in which a creature conditioned as I am bound to feel—how shall I trust my mind when it tells me about Evolution?[6]

Thus what Lewis is rejecting is not reality nor even reason, for his own reason led him to both Christianity and romanticism, but what he is rejecting is a reality that is superficial, misleading, or both. He goes on to note in *An Experiment in Criticism* that almost all stories before the nineteenth century, when the novel assumed real dominance, were true to life, but only when given an improbable set of original circumstances. Tales related what was unusual rather than what was usual. As Lewis says, "On the one hand, we can say that the only good fictions are those which belong to the second type, the family of *Middlemarch*: fictions of which we can say without reservation 'Life is like this.' If we do that we shall have against us the literary practice and experience of nearly the whole race."[7]

If we accept this kind of realism, we must reject myth, allegory, and all that they embody as well as rejecting experience itself in favor of an abstraction about experience. That, of course, is precisely what Lewis was unwilling to do, since he felt that myth and experience held ultimate reality rather than the kind of realism portrayed in the traditional novelistic patterns. As he puts it in a letter of February 8, 1956:

Actually, it seems to me that one can hardly say anything either bad enough or good enough about life. The one picture that is utterly false is the supposed realistic fiction of the XIX century where all the real horrors and heavens are excluded. The reality is a queer mixture of idyll, tragedy, farce, melodrama: and the characters (even the same character) far better *and* worse than ever are imagined.[8]

Formal nineteenth century realism, then, is simply the worship of a false god, the worship of appearance rather than what is portended or signified.

Lewis's attempt to arrive at a definition of true myth marks the war between the rationalist, the romantic, and the Christian, a war that continues throughout his career and forms one of the major sources of tension in his novels. But the dominance of the romantic is really never in doubt, for Lewis began his writing, as he notes in *Surprised by Joy*, with beast fables and created kingdoms and ended his career with a space trilogy and an ancient Greek myth recast in Christian form. As he himself said, "The imaginative man in me is older, more continuously operative, and in that sense more basic than either the religious writer or the critic."[9]

LEWIS AND THE ROMANTIC NOVEL

To embody this combination of myth, romanticism, and orthodox Christianity, Lewis created a new kind of novelistic form, for, as he noted in *Allegory of Love*, the traditional form of the novel had become a "stereotyped monotony" because of its "threadbare motives." The new form was a type of prose fiction similar to the novel, but to the novel that might have emerged from a romantic or comic tradition rather than from an eighteenth-century rationalism. The requirements for the new form were that it be prose fiction, that it provide the author with a popular format into which he or she could work the material, and that it offer ways to strip the veil of familiarity from common objects. Perhaps most important of all was Lewis's insistence that it be true to the total experience of humanity, a truth which went beyond superficial reality to point out those things that were intuitively and experientially true in the sense of being permanent. What he sought to create was an inner truth that was often strange and fanciful but was also inherently more faithful to reality than merely objective reality had ever been.

Now, Lewis did not care whether his creations were called novels or something else. As he says in "On Science Fiction," "It may very well be convenient not to call such things novels. If you prefer, call them a very special form of novels. Either way, the conclusion will be much the same: They are to be tried by their own rules."[10] Whether Lewis cared or not, it is important to understand that the Space Trilogy and *Till We Have Faces* are novels, fantasy novels, and that in their creation and critical justification Lewis makes a major contribution to the establishment of the fantasy novel as the kind of alternative that is so much the concern of this book. That the Space Trilogy and *Till We Have Faces* are novels is unquestionable, for, though they deal with myth, space, and magic, they are true to a vision of reality that begins with what Ian Watt has called formal realism, but which goes far beyond both it and the psychological pretensions of the stream-of-consciousness novel. They do so by affirming the total experience of humanity, thereby placing themselves at the heart of the comic, ecological tradition and squarely in defiance of both the tragic ideal and the false myths propounded by "scientism" and formal realism.

THE NOVELS AND EXPERIENCE

Perhaps the most surprising element of Lewis's novels is their unabashed emphasis upon experience rather than abstraction. In a slightly different way in each of the four novels, Lewis rejects abstraction, whether scientific, religious, or philosophical, because it leads to disaster on a number of levels. On one level it leads directly to environmental catastrophe; on another to physical death; and on still another to spiritual desolation. Obviously, then, Lewis's concept goes beyond the simpler phenomena of physical existence, for it includes those aspects of experience which Kant called *a priori*, things which we know but cannot demonstrate factually, things such as space, time, and even God. What is most amazing of all, however, is that Lewis renders everything in terms of physical being. Even in *Perelandra*, the most obviously allegorical and certainly the most didactic of all his novels in terms of Christian doctrine, all the characters come to act and believe (or to disbelieve) on the basis of their physical beings and experience. Likewise, they ultimately come to salvation and/or destruction based on the sum total of their actions.

In *Out of the Silent Planet*, Lewis makes it clear that the principal distinction between Ransom on the one hand and Weston or Devine on the other is one of preferring experience and what it teaches to abstraction and what it teaches. From the beginning of the novel, Ransom usually relies on experience and so long as he does so is capable of enjoying fully the world of which he is a part. This point is illustrated early in the novel, just after Ransom has been kidnapped and taken aboard the space ship bound for Mars. His initial reaction to his new environment is one of fear and disorientation, but even that is qualified by his sense of excitement which the various physical sensations provided: "Ransom was by now thoroughly frightened—not with the prosaic fright that a man suffers in a war, but with a heady, bounding kind of fear that was hardly distinguishable from his general excitement: he was poised on a sort of emotional watershed from which, he felt, he might at any moment pass into delirious terror or into an ecstasy of joy."[11] As his awareness grows, so ought his fears to grow, but once again his experiences militate against that approach, forcing him to acknowledge the difference between such abstractions as "ought" and the sensations surrounding him: "All this, as I have said, was sufficiently disquieting. The odd thing was that it did not very greatly disquiet him. It is hard for a man to brood on the future when he is feeling so extremely well as Ransom now felt." (pp. 30–31)

This same pattern of experience running squarely up against abstractions is carried throughout the novel. Ransom's imagining about the creatures of Malacandra, for example, paints them as horrible beyond belief: "Loathing of insects, loathing of snakes, loathing of things that squashed and squelched, all played their horrible symphonies over his nerves. But the reality would be worse: it would be an extra-terrestrial Otherness—something one had never thought of, never could have thought of." (p. 35) And yet when he meets and deals with some of those creatures, he learns the true difference between experience and abstraction or imagination:

They arose when the rationality of the *hross* tempted you to think of it as a man. Then it became abominable—a man seven feet high with a snaky body, covered, face and all, with thick black animal hair, and whiskered like a cat. But starting from the other end you had an animal with everything an animal ought to have—glossy coat, liquid eye, sweet breath and whitest teeth—and added to all these, as though Paradise had never been lost and earliest dreams were true, the charm of speech and reason. Nothing could be more disgusting than the one impression; nothing more delightful than the other. It all depended on point of view. (p. 58)

Abstraction and/or imagination had led Ransom to impose the same standards upon this new environment that he had applied to his previous ones, and yet experience had taught him that each environment on earth was different and might well require not only different mind sets but different actions to prosper. Thus, at least in the beginning, Ransom is as much a bringer of abstractions to Malacandra as are Weston and Devine, and the novel is as much about his growing awareness of the difference between abstraction and experience as it is about Malacandra as a symbol of the world prior to the fall. The difference between Ransom and the other two, however, is that Ransom is capable of learning from experience. Just as he finds beauty in the hross based on his experience of its physical presence, its kindness, and its courage, so too he can find beauty where he had never expected it because of the abstractions upon which he had relied:

But something he learned. Before anything else he learned that Malacandra was beautiful; and he even reflected how odd it was that this possibility had never entered into his speculations about it. The same peculiar twist of imagination which led him to people the universe with monsters had somehow taught him to expect nothing on a strange planet except rocky desolation or else a network of nightmare machines. He could not say why, now that he came to think of it. (p. 42)

But Ransom's experience on Malacandra does more than just make him more accepting of the physical attractiveness of the planet and its inhabitants. It also presents him with the full range of experiences which go into making up life, and it shows him that the acceptance of that range is essential to human happiness. It does not "justify" unpleasant experiences, as doctrine is wont to do, but it does demonstrate the role which all experience plays in the complex interrelationships between humanity and its environment. Consider the hross's explanation of the hnakra:

I long to kill this *hnakra* as he longs to kill me. . . . And if he kills me, my people will mourn and my brothers will desire still more to kill him. But they will not wish that there were no hneraki; nor do I. . . . The *hnakra* is our enemy, but he is also our beloved.
. . . And I say also this. I do not think the forest would be so bright, nor the water so warm, nor love so sweet, if there were no danger in the lakes. (pp. 74–75)

It is clear that this is not the Christian argument that without evil there can be no good. Rather, it is an argument based upon experience, upon an understanding that experience involves pleasant and unpleasant things and that the acceptance of both is more important than the justification of either. It is also an argument perfectly in tune with the conditions of a climax ecosystem, where stability results from the continual tension between the life, death, decay, and birth of the actors in the drama.

Yet it is not ever suggested that death be sought or welcomed, only that it not be feared. Avoiding it is the natural goal of a creature whose capacity for enjoyment of its environment is as substantial as that of the various creatures of Malacandra. The Sorns make this clear after Ransom attempts to defend the hross's lack of fear of death: "They are right not to fear it, Ren-soom, but they do not seem to look at it reasonably as part of the very nature of our bodies—and therefore often avoidable at times when they would never see how to avoid it. For example, this has saved the life of many a *hross*, but a *hross* would not have thought of it." (p. 97) Thus Ransom's visit to Malacandra is part of an educational process in which he learns the value of experience, the dangers of abstraction, and the necessity for action that this difference imposes. Set in stark contrast to Weston's determined defense of progressive evolution and Devine's single-minded pursuit of wealth and power, Ransom's experience allows the reader to see the beauty of Malacandra and to admire the distinctly hierarchical but innately satisfactory society in which the hrossa, sorns, and pfifltriggi play very different but mutually necessary roles.

Perelandra is in many ways the most problematic of Lewis's novels. With its long dialogues which become theological debates over the central concerns of Christianity, it would seem to lie totally outside the comic and ecological tradition, but in fact it does precisely the opposite, for it completes, in the most dramatic terms possible, the educational process which Ransom began on Malacandra.

Experience is as important on Perelandra as it was on Malacandra, but, because of what he learned previously, Ransom's experiences are intensified. In his taste of the yellow, globelike fruit, for example, Ransom finds a physical pleasure so extraordinary that it becomes a spiritual and emotional one as well. In spite of that, however, Ransom immediately understands that he does not want to gorge himself to gluttony:

As he let the empty gourd fall from his hand and was about to pluck a second one, it came into his head that he was now neither hungry nor thirsty. And yet to repeat a pleasure so intense and almost so spiritual seemed an obvious thing to do. His reason, or what we commonly take to be reason in our world, was all in favour of tasting this miracle again; the childlike innocence of fruit, the labours he had undergone, the uncertainty of the future, all seemed to commend the action. Yet something seemed opposed to this "reason." It is difficult to suppose that this opposition came from desire, for what desire would turn from so much deliciousness? But for whatever cause, it appeared to him better not to taste again. Perhaps the experience had been so complete that repetition would be a vulgarity—like asking to hear the same symphony twice in a day.[12]

Though it is phrased in terms of a rational or spiritual decision, a "vulgarity," it is in fact the experience itself that determines Ransom's response. He was no longer hungry nor thirsty; therefore, to repeat the experience would not be likely to satisfy the physical needs that formed the basis for the emotional and/or spiritual satisfaction. It is this same rule which operates in animals that kill only what is necessary to satisfy their hunger or in human hunter-gatherer cultures which have such strong taboos against killing more than the tribe or the individual can use.

Ransom's growing awareness of the imperatives of experience is heightened by the contrast between those imperatives and the theological debates that occur over whether the Green Lady should sleep on the fixed land. As those debates grow lengthier, several things become apparent. First, Ransom is losing the debates, not because of a lack of reason to his arguments, but because of his physical inability to maintain consciousness on a continual basis. He must sleep, while Weston seems never to need either food or rest. Second, the one argument that Ransom seems to be most unsuccessful in countering is that based on the tragic conception of humanity. The Lady begins to respond to the image that Weston/Un-man presents—"the picture of the tall slender form, unbowed though the world's weight rested upon its shoulders, stepping forth fearless and friendless into the dark to do for others what those others forbade it to do yet needed to have done." (p. 126) As Weston/Un-man teaches her more of the tragic duty that she must bear and invites her to develop the vanity and pride by which she can become martyred "savior" of the King and her own children, and as Ransom becomes more and more physically tired and less able to counter the effects of Weston/Un-man's arguments, he comes unexpectedly and most unwillingly upon the only way to stop what is going on: to physically attack and kill the enemy.

Few things in the novel are presented more compellingly than this solution. It is not a rational decision, but one to which Ransom comes out of desperation, out of his own physical inability to keep up with Weston/Un-man as much as out of his inability to counter arguments which place man in such a "noble" position. Moreover, the solution is one that runs counter to all of Ransom's ideas. Theological debates are fought on spiritual or intellectual planes, and the very idea of bringing physical experience into the fray frightens and disgusts Ransom. Yet he is brought inescapably to the conclusion that that is precisely what he must do: he must preserve the world of Perelandra because he has the physical ability to do so. As Ransom acknowledges, "And thinking of these things he perceived at last, with a sinking of heart, that if physical action were indeed demanded of him, it was an action, by ordinary standards, neither impossible nor hopeless. On the physical plane it was one middle-aged, sedentary body against another, and both unarmed save for fists and teeth and nails." (p. 146) And so in violation of his own instinctive fear of death, Ransom decides to do battle with and to kill Weston/Un-man.

Nor is the battle itself spiritual. It is a battle of fists, nails, and teeth that takes place on the floating islands, on the sea, and in the bowels of the land itself. In the battle, Ransom is aided by two things, rage and a certainty that he can win because he is indeed stronger. As Ransom thinks to himself: "His former certainty of death now seemed to him ridiculous. It was a very fair match. There was no reason why he should not win—and live." (p. 155) And Ransom does win, but only by first strangling and later bashing in Weston/Un-man's head with a rock.

Thus, in spite of the allegorical trappings of the novel, it is clear that Ransom himself is a part of the physical world and that that world depends upon its creatures' actions, not their spirituality. Ethical and natural concerns are united as are actions and ideas. Of even more importance, the distinction and separation between humanity, animal, and angel ultimately disappear in the persons of the King and Queen:

On the one side, the crystal, bloodless voice, and the immutable expression of the snow-white face; on the other the blood coursing in the veins, the feeling trembling on the lips and sparkling in the eyes, the might of the man's shoulders, the wonder of the woman's breasts, a splendour of virility and richness of womanhood unknown on earth, a living torrent of perfect animality— yet when these met, the one did not seem rank nor the other spectral. *Animal rationale*—an animal, yet also a reasonable soul: such, he remembered, was the old definition of Man. But he had never till now seen the reality. For now he saw this living Paradise, this Lord and Lady, as the resolution of discords, the bridge that spans what else would be a chasm in creation, the keystone of the whole arch. By entering that mountain valley they had suddenly united the warm multitude of the brutes behind him with the transcorporeal intelligences at his side. They closed the circle, and with their coming all the separate notes of strength or beauty which that assembly had hitherto struck became one music. (p. 207)

The role of experience, then, in *Perelandra* is paramount. Men and women create their environment through their actions, they protect it with their physical beings as well as with their ethical decisions, and they enjoy it through their physical sensations. These facts, when combined with the concepts of the Great Dance and the affirmation that emerges from that dance, place *Perelandra* squarely in the center of the fantasy tradition which is the subject of this book.

If *Perelandra* is the most allegorical novel in Lewis's Space Trilogy, then *That Hideous Strength* is his most "realistic," at least insofar as it deals with the experiences of humanity and creatures of Earth itself. Perhaps for that reason, however, the treatment of experience is more apparently contradictory than in any other of Lewis's novels. On the one hand, Lewis presents experience as it is seen by Curry, Feverstone, Fairy Hardcastle, and Frost; on the other, he presents it as understood by Ivy Maggs, Mother Dimble, MacPhee, and Ransom. Finally, using Mark and Jane as the characters who come to understand the differences betweeen experience and abstraction as a direct result of their own actions, Lewis completes the description which he began in *Out of the Silent Planet*.

Curry, Feverstone, Fairy Hardcastle, and Frost all see experience as a mildly unpleasant nastiness that is necessary for the conduct of life's daily business. That is not to say that they are all equally aware of its significance, but their ultimate treatment of it results in similar kinds of things. Only the degree of those things changes. Curry, for example, sees experience from the beginning of the novel to its conclusion as being defined by getting things done. Whether he is stage-managing the sale of Bragdon Wood for the Progressive Element or nobly preparing himself to replace the destroyed Bracton College, he sees reality in terms of doing business. The fact that that business was never connected with concrete, sensual experience nor with actual utility is of little importance to him; rather, it is the act of doing, not the significance of the acting, that matters. Thus he can misread a letter to the Fellows of the College, vaguely threaten Mark with expulsion from the Progressive Element, or consider "providential" the destruction of the college and his own colleagues without ever doing anything more than reacting on the most superficial of levels: "All the time, without the least hypocrisy, habit and instinct had given his shoulders just such a droop, his eyes such a solemn sternness, his brow such a noble gravity, as a man of good feeling might be expected to exhibit on hearing such news." [13]

Feverstone's treatment of experience is one step above Curry's. Feverstone (Devine in the earlier novels) knows that Curry and the Progressive Element are utterly ridiculous. He also knows, for example, that "Glossop and Bill the Blizzard, and even old Jewel, have ten times their (the Progressive Element's) intelligence." (p. 39) He also understands that Curry and the other people like him know nothing at all about what they are really doing or why they are doing it: "It really is rather devastating . . . that the people one has to use for getting things done should talk such drivel the moment you ask them about the things themselves." (p. 39) Nor is Feverstone ever willing to embrace the kind of abstraction that destroys so many people in the novel. His every action is dedicated to two things: avoiding being a pawn, and fighting on the winning side. He never worships the Head and never really commits himself to Belbury any more than he had ever committed himself to Weston in the earlier novels. Feverstone is the very portrait of the opportunist and may appear at first to be the perfect portrait of experience totally rejecting abstraction. Such is not the case, however, for at the conclusion of the novel he dies simply because of his inability to understand what he himself had helped to bring about. He had helped to arrange the riots at Edgestow, had conspired with N.I.C.E. to have himself named special commissioner of the riot-torn area, and had experienced first hand the destruction at Belbury. Yet, in spite of these things, he persists in going to Edgestow until it is too late, until he is caught in the earthquake that swallows that unfortunate town and all its remaining inhabitants. Feverstone, then, dies because of his inability to understand what experience has taught him, dies because ultimately he is unable to understand that experience encompasses more than he has ever before imagined and because he is totally incapable of acknowledging and adapting to that new range of experience.

Fairy Hardcastle's understanding of experience is like that of Feverstone, but exaggerated to a still greater extent. She understands physical torture and physical compulsion, she understands lust and the gratification of physical desires, but she is totally unable to conceive of anything more. The fear she engenders in Mark and Jane is a physical fear, and, while the threat she poses is real, it is also clearly less than that posed by Frost, Wither, and their masters. Moreover, her inability to understand anything about the minds of her opponents leads her into making two fatal errors. First, she neglects to follow Dimble, thereby missing the chance to find Jane and the entire headquarters of the enemy camp. Her failure to follow him is a sole result of her misjudgment of who and what is dangerous: "Both these are dangerous men. They are the sort of people who get things done—natural leaders of the other party. Dimble is quite a different type. He's purely academic. I shouldn't think his name is much known, except to other scholars in his own subject. Not the kind that would make a public man. Impractical . . . he'd be too full of scruples to be much use to them." (p. 237) This failure prepares the reader for Fairy's participation in the destruction of Belbury. When, at the dinner, she receives the note from Frost, her action is characteristic. First she locks the door so that no one may escape, then she shoots Jules, and finally she falls prey to the tiger that she has forced to remain within the room. Thus, like Feverstone, she dies because her experience is incomplete, just as she had misjudged the enemy because her experience had not acquainted her with any real understanding of the events of which she was a part. This failure to understand the system, this failure to accurately perceive her own role in a much more complicated ecosystem than her self-limited experience would allow her to acknowledge, is typical of the majority of those both at Belbury and at the College, a majority which did not want the horrors at Belbury but which sanctioned those horrors by a stubborn refusal to move beyond immediate needs.

Frost, more than any other character, represents the natural end to which the limited kind of experience present at Belbury will come. Claiming to be totally objective, he attempts to train Mark in understanding that all experience is chemical phenomena, that actions are the justifications of themselves, and that cause and effect reasoning is absurd. As he tells Mark:

Motives are not the cause of action but its byproducts. You are merely wasting your time by considering them. When you have attained real objectivity you will recognize, not *some* motives, but all motives as merely animal, subjective epiphenomena. You will then have no motives and you will find that you do not need them. Their place will be supplied by something else which you will presently understand better than you do now. (p. 296)

What is not immediately clear is that this apparent objectivity, this apparently total reliance on experience, is itself an enormous abstraction, and one that is less true to experience than anything else in the novel. And, as in the case of every other character who follows an abstraction to its logical conclusion, Frost dies. That his death is more memorable than that of any other character is consistent with the degree of his belief in the abstraction and his unwillingness to acknowledge, even at the last moment, that it is the abstraction combined with his own inability to look clearly at the products of actual experience that dooms him:

Escape for the soul, if not for the body, was offered him. He became able to know (and simultaneously refused the knowledge) that he had been wrong from the beginning, that souls and personal responsibility existed. He half saw: he wholly hated. The physical torture of the burning was not fiercer than his hatred of that. With one supreme effort he flung himself back into his illusion. In that attitude eternity overtook him as sunrise in old tales overtakes and turns them into unchangeable stones. (p. 358)

It is in Ransom's camp that the importance of experience becomes apparent. Ivy Maggs understands the nature of experience, for example, when she freely acknowledges the need for her own obedience and service to the Director, raises objections to Mr. Bultitude being in her kitchen only because he sometimes makes a mess, and treats MacPhee, Jane, and the rest of the people with the combination of civility and cheek necessary to keep a widely diverse household running with some degree of both grace and efficiency. Mother Dimble is just an extension of Ivy Maggs's attitude, though an extension into a clearly more complex state. Tied by the image of the flame-colored dress to the inherent sexuality and passion inherent in all of experience, Mother Dimble relies on instinct and reason to understand and operate comfortably in her world. Jane begins to understand something of the connection between sexuality and experience when she helps Mother Dimble and Ivy Maggs prepare the lodge for the meeting between Ivy and her husband:

Mother Dimble, for all her Nineteenth-Century propriety, or perhaps because of it, struck her this afternoon as being herself an archaic person. At every moment she seemed to join hands with some solemn yet roguish company of busy old women who had been tucking young lovers into beds since the world began with an incongruous mixture of nods and winks and blessings and tears—quite impossible old women in ruffs or wimples who would be making Shakespearian jokes about codpieces and cuckoldry at one moment and kneeling devoutly at altars the next. (p. 301)

Mother Dimble had already revealed earlier her basic acceptance of the differences between the way men and women did things when she had organized women's and men's day in the kitchen according to the

Director's orders, though noting that the whole thing is "so simple and natural that it oughtn't to need saying at all." (p. 168) She also accepts the fact that men and women frequently have to put up with the things each other do just as a matter of course, which has nothing to do with abstractions at all, but rather with the practical necessity of getting along:

I remember one day—it was before you came—Mother Dimble was saying something to the Doctor; and there he was sitting reading something, you know the way he does, with his fingers under some of the pages and a pencil in his hand—not the way you or I'd read—and he just said, "Yes, dear," and we both of us knew he hadn't been listening. And I said, "There you are, Mother Dimble," said I, "that's how they treat us once they're married. They don't even listen to what we say," I said. And do you know what she said? "Ivy Maggs," said she, "did it ever come into your mind to ask whether any-one *could* listen to all we say?" (p. 302–303)

This curious blend of the practical and the sexual is never more clearly revealed than in the last night at St. Anne's. When Mother Dimble is dressed in the flame-coloured gown and many-cornered cap, she becomes an explicit symbol of the sexuality which surrounds St. Anne's: "For now this provincial wife of a rather obscure scholar, this respectable and barren woman with grey hair and double chin, stood before her, not to be mistaken, as a kind of priestess or sybil, the servant of some prehistoric goddess of fertility—an old tribal matriarch, mother of mothers, formidable and august." (p. 363) But there is never any attempt to maintain her on this plane, for experience suggests that men and women are not gods. They are humans who assume different roles and attitudes in an often bewildering complexity. It is, after all, this same "pre-historic goddess of fertility" who must leave because she cannot tolerate the bats getting in her hair. Leave she does, taking her husband with her, and thereby avoiding the long good-byes in which he would be wont to engage. Thus Ivy Maggs with her common sense and Mother Dimble with her innate acceptance of humanity, her understanding of the role of sexuality in the lives of human beings, and her reliance on instinctive knowledge together set forth a view of experience distinctly at odds with that held at Belbury.

MacPhee plays a relatively minor role in Ransom's camp, and yet in the consideration of experience it is useful to note the difference between his "scientific" attitude toward experience and that at Belbury, at least as advanced by Frost and Wither. Frost insists that objectivity consists of getting entirely outside of subjective emotions, reconstructing the human race in the direction of increased efficiency, and acknowledging the total absence of values of any kind. MacPhee also insists on observation, on accuracy, and on the necessity for examining the role that emotions play in evaluating a system. In addition, however, he insists upon the necessity of values, the values imposed by truthful observation, even when it does not agree with one's preconceptions. As MacPhee points out, "I will not deny that I have observed a class of phenomena in this house that I have not yet fully accounted for. But they never occurred at a moment when I had a notebook handy or any facilities for verification." (p. 192) Thus MacPhee will not deny any experiences, though he may doubt those that lie outside the normal range of observation. Given this fact, it is not surprising that his limitations are clearly revealed, as when he cannot be allowed to go out to search for Merlin and is so easily conquered by Merlin when he arrives in the house. Neither is it surprising that upon taking leave of Ransom he acknowledges implicitly what Ransom has suggested to him all along, that there is more to life than his limited observations have been able to tell: "And I'll say this, Dr. Ransom, that with all your faults (and there's no man alive knows them better than myself), you are the best man, taking you by and large, that ever I knew or heard of. You are . . . you and I. . . ." (p. 379)

It is Ransom who finally must summarize the meaning of experience, for it is he who has learned first on Mars and then on Perelandra of its content and its importance. Experience, for Ransom, encompasses everything from Ivy Maggs's common sense to Mother Dimble's innate sexuality to MacPhee's dry observations to the riotous descent of the gods on St. Anne's. It includes the knowledge of the proper relationship between all the creatures of the earth, but it also includes the angels of heaven, for they too are a part of humanity's experience. And that is perhaps the most remarkable thing of all about the novel, for the eldils and the gods themselves are, in Lewis, made more physically appealing than could ever be thought possible. As Ransom puts it, "Perelandra is all about us and Man is no longer isolated. We are now as we ought to be—between the angels who are our elder brothers and the beasts who are our jesters, servants and playfellows." (p. 378) Earlier, when the gods had originally descended to invest Merlin with the powers with which he destroyed Belbury, Lewis identifies even more clearly the fact that the descent and the feelings and sensations associated with it are natural parts of the experience of life: "They felt themselves taking their places in the ordered rhythm of the universe, side by side with punctual seasons and patterned atoms and the obeying Seraphim." (p. 325) But it is in the final descent onto St. Anne's that the total range of experience is brought together. As one critic suggested, there is here no "undersexed god of the seminarians." Rather there is what John Phelan called "a wild joy in nature, an ecstatic awe before the glories of creation, a profound respect for man's ability to love and give of himself."[14] There are elephants and mice and bears and birds making love. Ivy Maggs is going to her husband to bring him comfort, Jane is going to Mark in love and obedience, and Ransom's last words to Jane imply the kind of experience that is involved in all these activities: "Go in obedience and you will find love. You will have no more dreams. Have children instead. *Urendi Maleldil.*" (pp. 379–380)

If Ransom summarizes the meaning of experience, however, it is Jane and Mark who illustrate it completely. From the beginning of the novel, these two characters rely heavily on abstractions. Jane wrote a thesis on Donne, but she was so concerned with his intellectuality that she completely missed or was able to ignore the sexuality that formed so important a part of his poetry, secular or sacred. She so completely rejects the giving up of her own control that she rejects Mark, children, sexuality, and all other intrusions upon what she calls "her own life." In short, she lives an abstraction, at least until she goes to St. Anne's. Even then, it is not until the last page of the novel, when she sees Mark's sleeve hanging out the window, that she decides that it is truly "high time she went in." (p. 382) Mark's movement in the novel is even more dramatic. From an eager toady to Busby, Curry, Feverstone, and the host of characters at N.I.C.E. at the beginning of the novel, Mark moves to a realization of the falsity of their ideas and the viciousness of their persons. Toward the beginning of the novel, Mark had observed the charm and beauty of the English village, but that observation did not influence at all his notion of reality:

All this did not in the least influence his sociological convictions. Even if he had been free from Belbury and wholly unambitious, it could not have done so, for his education had had the curious effect of making things that he read and wrote more real to him than things he saw. Statistics about agricultural labourers were the substance; any real ditcher, ploughman, or farmer's boy, was the shadow. Though he had never noticed it himself, he had a great reluctance, in his work, ever to use such words as "man" or "woman." He preferred to write about "vocational groups," "elements," "classes" and "populations": for, in his own way, he believed as firmly as any mystic in the superior reality of the things that are not seen. (p. 87)

It is not until Mark is thrown into prison at Belbury and threatened by Fairy Hardcastle, Frost, and Wither that he comes to understand the nature of the abstraction under which he has been living. Frost is evil, as Mark points out when he notes that he could not understand "how he had ever managed to overlook something about the man so obvious that any child would have shrunk away from him and any dog would have backed into a corner with raised hackles and bared teeth." (p. 248) Mark's final capitulation to experience comes, not in intellectual argument, but in a kind of emotional response to a very real attack. With that final capitulation, the stage is effectively set for his return to Jane at the end of the novel, but a return that is marked by a humility, by a desire for Jane that recognizes her own richness and strangeness, and by a complete "physicalness" which is at the opposite extreme from the abstraction with which he began: "He did not dare disobey ('Surely,' he thought, 'I must have died'), and he went in: found himself in some place of sweet smells and bright fires, with food and wine and a rich bed." (p. 382) Thus it is experience to which he has come, physical experience that is but one part of a total experience which he knows, not out of ideas, but out of feelings and occurrences. Ransom's semispiritual quest and experiences are completed, then, in *That Hideous Strength*, completed in and around a quite ordinary man of Earth who has learned to trust, not in abstractions, but in actual experience which makes the kind of practical and objective sense which Hingest had referred to early in the novel: "Eh! Two views? There are a dozen views about everything until you know the answer. Then there's never more than one." (p. 72)

If the Space Trilogy is an education into the meaning of experience for Ransom and modern humanity, *Till We Have Faces* is the application of that education to western history and mythology. A story based on the Cupid/Psyche myth, it is more realistic in tone and style than any other of Lewis's novels despite its apparently fairy-tale subject matter. The major difference between *Till We Have Faces* and the novels of the Space Trilogy, however, is that they are more concerned with the false myth as it is currently being expressed, while *Till We Have Faces* addresses itself directly to the tragic concepts which lie behind so much of the falseness of the myth. And, rather than science as the cause of that false myth, *Till We Have Faces* suggests that it is the kind of false rationalism that separated body and spirit and suggested that the mind ought to construct its own reality rather than relying on the physical and emotional experiences which must be taken together if actual reality is to be determined.

The reliance on rationalism is, interestingly enough, presented by the most attractive characters in the novel, Fox (the tutor) and Orual (the elder sister and narrator). Fox understands them all. Even the gods are subject to human reason, for they are not "jealous;" and the kind of gods who are either jealous or not subject to reason are "all folly and lies of poets."[15] Throughout the novel, Fox advises Orual to depend on her reason, to reject the folly of emotionalism and/or experience. So strong is his advice that Orual won't even tell him about the glimpse of the palace she has had for she knows he will ridicule it. His analysis of Psyche's condition is that of the scientist who knows that his "theory" is right and who is willing to look only at the evidence which supports it. But, since that refusal is couched in terms that seem reasonable and since that reasonableness agrees with the myth which we have agreed to believe, we have no more hesitation about accepting it than does Orual. Fox comes to represent, for Orual, knowledge. He gives her information about nature in its physical sense, in its rational sense, and in the relationship between these physical elements and humanity's ethics.

If Fox's advice is at the heart of Orual's philosophy, however, it is Orual herself who makes the philosophy so attractive. In one of the most psychologically accurate portraits in all of his works, Lewis presents Orual as a woman who examines honestly and skeptically, who is honest enough to admit doubts and fears, and who ultimately comes to a decision based on her best reason. Orual's childhood unhappiness, her love and devotion to Psyche, and her own constantly employed critical intelligence set her up as a character whose judgments are likely to be valid. Orual even notes that she wanted to believe in the valley because she recognized the possibility of there being in it things she could not see. Yet ultimately Orual rejects Psyche's valley and her lover, for she is not sure that the vision of the palace was real nor that it was a sign of any kind. As she so poignantly asks: "What is the use of a sign which is itself only another riddle?" (p. 133) Even following her decision and the destruction of Psyche's worlds, however, Orual's attractiveness does not cease, for she acknowledges her fault and goes on to direct the world of which she has become queen with courage, directness, and good sense.

Perhaps the most compelling argument for the rationalism of Fox and Orual is made, not by either of them directly, but by the complete unattractiveness of their opposite, Ungit. The goddess of Glome, Ungit and those who act for her seem repulsive in every aspect. The priest is a "gaunt bird," an old, blind man who smells of oils and essences and whose effect is that of a vulture who continually seeks sacrifices. His very presence brings "the holiness and horror of divine things continually thickening in that room" (p. 49), and the house of Ungit herself is a foul and ugly place marked by the smells of sacrifice, sweat, and humanity. Ungit is physical; her house is full of the experience of life in all its aspects; the demands made upon those who understand those experiences are complex and complete, not simple, clean, and neat. Thus Orual rejects them, just as does Fox, because they complicate experience beyond the willingness of either to deal with.

And yet in the midst of all these remarkably attractive reasons to reject experience in its totality for experience in its neatly tied-up abstraction, Lewis is careful to preserve the portrait of what real experience involves. For example, when Orual returns from her disastrous attempt to save Psyche, Bardia tells her to exercise, not because it will cure her sadness, but because it will give her another dimension on which to focus her attention. "No one can be sad while they're using wrist and hand and eye and every muscle of their body. That's the truth, Lady, whether you believe it or not." (p. 90) An even clearer comment is made by Psyche, however, in what is the most direct refutation of this false rationalism before the conclusion of the novel and Orual's realization of the nature of her complaint:

Do you know, Sister, I have come to feel more and more that the Fox hasn't the whole truth. Oh, he has much of it. It'd be dark as a dungeon within me but for his teaching. And yet . . . I can't say it properly. He calls the whole world a city. But what's a city built on? There's earth beneath. And outside the wall? Doesn't all the food come from there as well as all the dangers? . . .

things growing and rotting, strengthening and poisoning, things shining wet
. . . in one way (I don't know which way) more like, yes, even more like
the House of—. (pp. 70–71)

What Psyche is referring to here, of course, is the total range of experience that constituted what Ransom had learned on Perelandra,
where he had wanted to divide the spiritual from the physical. The
problem is that both constitute parts of experience, and to ignore either
is to falsify an understanding of what either humanity or the world is
about and, thereby, to invite humanity's own destruction.

The difference, finally, which Lewis portrays between abstract, scientific experience and experience in its totality is remarkably similar
to that outlined by Flannery O'Connor in her grotesque exaggera-
tions. It is the difference between what reality *seems* to be and what
reality actually *is*. What seems to be sane and rational reality is in fact
nothing but the false myth of "scientism." The old way of doing things,
the reliance on experience instead of rationality, however, is what Orual
finally learns to accept. When she hears from the old priest of Psyche
the story that the gods have so "distorted," she writes her complaint
against them claiming that what they have done is to ask her to con-
tradict what her senses had told her to believe. In fact, however, Orual saw the palace, she saw Psyche's blooming health, and she heard
the voices singing from the palace. Because she could not repeat those
experiences, however, and because she was confronted with contradictory kinds of evidence, she chose to reject one experience and to
accept another. But, as Lewis has shown throughout his four novels,
to reject any part of experience is to distort reality, and distortion of
reality leads to unhappiness, to destruction of the physical environment, and ultimately to death.

THE NOVELS AND "SCIENTISM"

Throughout each of the novels of the Space Trilogy is an explicit
debate between scientism and experience, and an implied one in *Till
We Have Faces*. And the doctrine of scientism is one of which Lewis
spoke directly in response to a suggestion that his books libeled science, particularly *Out of the Silent Planet*:

It certainly is an attack, if not on scientists, yet on something which might
be called "scientism"—a certain outlook on the world which is casually con-

nected with the popularization of the sciences, though it is much less common among real scientists than among their readers. It is, in a word, the belief that the supreme moral end is the perpetuation of our own species, and that this is to be pursued even if, in the process of being fitted for survival, our species has to be stripped of all those things for which we value it—of pity, of happiness, and of freedom.[16]

Now what is remarkable in this description is that it appears to be directly opposed to the basic ecological principles, but in face the precise opposite is true. As Lewis points out, scientism insists that it is the preservation of *our species* that is paramount, not the preservation of the whole system nor the awareness that unless the whole system survives both the species and the individuals within it will perish. In other words, preservation of the species becomes simply another abstraction, an abstraction so far removed from reality and experience as to guarantee destruction for any who follow it. Weston's words at the beginning of *Out of the Silent Planet* clearly indicate that it is an abstraction, and an abstraction every bit as dangerous as every other abstraction has been:

My only defense is that small claims must give way to great. As far as we know, we are doing what has never been done in the history of man, perhaps never in the history of the universe. We have learned how to jump off the speck of matter on which our species began; infinity, and therefore perhaps eternity, is being put into the hands of the human race. You cannot be so small minded as to think that the rights or the life of an individual or of a million individuals are of the slightest importance in comparison with this. (pp. 26–27)

He continues this notion at the conclusion of the novel in his argument before Oyarsa:

. . . the right, or, if you will, the might of Life herself, that I am prepared without flinching to plant the flag of man on the soil of Malacandra: to march on, step by step, superseding, where necessary, the lower forms of life that we find, claiming planet after planet, system after system, till our posterity—whatever strange form and yet unguessed mentality they have assumed—dwell in the universe wherever the universe is habitable. (p. 137)

Oyarsa rejects the argument in words that strongly resemble the suggestions of ecologists like Shepard and Dubos and Bateson: " 'Strange!'

said Oyarsa. 'You do not love any one of your race—you would have let me kill Ransom. You do not love the mind of your race, nor the body. Any kind of creature will please you if only it is begotten by your kind as they now are. It seems to me, Thick One, that what you really love is no completed creature but the very seed itself: for that is all that is left.' " (p. 138) What Weston fears, of course, is death. What he argues for is a "scientific" way to gain immortality. What he cannot accept is experience, which tells him that he and eventually his kind will pass from existence. The result is that he can kidnap and kill and destroy, all in the name of objective science. The problem is that it is neither objective nor is it science. There is in it no humility, no respect for nature or its processes. Rather, there is the insistence that humanity is supreme, that it is its duty to rule and master nature, even to the extent of banishing death. That, from both Lewis's and the ecologist's perspectives, is what lies at the heart of the false myth.

In *Perelandra* Weston/Un-man propagates the same false myth, but this time wearing a new face and different clothing. The falseness of the myth is more apparent here, in line with the novel's more allegorical quality, for it is, more explicitly stated, "a dream begotten by the hatred of death upon the fear of true immortality, fondled in secret by thousands of ignorant men and hundreds who are not ignorant." (p. 82) But with this increased authorial intrusion comes an increased level of abstraction and moralizing to justify the false myth as well. Weston puts it this way in outlining the sort of "emergent evolution" concept which is nothing but the false myth decked out in new clothes.

The majestic spectacle of this blind, inarticulate purposiveness thrusting its way upward and ever upward in an endless unity of differentiated achievements towards an ever-increasing complexity of organization, towards spontaneity and spirituality, swept away all my old conception of a duty to Man as such. Man in himself is nothing. The forward movement of Life—the growing spirituality—is everything. (p. 91)

Weston spends his time with Ransom in trying to convince him of the similarity of their ideas, using this scientism as the basis of his argument. Weston insists that both God and the devil are parts of the life force that leaps forward and demands all sacrifices of those who would serve it, and he invites Ransom to consider it as a commitment which "utterly overrides all our petty ethical pigeon-holes." (p. 95) When

Ransom attempts to tie this idea to experience and action, however, Weston reveals the true nature of the false myth when he says: "In so far as I am the conductor of the central forward pressure of the universe, I am it. Do you see, you timid, scruple-mongering fool? I *am* the Universe. I Weston, am your God and your Devil." (p. 96) With this remark, Weston unmasks the falsity of the myth completely, and he clearly establishes the difference between it and the humility of the true scientist. The false myth puts humanity at the center. It makes the continuation of its wishes and desires supreme to everything else in the universe, including the universe itself, and it reduces everything else in the universe to an object designed for no purpose other than being subject to humanity's will, to an object which humanity must bend to its will simply because it wishes it so. Ultimately, of course, it must consume humanity, for by consuming all within its system, it must thereby ensure its own demise, for what it really seeks is death for itself as well as for the rest of the universe. It is no surprise when Ransom defeats the false myth on Perelandra, for he does so by relying on experience, the complete experience, which teaches humility before the natural processes and an acknowledgment of the interdependent roles which humanity and nature play in scientific, moral, and ethical systems which are inextricably intertwined.

That Hideous Strength concludes the scientism/experience debate for the Space Trilogy by putting the abstractions of the false myth into practical effect on earth itself. The arguments are not new, though the effects are perhaps more striking than even the proponents of the arguments had ever expected. Feverstone (Devine of the first novel) puts it this way: "It does really look as if we now had the power to dig ourselves in as a species for a pretty staggering period, to take control of our own destiny. If Science is really given a free hand it can now take over the human race and re-condition it: make man a really efficient animal. If it doesn't—well, we're done." (p. 41)

What is most remarkable about the myth as it appears in *That Hideous Strength*, however, is the manner in which it outlines the relationship between nature and humanity in this new, scientific world. Filostrato suggests that it will be necessary to "shave the planet," to abolish all organic life, and to eliminate sex entirely in order to force humanity to "become finally governable." (pp. 172–173) He concludes that the purpose of N.I.C.E. is to finally abolish "nature" altogether: "It is for the conquest of death: or for the conquest of organic life, if you prefer. They are the same thing. It is to bring out of that cocoon of organic life which sheltered the babyhood of mind the New Man, the man who will not die, the artificial man, free from Nature. Nature is the ladder we have climbed up by, now we kick her away." (p. 177) Straik insists that it is the resurrection come to life, the "beginning of Man Immortal and Man Ubiquitous." (p. 178) The end result of all the efforts and philosophies of Filostrato, Straik, Wither, Frost, Feverstone, and the others is remarkably apparent, and Lewis does not hesitate to enter as the omniscient author and describe it directly:

The time was ripe. From the point of view which is accepted in Hell, the whole history of our Earth had led up to this moment. There was now at last a real chance for fallen Man to shake off that limitation of his powers which mercy had imposed as a protection from the full results of his fall. If this succeeded, Hell would be at last incarnate. Bad men, while still in the body, still crawling on this little globe, would enter that state which, heretofore, they had entered only after death, would have the diuturnity and power of evil spirits. Nature, all over the globe of Tellus, would become their slave; and of that dominion no end, before the end of time itself, could be certainly foreseen. (pp. 203–204)

Clearly, here is scientism at its most rampant, and here is the rejection of experience for the most abstract of all abstractions. Here is the old tragic conception of humanity taken to its logical extreme, the point at which its ethical and moral judgments are removed completely from the natural world and put entirely into the world of abstractions, with the consequent loss of all humanity as well as all of nature. When this is contrasted with the figure of Merlin, the life of the company at St. Anne's, or the descent of the gods in the remarkable last chapter, the debate has been completed; and it is clearly experience that has been the victor literally in terms of the novels themselves and figuratively in terms of its emotional impact upon their readers.

Scientism as such is not discussed directly in *Till We Have Faces*, but there is more clearly a distinction between true and false myth in this work than in any other of Lewis's novels. As already noted in the discussion of experience in *Till We Have Faces*, what Lewis is presenting is the difference between the appealing reason of Fox, which is tied to rationalism, and the appalling demands of Ungit, which are tied to physical and emotional as well as to mental processes. This difference is, of course, just another form of the debate between scientism and ecology, though it is portrayed in its infant form without any of the more disturbing, troublesome, and practical questions which appear in *That Hideous Strength*. The scientism of the Space Trilogy is the natural end result of Fox's rationalism. Fox summarizes both the argument and its error when he speaks in Orual's defense before the gods whom she has accused:

Of course I didn't know; but I never told her I didn't know. I don't know now. Only that the way to the true gods is more like the house of Ungit . . . oh, it's unlike too, more unlike than we yet dream, but that's the easy knowledge, the first lesson; only a fool would stay there posturing and repeating it. The Priest knew at least that there must be sacrifices. They will have sacrifice—will have man. Yes, and the very heart, center, ground, roots of a man; dark and strong and costly as blood. (p. 295)

As Orual had realized earlier, the false myth—scientism in the earlier novels—was based on egotism of the most arrant kind. Just as Orual's love for Psyche had been not love at all but rather a pride in possession and an assertion of her superiority to everything else in the universe, so Fox's rationalism has been based on the assumption that humanity's reason is supreme to the body and its theories more significant than experience or observation. When she learns these things, Orual's complaint against the gods is answered, and for the first time she can begin to trust in what her experience tells her; for the first time she can begin to see, as she does when she beholds Psyche with this new concept. She sees that Psyche is her old self, but that she is also new and more beautiful, that in fact she is, for the first time, the image of what a woman truly is. Thus Lewis concludes the debate between scientism and experience by taking the reader back to the origins of that debate and forcing him or her to acknowledge the implicit assumptions of scientism, which must ultimately prove so false as to arrive at the "shaved" planet and the "objective," impotent, deadly fools whose creation of Belbury becomes such a senile parody of science, objectivity, and experience.

THE NOVELS AND THE GREAT DANCE

The Great Dance is the symbol that Lewis uses to illustrate the complex interdependence of all things in the universe. Closely related to the system portrayed by Dante in the "Paradiso" and to the great chain of being, the Great Dance is Lewis's image of the proper integration of all things. Victor Hamm noted this very early when he described Lewis's hierarchy of values:

In a fall-less world, Lewis seems to say, there could be continuous development of knowledge: physics, chemistry, all the rest. Such a world need not remain primitive. But the true hierarchy of values would be undisturbed: not only would science stay in its proper place as a means, but scientists would preserve their sense of proportion as well, and realize that the world is made up of a number of kinds and degrees of knowledge, all of them oriented and integrated by that reason which is metaphysical and religious. It is this proper integration that has been destroyed or at least badly bent out of shape by the Fall and its consequences.[17]

Though the symbol is present in all of the novels, it is in *Perelandra* that it is presented most explicitly.

The Great Dance is presented at the conclusion of Ransom's experiences on Perelandra, where it clearly illustrates the proper relationship between all things in a world not distorted by false pride or other logical consequences of the tragic concept. The Great Dance, according to the eldils who describe it, has always been and contains all things: "The edge of each nature borders on that whereof it contains no shadow or similitude. Of many points one line; of many lines one shape; of many shapes one solid body; of many senses and thoughts one person." (p. 214) Thus the Great Dance is all encompassing, and it links every piece of creation to every other piece of creation in a complex interrelationship in which there are differences and degrees but not ranks of superiority:

In the plan of the Great Dance plans without number interlock, and each movement becomes in its season the breaking into flower of the whole design to which all else had been directed. Thus each is equally at the centre and none are there by being equals, but some by giving place and some by receiving it, the small things by the smallness and the great by their greatness, and all the patterns linked and looped together by the unions of a kneeling with a sceptred love. (p. 217)

Very much like the medieval chain of being, which Lewis had used and described so explicitly in *Allegory of Love*, the Great Dance might well be a description of the complex ecosystem discussed earlier. Animals, plants, humans, and all other parts of creation play a role in which they are both ruler and ruled, each contributing to the cycle which is itself the continuation of the system. And yet the plan is so complex, so varied, that it often seems formless and chaotic. That seeming is false, though, just as those theories which would order and simplify the plan to logical absurdity are false: "So with the Great Dance. Set your eyes on one movement and it will lead you through all patterns and it will seem to you the master movement. But the seeming will be true. Let no mouth open to gainsay it. There seems no plan because it is all plan: there seems no centre because it is all centre." (p. 218) Now there is no question that in Lewis's terms, the Great Dance is Christian, that it is a central part of traditional religious theology. And yet clearly his description is related more to the doctrines of St. Francis and St. Benedict than to the more traditional views of Christianity.

The Great Dance appears in the other novels in a more muted form, one that emphasizes the interrelatedness of all things and contrasts starkly with the false myths of scientism and/or rationalism which one or another of the major characters has advocated. In *Out of the Silent Planet* the idea of the Great Dance is expressed by Oyarsa in his conversations with Weston, but it is perhaps illustrated best in the letter written by Ransom concerning the relationship between the various species on Malacandra. Talking about pets and why the relationship between Malacandrians and "lower animals" differs from that between people and animals on Earth, Ransom says:

Each of them is to the others *both* what a man is to us *and* what an animal is to us. They can talk to each other, they can cooperate, they have the same ethics; to that extent a *sorn* and a *hross* meet like two men. But then each finds the other different, funny, attractive as an animal is attractive. Some instinct starved in us, which we try to soothe by treating irrational creatures almost as if they were rational, is really satisfied in Malacandra. They don't need pets. (p. 156)

Having already been told by the Malacandrians that death is a part of life, that conflict and strife between various creatures is natural and essential to the continuation of the system (as the conflict between the hrossa and the hnakre illustrates), and that all of these things constitute part of a total pattern in which experience rather than abstraction plays the most important part, we see set up in the novel the model upon which the Great Dance is to be built in *Perelandra*.

In line with its more satirical, realistic tone, *That Hideous Strength* presents the concept of the Great Dance indirectly by the contrast between the company at Belbury and that at St. Anne's and directly through the words of Ransom and the symbolism of the remarkably sensuous last chapter. The contrast between the two companies is a clear indication of the self-destruction brought on by denial of the Great Dance and at the same time an even clearer indication of the regenerative life engendered by recognition of and obedience to it. The company at Belbury, from its inception, is engaged in self-destruction, feeding upon its members in a kind of collective suicide. Jules is the spokesman, but he is a fool who knows nothing about N.I.C.E.; Filostrato is the scientific genius who has kept Alcasan's head alive, but he does not understand the nature of the intelligences which are using it; Feverstone is the front man, and he is to be sacrificed because he does not have a sufficient commitment to the project. Straik and Wither kill Filostrato, Wither kills Straik, and Mr. Bultitude (the bear imprisoned on Wither's orders) kills Wither. Frost, the last of that company, kills himself and destroys all of Belbury in despair at the truth of all those things that he had for so long denied. In contrast, the company at St. Anne's is marked by obedience, willingness to play different roles as part of a complex plan (the full extent of which is more felt than rationally understood), and acceptance of emotion and instinct as necessary parts of the total experience. Ivy Maggs is reunited with her husband, Camilla and Denniston go off to make love, Mother Dimble and Dimble leave to make a new home in the midst of unabashed sexuality and the attractions of domesticity, Jane goes to Mark in obedience, innocence, and an awakened passion, and Ransom joins Venus on Perelandra. Death comes from Belbury; life and sexuality come from St. Anne's; and both are the result of understanding and accepting or misunderstanding and rejecting the Great Dance in all its implications. Ransom had indicated clearly the nature and importance of the Great Dance relatively early in the novel when he had invited Jane to watch the mice picking up crumbs in his room. Jane, who was not too fond of mice, especially "in the neighborhood of her feet," saw them from a different perspective after Ransom commented: " 'There', he said, 'a very simple adjustment. Humans want crumbs removed; mice are anxious to remove them. It ought never to have been a cause of war. But you see that obedience and rule are more like a dance than a drill—specially between man and woman where the roles are always changing.' " (p. 149) In this small incident we see the full meaning of the Great Dance which has been symbolized so completely in *Perelandra*. All things work together; to the extent to which each recognizes and accepts that interdependence, the system continues; to the extent to which each attempts to dominate the system and to rule it solely for him or herself, as the company at Belbury has done, the system destroys itself and all those in it.

Till We Have Faces, like *That Hideous Strength*, presents the idea of the Great Dance indirectly, though perhaps in more clearly ecological terms than in any of the other novels. The portrayal, interestingly enough, comes largely through Fox, even in the early parts of the novel, for unlike the abstraction worshippers of the earlier novels, his dependence on rationalism is neither so immediately crippling nor so devoid of understanding as its logical extreme later becomes. Early in the novel when Orual fears the death of the Queen, Psyche's mother, Fox tells her that it is necessary to accept rather than fear the operations of nature. Later, in attempting to console her about Psyche's death, he notes that life and death are equal parts of loving and that bearing the latter is an important part of our learning about life. Still later, when announcing his decision to stay in Glome, Fox says, "For I have won a battle. What's best for his fellows must be best for a man. I am but a limb of the Whole and must work in the socket where I'm put." (p. 210) Finally, in Orual's dream and complaint against the gods at the conclusion of the novel, Fox summarizes the truth of what he had been saying earlier and extends that to the knowledge he had gained about Ungit and her participation in the whole when he insists again that all people are part of one whole and, therefore, part of nature, humankind, and the gods at once. What Fox has outlined is the practical application of the Great Dance to human participation in the whole system of which he is but one part. Life, death, sorrow, pain, joy, love, sweat, food, drink, and everything else have value. No thing is separate from any other thing. As Orual learns that she too is Psyche, so she learns that she has been a part of everything that has occurred. Just as the mice had been a part of the system which Jane's distorted perspective had not allowed her to see, so Orual's distorted perspective and Fox's confused rationalism had not allowed them to see that Ungit was also a way into the Great Dance, and that to ignore her would be to deny and therefore to invite destruction of a part of the system.

THE NOVELS AND AFFIRMATION

By this time it should become clear that Lewis is working in the comic, ecological tradition even though he is also working within the Christian perspective. The case is very much like that of Dante, who created a vast system largely interpreted as being a showplace of medieval theology but which Meeker has shown to be equally a vision of felicity which "becomes possible as the eye learns to see the millions of fragments which make up the universe interacting with one another to create a cosmos."[18] Lewis's affirmation in each of the novels of the Space Trilogy and in *Till We Have Faces* is a statement of faith in experience over abstraction, of trust in the emotional and instinctual side of nature as well as in the rational processes of the mind, and of acceptance of all creatures in the system as essential to the emergence of a total picture which is so complex that any attempt to impose a single abstraction or creature as dominant would result both in distortion and destruction of the whole.

The affirmation in *Out of the Silent Planet* is more implicit than in any other of Lewis's novels, for here Ransom is learning what it means to be a part of a larger system. His education is carried out in terms of extraterrestrial creatures who are unlike him in form and in terms of a geography that is different from anything else he has known. Just as he had learned in the space ship of the falsity of his notions about the ugliness and darkness of deep space, so on Malacandra he learns of the essential unity of all creatures which, in harmony with the natural world of which they are a part, brings an enormously physical as well as spiritual joy: "He felt the old lift of the heart, the soaring solemnity, the sense, at once sober and ecstatic, of life and power offered in unasked and unmeasured abundance. If there had been air enough in his lungs he would have laughed aloud." (p. 99) Moreover, it is significant that Ransom chooses life among his own creatures on his own planet over life on Malacandra. He will not willingly die to serve the scientism of Weston, nor will he sacrifice himself on the return trip so that Weston and Devine may live. Neither will he yield himself to abstractions and remain in a world of which he is not a part. He has also learned that facts and information are relatively useless unless the pattern to which they belong can be found: "But what can one do with these scraps of information? I merely analyze them out of a whole living memory that can never be put into words, and no one in this world will be able to build up from such scraps quite the right picture." (p. 156) The affirmation in *Out of the Silent Planet*, then, is simply that of the interconnectedness of all species and of the distortions of perspective that occur whenever any one part of the pattern sees itself as the center, as the ruler, who directs the whole. Moreover, the book clearly implies, Thulcandra (Earth) has come to its present condition precisely because of its disregard of that simple but essential knowledge.

In *Perelandra* the affirmation is much more explicit, for in this novel the education of Ransom is completed with the presentation of the Great Dance. Here Ransom is not concerned with the strangeness of the plant and animal species, for he has already learned that part of the pattern on Malacandra. The principal concern here is that he still makes the distinction between physical and spiritual which is a result of the fall on Earth, and that distinction leads him to a false notion of what his responsibility is to the system of which he is a part. Having learned that, however unwillingly, and finally bringing the two items together in his battle with Weston/Un-man, he is then capable of seeing and understanding the Great Dance itself:

And by now the thing must have passed together out of the region of sight as we understand it. For he says that the whole solid figure of these enamoured and interanimated circlings was suddenly revealed as the mere superficies of a far vaster pattern in four dimensions, and that figure as the boundary of yet others in other worlds: till suddenly as the movement grew yet swifter, the inter-weaving yet more ecstatic, the relevance of all to all yet more intense, as dimension was added to dimension and that part of him which could reason and remember was dropped farther and farther behind that part of him which saw, even, at the very zenith of complexity, complexity was eaten up and faded, as a thin white cloud fades into the hard blue burning of the sky, and a simplicity beyond all comprehension, ancient and young as spring, illimitable, pellucid, drew him with cords of infinite desire into its own stillness. He went up into such a quietness, a privacy, and a freshness that at that very moment when he stood farthest from our ordinary mode of being he had the sense of stripping off encumbrances and awakening from a trance, and coming to himself. (p. 219)

The affirmation is a complete one. It is an affirmation of life, of experience, and of limitless joy. At the same time, it is an acknowledgment of the pain, suffering, and death that is a part of that life. But what seems most important of all for our purposes, it is an affirmation that comes through the union of the senses and an understanding that the very complexity of the pattern makes each part of that pattern so immeasurably important that no part can claim dominance or superiority. It does not deny, indeed it affirms, rules and obedience, but it does so in terms of function rather than in terms of moral superiority or merit. Thus it is paradoxically Christian and comic at the same time, precisely in the sense that the "Paradiso" is Christian and comic as Dante gazes at the source of light directly and makes out new images within it.

In spite of the fact that perhaps it is the most flawed of the novels in the Space Trilogy, *That Hideous Strength* contains in many ways the most convincing and satisfying affirmation of all, for it is an affirmation of the possibilities of life so strong and so vital that it almost compels belief. First, like the "Paradiso," it is an overwhelming blend of the sexual and the spiritual. Lewis doesn't let his readers forget the Christian perspective, for he reminds them, through Ransom, of the Great Dance, of the hierarchy of obedience, and of the impossibility of understanding the absolutely powerful nature of God. At the same time, however, he reminds the readers even more forcefully of the physical and emotional pleasures possible when one is in harmony with the system of which one is a part. Lovemaking seems to be virtually the only thing happening in the amazing last chapter of the novel, and it is even more significant because the lovemaking is going on throughout the animal as well as the human kingdom at St. Anne's. Mr. Bultitude, the bear, and his prospective mate begin to court in the kitchen, with Ivy Maggs's only comment being that it's "only natural for her." (p. 376) Bats begin to mate, birds begin to sing prior to mating, elephants perform a ceremonial dance prior to their mating in an act as "private as human lovers," (p. 379) and even the mice in the house revel in a mating ceremony. The human inhabitants of the household depart, one by one, to do the same thing. These events combined with the image of the woman "divinely tall, part naked, part wrapped in a flame-coloured robe" (p. 382) (who is like the figure of Vir-Vichal in Chant's *Red Moon and Black Mountain*) constitute the final affirmation of life, and not life lived for the dry abstractions of spirituality. Rather, it is life lived in the most directly sensuous and overwhelmingly physical sense possible, and equally important, life that is a part of the natural world, and not apart from it. Grace Ironwood sums up most clearly what all in the company have learned about nature:

"It is not contrary to the laws of Nature," said a voice from the corner where Grace Ironwood sat, almost invisible in the shadows. "You are quite right. The laws of the universe are never broken. Your mistake is to think that the little regularities we have observed on one planet for a few hundred years are the real unbreakable laws, whereas they are only the remote results which the true laws bring about more often than not; as a kind of accident." (p. 368)

Denniston completes that knowledge when he remarks that "nothing in Nature is quite regular. There are always exceptions. A good average uniformity, but not complete." (p. 368) Thus the cycle begun by Ransom on Malacandra has been completed on Thulcandra, where life has finally asserted itself in reaction to the "objective death" preached by Frost and the company at Belbury.

Till We Have Faces is the most complex of Lewis's novels in terms of its affirmation, largely because the central figure in the novel, Orual, dies at the conclusion. Her death has brought her knowledge, but nevertheless that death seems to be very much in the old tragic tradition which affirms a human morality and superiority drawn from something outside of and superior to nature—more carefully considered, however, that death is the natural conclusion to a long-lived life. It is a part of a natural process, and it is not knowledge which has caused Orual's death, but rather the lack of it previously. The fact that her book ends as it does reflects the kind of affirmation which is being made. It is an affirmation of instincts, nature, emotions, and experience over the abstractions of words battling against words. The rejection of words is the rejection of abstractions, just as the acceptance of Ungit as part of the truth of the gods is the acceptance of the system of instinctual, physical, and emotional needs which must complement rationalism. Just as Orual must accept the fact that she is Ungit, so too she must accept that she is Psyche. She is, in herself, all things, and she is thereby tied to all other things. It is almost as if Lewis had used *Till We Have Faces* to summarize and exemplify all that had occurred in the Space Trilogy, but transforming the "arresting strangeness" that had been present there into work-a-day reality which, in its turn, artificially distinguishes between true and false myth. The true myth is infinitely complex, and any attempt to reduce that complexity results in disaster for the individual as well as the system. The only way out is integration, an integration which Orual achieves too late. And in that fact, perhaps, Lewis has been most realistic of all. Orual *was* the tragic heroine, and, as is the wont of tragic heroines, she dies. Just as an animal cast from its group is unlikely to survive, so Orual was unlikely to survive. What does survive, however, is the book in which she catalogues her experience, and from that experience the reader comes to realize the possibilities of both life and death, but most of all the difference between meaningless words (abstractions) and specific actions (experiences).

CONCLUSION

What Lewis accomplished for the fantasy novel is significant: he contributed an aesthetic which set the stage for critical understanding of the relation between the fantasy tradition and the tradition of the novel as a whole. He also, however, did something considerably more difficult, for he integrated the comic, ecological tradition with the traditions of an almost medieval Christianity in a way that had not been done since Dante's *Comedy*. Chad Walsh sums up well the potential effects of Lewis's work:

Quite possibly, at some time that no one can predict, the Ego-searching and Id-probing of our time will lose its fascination, and men will suddenly see an interesting world outside themselves, a world with which they can enter into significant relations. With a sigh of relief, they may turn from the ever-receding self to the non-self and in joyfully accepting it, know themselves at last. If this happens, Lewis may serve as a spiritual mentor for many of them. He is the specialized guide through a world that is simply there because God put it there.[19]

While comedy and ecology may not require the "guide to God" that Walsh sees in Lewis, they may be very well served by the vision of the complex, integrated system of existence which his novels portray, the affirmation of the possibilities of life which his characters experience, and the inextricably close connection between literary theory and ecological practice which his criticism postulates and his fiction demonstrates.

4

CHARLES WILLIAMS

T. S. Eliot may have been right about Charles Williams when he noted that "what he had to say was beyond his resources, and probably beyond the resources of any language, to say once for all through any one medium of expression."[1] His novels are, on the whole, less satisfactory than any of the other fantasy novels considered in this book, and yet they are essential to an understanding of the development of the fantasy tradition in the twentieth century and of the centrality of the comic, ecological processes in that development. The novels fail for several reasons: the lack of consistent character development; the uneasy marriage of psychological, theological, and supernatural elements; the reliance on abstract rhetoric instead of concrete symbol and/or incident to develop plot, character, and theme; and the combination of what Ian Watt would call the formal realism of the setting with the basically fantastic style, story, and theme. Yet, with all of these failings, the novels tell us still a great deal about the fantasy tradition and condition, in precisely the same way Frank Herbert's ultimate failure in the *Dune* series does, for they illustrate clearly both the necessary conditions and limitations of the form. And again like Herbert's work, they are frequently compelling and moving as they insist upon the integration and joy that are hallmarks of twentieth-century fantasy and the basic theme of the ecological comedy.

Before turning directly to the novels, I want to explore the last of the reasons noted above for the novels' failure. Williams's work is the only work considered in this volume that does not make use of the created world setting. Herbert, Chant, and Tolkien all make the created world a setting with no reference to the primary world, and Lewis makes only passing reference to the primary world in the first two novels of the Space Trilogy and none in *Till We Have Faces*, though he is concerned with a kind of primary world in *That Hideous Strength* (see the Lewis chapter for further discussion of this matter). Williams, however, uses the primary world as his setting, though he enlarges that world by the inclusion of the supernatural as a natural part of it. The result is a loss of credibility which is more harmful to Williams's work than any other single flaw except for its rhetoric. The reasons for this can be illustrated best by a brief comparison of what I believe to be the best and the worst of Williams's novels, a judgment which is at odds with those of other critics (Spacks and Eliot, for example).

The best of Williams's novels are *War in Heaven* and *All Hallow's Eve*. In them less contradiction exists between external and internal reality, and, as a result, the characters and themes are more fully and completely realized. *War in Heaven* takes place in the very real London publishing world, in the quiet English countryside in and around Castra Parvulorum, and in the townhome of the Duke and the shop of Manasseh. And, though there is certainly the fantastic element of the war over the Grail which influences each of these places, it does not require the simultaneous acceptance of two contradictory realities. In short, the created world of the novel is consistent with the characters and the situations that Williams proposes. And, if the imaginatively compelling richness of Tolkien, Lewis, Chant, and others is not there, there is a compelling power of belief that enlarges rather than infringes upon the reality of the novel itself.

All Hallow's Eve is perhaps even more compelling because there is here a created world that compels respect because of the precision of its creation. The parallel worlds of the living and the dead and the again-parallel worlds of time succeed in the novel because they are so specifically realized. From the moment at the beginning of the novel when Lester discovers herself walking in a silent, empty world furnished with all the items of London except its people to the image of Betty joyfully reading the newspaper or meeting with Lester as Father Simon seeks to "murder" her and seize permanent control of her soul, the created world is real. There is no attempt at a psychological explanation; there is simply the creation of a world that compels belief on its own terms, terms which are similar to those outlined by Tolkien in his essay "On Fairy Stories." Moreover, there is a clear connection between the "co-inherent" worlds, and the characters who assume the reality pertinent to each.

Such is not the case with *Descent into Hell* and *The Place of the Lion*, for in neither of them is a reality present that is consistent with itself. Instead, Williams turns setting into a symbolism of ideas and combines discordant elements which war so constantly with each other that they destroy both realities they are intended to suggest. In *Descent into Hell*, Williams offers, on the one hand, the smugly comfortable world of the Hill. Its petty jealousies, its superficial culture, and its patina of respectability would be convincing in a novel by Evelyn Waugh or Anthony Powell, but Williams is not writing their kind of novel. Instead, he combines these elements with the ghost of the unskilled workman, whose world is similar to that which Lester first notes in *All Hallow's Eve*, and the succubus of Wentworth's self-centered imagination. These two might even be unified with each other as Dante had unified the blessed damned (Socrates, et al.) with the eternally damned, but they cannot be tied back to the Hill without sacrificing the credibility of both, particularly since the plot which unites them suggests that neither is important, that only the ideas are important.

The Place of the Lion strains credibility in a similar fashion. Platonic realities coming to life in a created world (Lewis's, for example) are one thing; platonic realities coming to life in Smetham and heralding a kind of physical as well as psychological last judgment are quite something else. The lion and the snake are simply not real in either world, nor are Mr. Tighe's butterflies. Richardson's small bookstore simply does not fit with Foster's rabid pursuit of Quentin and his rescue by Damaris. Neither does Ms. Wilmot's physical transformation into the snake correspond with the world in which Quentin and Anthony engage in light-hearted philosophical debate or in which Damaris engages in scholarly pedantry which obscures rather than clarifies her subject. What Williams seems to be asking is that his readers suspend their belief at the same time that they exercise their critical faculties to an even greater degree. The result is that readers can believe in neither world.

Thus one of the major reasons why Williams's novels are problematic is that he has failed to recognize an inherent quality of fantasy, the necessity for compelling belief in a world that is internally and externally consistent, even though that consistency may violate the consistency of formal realism which the novel usually claims as its purview. And that is, I think, the most important point to be made here. Fantasy begins with a created world that is itself complex and multifaceted, just as is any higher ecosystem, and it survives only so long as that created world maintains itself. Intrusions from the primary world (Tolkien's term), must either be integrated into the created world as Chant and Lewis do, for example—or the work itself must be changed into something other than fantasy as Swift does with his use of Menippean satire in *Gulliver*. Such a change is consistent with the laws of comedy, art, and ecology; the principle behind it is a constant reminder of the inseparable tie between form and theme in literature and between environment and individual in nature.

WAR IN HEAVEN

War in Heaven is the most conventional of Williams's novels. A kind of detective thriller which centers first around the murdered man whom Lionel Rackstraw finds in his office and only later around the struggle for possession of the Grail, it is successful precisely because it has two characters who are well within the comic tradition in their refusal to take themselves too seriously, in their understanding of the importance of honoring instinct as well as reason, and in their rejection of abstractions.

The first and most important of these characters is the Archdeacon. The leading figure in the war for the Grail, he is perhaps the only one who understands that the Grail itself is of as little importance as the demonstrably evil desires of Gregory Persimmons. Things occur according to their own predisposition, and to assert ultimate control over them or to attempt to shape them to individual will is to overstate the importance of the individual and to understate the importance of the system. The result is the kind of foolishness which the Archdeacon notes just before stealing the cup back from Gregory:

But this enlargement was as unreal as it was huge; the sentences which he had uttered a few days back on denying and defying Destiny boomed like unmeaning echoes across creation. Nothing but Destiny could deny Destiny; all else which sought to do so was pomposity so extreme as to become merely silly. It was a useless attempt to usurpation, useless and slightly displeasing, as pomposity always is. In the universe, as in Fardles, pomposity was bad manners.[2]

Now clearly Williams is suggesting a kind of dance like that suggested by Lewis's Great Dance at the conclusion of *Perelandra*, and equally clearly that dance is Christian at its center; but the Archdeacon at least understands and presents it as a kind of natural law that nourishes humans as they subordinate themselves to it in order to survive with some degree of happiness and freedom. He also understands that his own position is more like that of the comic than that of the tragic man. This fact comes across most clearly when he is listening half-heartedly to Mr. Batesby's foolish and self-important chatter:

. . . knew too that his guest and substitute would rather have been talking about his own views on the ornaments rubric than about the parishioners. He wished he would. He was feeling rather tired, and it was an effort to pay attention to anything which he did not know by heart. Mr. Batesby's ecclesiastical views he did—and thought them incredibly silly—but he thought his own were probably that too. One had views for convenience' sake, but how anyone could think they mattered. (WH, p. 70)

Holding "views for convenience' sake" is far from the usual attitude of the church toward its creeds or doctrines, but throughout the novel the Archdeacon is more concerned with practical matters of behavior than with abstract notions. He tells the Duke, for example, that one can't insult God any more than one can pull his nose, and after their ultimate victory in the war for the Grail, instead of keeping a watch over the Grail as the Duke wishes, the Archdeacon insists that what he really wants to do is to sleep. Even the Archdeacon's death at the conclusion of the novel becomes part of this process by joyous reintegration with all of nature. Word and act become one, and humanity becomes part of the Great Dance wherein each element knows its place and seeks the continuation of the system which is essential to its own well-being:

The thoughts with which he approached the Mysteries faded. He distinguished no longer word from act; he was in the presence, he was a part of the Act which far away issues in those faint words, "Let us make man"—creation rose and flowed out and wheeled to its august return—"in Our image, after Our likeness"—the great pronouns were the sound of that return. Faster and faster all things moved through that narrow channel he had before seen and now himself seemed to be entering and beyond it they issued again into similar but different existence—themselves still, yet infused and made one in an undreamed perfection. (WH, pp. 253–254)

Thus, though what he is describing is death and resurrection, Williams makes of it an expansion of consciousness and awareness, not merely a putting aside of the physical and worldly in favor of the spiritual. Moreover, in his refusal to make the Archdeacon a tragic figure, whether in his confrontations with Gregory and Manasseh or in the moment of his death, Williams suggests the same kind of comic tradition that Lewis does at the moment of Venus's descent to earth and Ransom's passing from earth in *That Hideous Strength*.

Lionel Rackstraw's role is a different one from that of the Archdeacon, who possesses the essential comic knowledge throughout the novel. Lionel has to learn that such knowledge and experience are possible, for he begins with a tragic attitude that proceeds from a kind of romantic existentialism. Terrified of a world he can neither understand nor control, Lionel believes in and denies nothing, revealing his attitude by his question, "What mightn't be true, in this terrifying and obscene universe?" (WH, p. 19) Flattered by Gregory Persimmons's attentions to Lionel and frightened by Barbara's strange attack, Lionel nevertheless avoids the trap of his own ego by a curiously stubborn skepticism which also enables him to avoid Gregory's open invitation to indulge in ultimate power. Replying that "there is no satisfaction and no delight that has not treachery within it," (WH, p. 167) Lionel dismisses the idea that there is any more possibility of ultimate rapture in the worship of evil than of good, insisting that "Satanism is the clerk at the brothel" (WH, p. 168) and that "there is no way to delight in the horrible." (WH, p. 168) In this dismissal, then, he reduces both evil and himself to the proper proportions, while not yet understanding the possibilities for joy in his daily experiences.

This lack of understanding continues until after Adrian has been rescued and Gregory arrested and charged with murder, though again the lack of understanding is tempered by Lionel's refusal to make an absolute out of what is despair over a world that he cannot control or understand. When Prester John points out, however, that Lionel loves his fears precisely because he feels himself so alive that he fears losing life in the business of daily existence, Lionel suddenly realizes that what he has been seeking is "annihilation," but annihilation of the kind brought on by the hope of heaven. Prester John puts it this way: " 'Death you shall have at least,' the other said. 'But God only gives, and He has only Himself to give, and He can give it only in those conditions which are Himself. Wait but a few years, and He shall give you the death you desire. But do not grudge too much if you find that death and heaven are one.' " (WH, p. 251) The effect of what Lionel experiences, then, in the moments following the Archdeacon's death is to redefine his concept of life in such a way as to make a place for joy: "He felt suddenly the joy of the fantasy rise in his mind." (WH, p. 256) He does not and is not willing to adopt a Christian abstraction, but his experience has brought him to recognize the possibilities for joy in his own life because he has now experienced it in precisely the same manner as he has experienced the despair. Very much like Bellow's *Herzog* in a novel of an entirely different kind, Lionel too is content "to be just as it is willed, and for as long as I may remain in occupancy."[3]

The abstractions usually so prominent in Williams's novels are in relatively short supply in this one. The Graal, the first and most evident, is finally relegated to a secondary spot largely due to the attitude of the Archdeacon. Though he steals it from Gregory and though he acknowledges that "of all things still discoverable in the world the Graal had been nearest to the Divine and Universal Heart," (WH, p. 137) he also understands that it is creation itself that is important rather than its symbol, and he understands even more clearly that creation manifests itself far more through the "thousand dutifully celebrated Mysteries in his priestly life" (WH, p. 137) than through any symbol. He illustrates the difference between his attitude and that of Mornington and the Duke towards the Graal when he gives it to Manasseh for "curing" Barbara: "For myself, I would not have delayed so long. I would give up any relic, however wonderful, to save anyone an hour's neuralgia—man depends too much on these things." (WH, p. 184) This pragmatic emphasis upon life and joy rather than martyrdom for oneself or for others contrasts sharply with Mornington's worship of the Graal as the essence of poetry or the Duke's adoration of its ancient ecclesiastical functions. Precisely for this reason, then, the Graal is subordinated throughout the novel to the central characters, their experiences, and their actions.

The only other major abstraction in the novel is that of power, the power sought by Gregory Persimmons. Power, for Persimmons, is far more than simply control over his own affairs or even those of other people. It is the adoration of power and strength as a god, not for what it can do, but as an abstraction sufficient unto itself. It is, of course, a power based on denial and rejection rather than on affirmation, and its ultimate rejection is that of life itself:

> He found that by chance he was now in touch with two or three persons who found no satisfaction in desire and possession and power. No power of destruction seemed to satisfy Manasseh's hunger; no richness of treasure to arouse the Archdeacon's. And as he moved in these unaccustomed regions he felt that what was lacking was delight. It had delighted him in the past to overbear and torment; but Manasseh's greed had never found content. And delight was far too small a word for the peace in which the Archdeacon moved; a sky of serenity overarched Gregory when he thought of the priest, against which his own arrows were shot in vain. He saw it running from the east to the west; he saw below it, in the midst of a flat circle of emptiness, the face of the Greek spewing out venom. Absurdly enough, he felt himself angered by the mere uselessness of this; it was something of the same irritation which he had expressed to his son on the proportion of capital expended on the worst kind of popular novel. Enjoyment was all very well, but enjoyment oughtn't to be merely wasteful. It annoyed him as his father had annoyed him by wasting emotions and strength in mere stupid, senile worry. Adrian must be taught the uselessness of that—power was the purpose of spiritual things, and Satan the lord of power. (WH, pp. 236–237)

What is significant here is that Gregory is not seeking life, joy, physical satisfaction, or anything else concrete through this abstraction. Instead he is seeking to make himself a god, one who rules over and is superior to his environment, or, alternatively, to become a servant of the god whose name is power. In any case, it is a rejection of what experience has taught him in the persons of Manasseh and the Archdeacon and an acceptance of the abstraction he holds within himself. The end result is, of course, a defeat for the abstraction, not because of a superior abstraction, but because of the fact of the Archdeacon's joy, Lionel's skepticism, and Adrian's unabashed delight in a world which he cannot begin to understand intellectually.

Thus *War in Heaven* is successful as fantasy precisely because it goes beyond its detective trappings and its attempts at a formally realistic setting to explore the experience of the Archdeacon and Lionel as contrasted with that of Gregory and Manasseh. Its clearly Christian overtones and myths, such as the Graal and Prester John, flow from rather than are imposed upon the novel itself, and the ultimate affirmation is of the importance of the kind of system that makes humanity's survival, with some degree of happiness and some degree of freedom, possible. Characters and events are preferred to symbols and rhetorical flights, and the reader is not forced to strain his or her credulity by any strong contradiction between fantastic and realistic elements.

ALL HALLOW'S EVE

All Hallow's Eve is the most successful of Williams's novels precisely because there is no contradiction between the two parallel worlds or the characters who inhabit them. It is clearly fantasy in the same sense that Lewis's, Tolkien's, Herbert's, and Chant's are, though in a different form. The difference is that Williams sets his novel on earth rather than moving it to a distant planet (as Lewis does), moving it to another time (as Tolkien does), or cutting entirely the specific ties between the present and the fantasy world (as Chant and Herbert do). Perhaps still more important, there is an even greater sense of the importance of character and event—as opposed to abstractions and theology—than in *War in Heaven*. Most important of all, however, is the unity between the two worlds and the manner in which that unity reinforces the validity of experience over creed of whatever kind.

It is significant that the relationship between the two worlds does not turn upon a physical object nor upon a specific doctrine. While Williams may well be exploring the meaning of "co-inherence," neither the term nor its theological/metaphysical implications are ever mentioned. Instead Williams presents Lester and Evelyn as inhabitants of one world, Richard and Jonathan as inhabitants of the other, and Simon and Betty as links between the two. Thus the focus is upon the characters, each of whom is credible in the world in which he or she participates, and upon the effect which actions in the one have upon the other. For example, Lester's opening account of her world emphasizes silence, loneliness, and despair, each of which is mitigated initially when she meets Evelyn. Shortly after that meeting, however, she discovers that Evelyn is as petty and boring as she was in the world of the living, that she is as little capable of being relied upon, and that she is more likely to entrap by obligation than by merit. That awareness forces Lester into an acknowledgment of her responsibility in creating joy or sorrow in her own life and subsequently allows her to move into Betty's life, to assist and to accept the pain that comes as a consequence of full participation in the system. She acknowledges that Betty's judgment of her is monumentally important, and she further acknowledges that Betty must judge on the basis of full knowledge. What she is seeking is not forgiveness or validity, but a joy that comes from a sum total of good which counterbalances the evil and/or harm she may have done: "The air she breathed was fresh with joy; the room was loaded with it. She knew it as a sick woman knows the summer. She herself was not yet happy, but this kind of happiness was new to her; . . . They belonged here, those times; yet those times were as true as those other sinful times that danced without . . . perhaps this hovering flicker of known joy might be permitted to go with her."[4] When Lester subsequently accepts the death Simon has aimed at Betty, when she enters voluntarily with Evelyn into the dwarf's body, and when she participates in the last dramatic scene with Simon, Lester gives further credibility to the City she inhabits and further amplification of its laws. She does not become a symbol of creeds or dogmas or philosophies; she is the embodiment of her own actions in a system to which she ultimately accommodates herself in actions that involve the petty as well as the heroic. Finally, she links her environment to her own actions just as clearly as Evelyn does. The difference between them is that Evelyn seeks to rule her world, and thus she is destroyed by it. Lester accommodates herself to the natural laws of hers and thereby enhances her own ability to partake of its joy as well as of its pain and sorrow.

If Lester and Evelyn illustrate clearly the reality of their City, then Jonathan and Richard illustrate equally as clearly the reality of theirs. Jonathan represents that reality perhaps most clearly in his two paintings. The painting of Simon with its face of "peculiar deadness" and the people whose "whole mass of inclined backs could be seen almost as a ranked mass of beetles" (AHE, p. 48) shows the evil present in its disgusting obscenity. The painting of the city with its light "concealed in houses and in their projected shadows, lying in ambush in the cathedral, opening in the rubble, vivid in the vividness of the sky" is "universal and lived." (AHE, p. 41) Full of the promise of joy arising from actions and experiences, it too is representative of its world. When these paintings are taken in conjunction with Jonathan's love for Betty and his ultimate acceptance of what she must do, the reality of his world is clearly established. Richard functions in a similar fashion, though by different means. Motivated by love and loneliness, Richard is the active counterpart of the more contemplative Jonathan. But this activity must be balanced by the contemplation, since contemplation and activity are parts of the system of which Lester is a part; indeed, they are like the two faces of Lester herself:

He had never before clearly understood that sense of Lester as now when that second line must be rationally untrue. But his sleep had restored to him something he had once had and had lost—something deeper even than Lester, something that lay at the root of all magic, that the body was itself integral to spirit. He had in his time talked a good deal about anthropomorphism and now he realized that anthropomorphism was but one dialect of divine truth. The high thing which was now in his mind, the body that had walked and lain by his, was itself celestial and it was only visible Lester. (AHE, p. 191)

Thus both Jonathan (in his paintings) and Richard (in his understanding of Lester) ultimately affirm the physical and spiritual character of the world they inhabit. Moreover, they affirm, by the conclusion of the novel, the importance of understanding both worlds through experience that acknowledges body and soul just as it does joy and pain, beauty and ugliness, life and death.

Simon and Betty, the evil and good forces in the novel, respectively, link the two worlds more directly than do any of the other characters. Simon's lust is for a power that is remarkably similar to what Gregory Persimmons wants in *War in Heaven*. He is a full participant in the "real" world of Jonathan and Richard in his attempts to amass money, political prestige, and physical control. However, he is equally a participant in the "other" world in his attempts to bind the spirits there to him in such a way as to "undo death." Thus Simon has both a physical power in the primary world—his ability to banish or cure people's ills—and a spiritual power in the secondary world—his ability to send Betty into it on her errands. His real interest, though, is in neither. His real interest lies in domination, as he indicates when he tells Jonathan, "I shall give all these little people peace because they believe in me. But these fancies of light would distract them. There is only one art and that is to show them their master." (AHE, p. 66) It is further revealed in his division of himself, in his entrapment of Evelyn and Lester in the dwarf's body, and in his ultimately unsuccessful struggle at the conclusion of the novel. Betty, by contrast, is the positive link between the two worlds. A girl who, at the beginning of the novel, is pictured as something of a pathetic, spiritless creature, Betty travels in both worlds, first by Simon's command and later by her own strength. The movement from one state to the other occurs partly as a result of her own inner strength and partly as the result of the love of Lester and Jonathan. During the first trip Simon sends her on in the novel, her own strength is heightened by her acceptance of herself as she is. "Someone had once told her that her mind wasn't very strong, and 'indeed it isn't,' she thought gaily, 'but it's quite strong enough to do what it's got to do, and what it hasn't got to do it needn't worry about not doing.' " (AHE, p. 82) Jonathan and Lester's love gives her the strength to resist Simon and ultimately to link the two worlds directly in the healing power she exhibits at the conclusion. A transmutation of Simon's apparent ability to heal, Betty's power is real. It comes from the other world, but it must be exercised fully in this one, where there is, as Plankin tells them, always "one more upstairs." (AHE, p. 239)

When these characters are taken together with the repeated assertions that the world is a whole, then the novel comes together in a remarkably compelling fashion. Lester's sense is that she belongs "to some great whole," (AHE, p. 168) and in that whole is every facet of experience, dirt as well as light. As she puts it: "The evacuations of the City had their place in the City; how else could the City be the City? Corruption (so to call it) was tolerable, even adequate and proper, even glorious. These things also were facts. They could not be forgotten or lost in fantasy; all that had been, was; all that was, was." (AHE, p. 198) The dirt is not to be disregarded; after all, Simon does cause pain and death, and Lester herself is separated from Richard. But in the face of the possibility of joy and love, then the dirt too was an experience worth having. "Neither of them took the word [tempt] seriously enough, nor needed to, to feel that this was what all temptations were—matter for dancing mockery and high exchange of laughter, things so impossible that they could be enjoyed as an added delight of love." (AHE, p. 166) In the final analysis, *All Hallow's Eve* is successful precisely because it creates worlds consistent with themselves and with the characters who inhabit them. Moreover, it creates for the reader the sense of joy that is possible through experience without ever denying the pain that also emanates from experience. Finally, its tragic figures, if Evelyn and Simon and Lady Wallingford can be called tragic, perish miserably, while its comic figures endure. They do not promise that miracles will always happen or that good will always triumph; they only suggest that it is possible in a world in which humanity becomes intimately aware of its total relation to its own environment.

THE PLACE OF THE LION

The Place of the Lion has clearly the most explicit ecological theme of any of Williams's novels, and yet it is also one of his most unsatisfactory works. The reasons are similar to those for Herbert's failure in *God Emperor of Dune*. First, Williams cannot reconcile the comic, ecological theme with either the tone or the abstract ideas that become his central concern. Second, he attempts to combine the physical and the spiritual world in such a way that neither can ever become credible. Finally, his preference for allegory and symbolism so overwhelms the novel that the characters themselves become secondary to what they represent and to the language used to present them. This is not to say that the novel is without merit. The description of the creature Damaris beholds in her father's house, the wolf's attack on Quentin, and Anthony's "naming" of the animals are scenes of as much descriptive power and imaginative clarity as any in fantasy literature. Unfortunately, however, they are not sufficient to overcome the heavy-handed manipulation of character, setting, and event that characterizes the rest of the novel.

Though the characters are not comic ultimately, despite some attempts to make both Damaris and Anthony so, the novel is heavily oriented toward ecological concerns, at least insofar as it emphasizes the importance of the system to uphold balance, the necessary interrelation between ideas and reality, and the power of humans to affect for good or ill their physical environment. With regard to the system and its balance, the entire novel centers around the disjunction which has been created between abstractions and actions. The lion, the snake, and all the other animals are nothing more than the concrete forms of various Platonic concepts which have been held over the ages. However, those animals as seen in the novel are divorced from their controlling feature, and the result is a kind of ferocity and destruction. As Anthony thinks just prior to his naming of the beasts: "The lion should lie down with the lamb. Separately they had issued—

strength divorced from innocence, fierceness from joy. They must go back together; somehow they must be called."[5] Nor is this theme limited to the conclusion of the text. It is carried throughout in the person of Damaris, who has been studying the ideas all along without believing that they had practical reality. It has formed the basis for the conversations of Anthony and Quentin, neither of whom knew precisely what they meant when they talked about the ideas. And what is clear in all these cases is that, divorced from the entire system of which they are a part, the creatures are fearsome, beautiful, evil, and/or disgusting in turn. Anthony notes rightly the importance of the system in preventing these disturbances when he comments on balance:

But some things were possible only to a man in companionship, and of these the most important was balance. No mind was so good that it did not need another mind to counter and equal it, and to save it from conceit and blindness and bigotry and folly. Only in such a balance could humility be found, humility which was a lucid speed to welcome lucidity whenever and wherever it presented itself. . . . Balance—and movement in balance, as an eagle sails up on the wind—this was the truth of life, and beauty in life. (PL, p. 187)

Finally, at the conclusion of the novel, the disturbances are ended when the balance is righted, when Anthony has named the animals and each has rejoined the system which made it possible in the first place. So the lesson is clear. Destroy the balance, destroy the system by elevating any abstraction out of its proper sphere, and the result is destruction of the entire system as well as destruction of the individuals within it, as the fates of Ms. Wilmot and Mr. Foster so clearly illustrate.

The problem is that this theme is at odds with both the tone and the central concerns of the novel. The tone is alternately lyric, as in the description of Mr. Tighe and the butterflies, and apocalyptic, as in Damaris's vision of the creature in her father's house. Moreover, it is essentially tragic in concept, insisting upon the sacrifice of the supremely important individual for a moral or ethical abstraction. Anthony becomes the tragic hero as he saves his world; Damaris brings a virginal innocence which eventually becomes a humble grace. Finally, the total emphasis is upon abstractions rather than action and/or characterization. Anthony's long deliberation concerning will and choice is but one example of this emphasis. Nor is this abstraction or any of the others in the novel integrated with the action. The abstractions remain the center of interest, thereby subordinating both plot and character.

A second major problem with the novel is that the attempted combination of the Platonic realities and the physical universe of Smetham does not work at all. A quiet, stodgy, nondescript English country town inhabited by the incarnation of the ancient gods, even if divorced from their sources, is simply unbelievable. Then, to suggest that the union be made more complete by the transformation of its people into animal-like creatures—all the while denying every aspect of their animality save that of ferocity, strength, and destructiveness—stretches the credulity of the reader even further. Of equal or perhaps even greater importance is the fact that there are no characters specifically to represent either world. In *All Hallow's Eve* the world of the City is represented clearly by Lester and is tied directly to the primary world by Simon and Betty. However, no one in *The Place of the Lion* represents the world of the abstractions; no one gives life or credibility to it or even suggests an understanding of it. Foster speaks of it, Quentin speaks of it, and none of them know it at all. Moreover, since they attempt to create the abstraction through another abstraction, an abstraction rising out of their own bias and confusion, the result is not clarity but confusion for the reader. Smetham is poorly created as well. We see virtually none of the village as a real world separate and distinct from its symbolic function. In *War in Heaven*, Castra Parvulorum was a fully realized place, and in *All Hallow's Eve* London of both the City and of the primary world was described in some detail. But the same is not true of Smetham. We see none of its ordinary people, we know nothing of its setting under ordinary circumstances, and there are none of its animals whom we see as anything more than symbols. Since neither the world of Smetham nor the world of the Platonic realities can compel belief, the reader is left holding little more than a set of abstractions which are themselves incredible without the structure to support them.

Williams's preference for allegory and symbolism gives the final blow to this novel. A lion that comes roaring out of a fire which erupts from a peaceful meadow for no other reason than to destroy a town and a people who are no better and no worse than many other towns and peoples needs a strong structure to support it, and there is no such structure here. Tolkien's Ents and Orcs are vital, alive, and eminently realistic precisely because he has created the world in which they are logical living creatures. The lion and snake are not. They are symbols, and they ought to mean something, as Williams has Anthony tell us: " 'I can't entirely disbelieve it without refusing to believe in ideas', Anthony answered, 'and I can't do that. I can't go back on the notion that all these abstractions do mean something important to us. And mayn't they have a way of existing that I didn't know? Haven't we agreed about the importance of ideas often enough?' " (PL, p. 63) The problem is that they don't mean anything in the context of the novel other than what Williams obviously manipulates them to mean. The butterflies seen by Mr. Tighe become a symbol which is then taken up by Anthony, and rather than leaving the marvelous characterization by Mr. Tighe alone—"I find that mutton helps butterflies and butterflies mutton" (PL, p. 26)—Williams must make the butterflies into a symbol of ineffable beauty through Damaris, Anthony, and the others. This is similar to the difference between the Hawthorne of "Young Goodman Brown" and the Hawthorne of "Egotism; or, The Bosom Serpent." The former is a marvelously controlled story which transcends its allegory and symbolism by the reality of its characters and the control of its tone; the latter is marked by overstatement, authorial intrusion, and overburdened diction. There is a similar contrast between the Williams of *War in Heaven* and *All Hallow's Eve* and the Williams of *The Place of the Lion*. His description of the naming of the animals should be sufficient to make the point clear:

A voice, crying out in song, went through the air of Eden, a voice that swept up as the eagle, and with every call renewed its youth. All music was the scattered echo of that voice; all poetry was the approach of the fallen understanding to that unfallen meaning. All things were named—all but man himself, then the sleep fell upon the Adam, and in that first sleep he strove to utter his name, and as he strove he was divided and woke to find humanity doubled. The name of mankind was in neither voice but in both; the knowledge of the name and its utterance was in the perpetual interchange of love. Whoever denied that austere godhead, wherever and however it appeared—its presence, its austerity, its divinity—refused the name of man. (PL, p. 191)

The language is noble with a nobility of high romance and tragedy. However, that nobility is rhetorical, not actual, for the abstraction itself is rendered in terms of abstractions. This is not the author creating an emotion in which the reader can share; it is the author telling the reader of an emotion that the author has had and which he wants the reader to accept, and in that process of naming emotion rather than showing it, Williams has violated one of the most basic rules of fantasy.

Thus *The Place of the Lion* fails both aesthetically and thematically. In spite of the emphasis on balance set up so clearly in the ecological theme, the remainder of the novel insists quite clearly that neither balance nor common sense is what is needed, Mr. Tighe's comment on mutton notwithstanding. Instead it pictures the tragic extremes and upholds them as the ideal which an imperfect man or woman will come to once having gone beyond his or her present limited state, and it does so in characters who are convincing neither as people nor as symbols.

DESCENT INTO HELL

Descent into Hell is perhaps the most curious of Williams's novels. Judged by many, including T. S. Eliot, to be his best work, it is none-theless unsatisfactory in almost every way. Its characters are remark-ably flat, its settings peculiarly unconvincing, and its language dis-tressingly overdone. And yet it has merits that cannot be denied. The merits lie largely in a consistent and compellingly simple portrayal of the interdependence of all elements of the universe and in occasional bursts of language that are eminently appropriate to the subject being described. It is almost as if Williams had chosen a subject and theme which, in their simplicity, could not be made to carry the burden of philosophical maunderings and abstract theological drivel which too often substitute for character and action in Williams's novels. Even its failure, however, tells a good deal about the limits of fantasy and the extent to which fantasy depends upon a basically ecological per-spective.

The ecological themes of the novel are, if taken in isolation, well handled and convincing. Perhaps the center of this theme is the em-phasis upon the interdependence of all things and the incredible de-struction which the tragic glorification of the individual wreaks upon both the individual and his or her system. Two examples make this clear. In the first, Pauline has been invited to allow Stanhope to help her with her fear. When she responds that she must be separate from everyone else and not depend upon anyone, Stanhope's reproof is un-mistakable:

If you want to disobey and refuse the laws that are common to us all, if you want to live in pride and division and anger, you can. But if you will be part of the best of us, and live and laugh and be ashamed with us, then you must be content to be helped.

If you want to respect yourself, if to respect yourself you must go clean against the nature of things, if you must refuse Omnipotence in order to respect yourself, though why you should want so extremely to respect yourself is more than I can guess, why, go on and respect.[6]

The universe lives by laws which apply to all creatures, and perhaps the chief of those laws is that of the necessity of depending on others and allowing others to depend on you. This is clearly beyond the role of tragic or culture heros who must sacrifice themselves for their country, their god, or their concept of morality. Rather, it is a concrete action taken upon the basis of experience which suggests that any other course of action is likely to lead to isolation and death. And this theme is carried out to some extent in the events of the play: Wentworth isolates himself and is lost; Pauline integrates herself with her fellow creatures and prospers, just as Mrs. Parry and her production of the play flourish precisely because of the successful interdependence of the author, actors, director, and producer.

The second example relates specifically to the play written by Stanhope and to the relation between poetry and language and those things it represents; I strongly suspect that it is the reason for the praise which so many critics have lavished on the novel:

The words she had so long admired did not lose their force or beauty, but they were the mere feel of the texture. The harmony of motion and speech, now about to begin, held and was composed by the pauses: foot to foot, line to line, here a little and there a little. She knew he had always spoken poetry against the silence of this world; now she knew it had to be spoken against— that perhaps, but also something greater, some silence of its own. She recognized the awful space of separating stillness which all mighty art creates about itself, or, uncreating, makes clear to mortal apprehension. Such art, out of "the mind's abyss," makes tolerable, at the first word or note or instructed glance, the preluding presence of the abyss. It creates in an instant its own past. Then its significance mingles with other significances; the stillness gives up kindred meanings, each in its own orb, till by the subtlest graduations they press into altogether other significances, and these again into others, and so into one contemporaneous nature, as in that gathering unity of time from which

Lilith feverishly fled. But that nature is to us a darkness, a stillness, only felt by the reverberations of the single speech. (DH, p. 180)

Like the naming of the animals, this idea suggests an integral connection between the otherwise divided aspects of the universe, a connection which can be made precisely because the processes of naming and creating become one, because the relation of thought to action and of both to words thereby becomes an explicit, almost physical entity. Now certainly this is an inherent part of the ecological perspective as well, for if the tensions between the various elements in a work of art are really similar to the tensions between creatures in a climax ecosystem, then it requires no great leap to suggest that poetry is a primary example of the interdependence of all of the created universe. Moreover, and perhaps most important of all, the whole idea suggests a system whose interdependence is so great that it makes tragic posturing a prelude to individual death and an omen of systemic disorder of enormous proportions.

The problem with these ecological themes is that they are treated only in isolation themselves, and they are subordinated entirely to Williams's principal concerns with individual damnation and isolation. The characters in the novel are, without exception, flat. Wentworth, the scholar who sells his soul for the physical pleasures of his Lilith-like succubus, should be the most completely developed character in the novel, but he is not. His dreams of climbing down the rope, his descent further into hell itself, his petty fears and jealousies are one-dimensional. Perhaps the choice between heaven and hell rests upon shoulderknots indeed, but if so then heaven and hell are both significantly less important than humans have been wont to believe or Williams to claim so ardently. And yet it is precisely upon that point that we are told Wentworth has consigned himself to hell. Moreover, we never see in Wentworth anything of the kind of intellectual honesty or rigor which Williams would have us believe makes his fall so tragic. What we see instead is a petty, self-important little man of irrelevant concerns who lusts in a minor fashion after a not-too-attractive girl until, disappointed, he turns to the equivalent of intellectual masturbation to satisfy himself.

Other characters are equally flat. Adela is the vain and silly beauty whose superficiality of mind and vapidness of spirit deserve neither the ideal Wentworth projects upon her nor the fate she meets at the conclusion of the novel. Pauline is the typical heroine of Williams's lesser novels: the basically good but originally misguided woman who comes to appreciate the awful grandeur of God and who ultimately accepts the sacrifice demanded of her. The problem is that Pauline is real in neither role. If she is as limited and fearful as Williams pictures her at the beginning of the novel, then it is simply not credible for her to accept her ancestor's fear of the flames or to feel and to understand the magnificent statement about poetry quoted previously. Peter Stanhope, the deus ex machina figure encountered under a different name (Prester John) in *War in Heaven*, serves as little more than an opportunity for Williams to introduce his musings on poetry and to save Pauline from the clutches of Lily Sammile. Finally, the murdered workman to whom so much space is devoted becomes neither convincingly parallel to Wentworth nor connected in any substantive way to the main story line. In fact, the only convincing character is Margaret Anstruther, whose vision of heaven is focused by her kowledge of hell and whose death is far more affecting than anything else in the novel. Nor is it unimportant that each of these characters is constructed on an either/or basis far more typical of tragedy than of comedy. Each comments at some point on the opposite extreme, but none ever experiences or acts out anything other than the singularly limited role demanded by Williams's relentless pursuit of his theological point.

The settings are equally unconvincing. The society of Battle Hill is seen only through its characters, and only in the person of Ms. Parry is there an interest in anything other than self. Unfortunately, however, Ms. Parry and her interest in the larger confines of her society are treated only peripherally. She is one who succeeds because of her devotion to duty, a fact which emphasizes her concern with the concrete as opposed to the abstract and which makes her the only character in the novel besides Margaret Anstruther who is anything more than a stick figure for ideas. The world of the dead—or of the hell which the workman and Wentworth and Lily Sammile all enter—is even less convincing, for it consists of one abstraction after another. The attempt is made to create a world similar to that developed later in *All Hallow's Eve*, but the lack of realization and the emphasis upon Wentworth's spiritual as opposed to his physical descent renders the entire scene in terms of psychological or theological analysis rather than artistic or fantastic creation.

Finally, the language of the novel, while occasionally as magnificent as indicated by the comment on poetry, is vague and dead. A typical example is this description of the workman's approach to his imminent suicide: "He went up as if he mounted on the bones of his body built so carefully for this; he clambered through his skeleton to the place of his skull, and receded, as if almost in a corporeal ingression, to the place of propinquent death." (DH, p. 29) Full of polysyllabic abstractions, the language conveys neither the horror of the act, the despair of the man, nor the terrible significance of the system in which it occurs. The same kind of language carries throughout the novel, as is illustrated when Williams attempts to make a significant connection between the workman and Wentworth:

The chamber of that dark fundamental incest had had the dead man for its earliest inhabitant, though his ways and Wentworth's had been far apart—as far as incest from murder, or as self-worship from self-loathing, and either in essence false to all that is. But the self-worship of the one was the potential source of cruelty, as self-loathing of the other was the actual effect of cruelty; between them lay all the irresolute vacillations of mankind, nourishing the one and producing the other. All who had lived, or did or could live, upon Battle Hill, leaned to one or the other, save only those whom holy love had freed by its revelation of something ever alien from and conjoined with the self. (DH, p. 132)

This language does not make the connection. Neither does it make either Wentworth or the workman matter in any significant emotional fashion to the readers. A final example from what should be the most dramatic point in the novel will complete the point:

Pauline saw her sitting, an old woman crouched on the ground. As the girl gazed the old woman stirred and tried to speak; there issued from her lips a meaningless gabble, such gabble as Dante, inspired, attributes to the guardian of all the circles of hell. The angelic energy which had been united with Pauline's mortality radiated from her; nature, and more than nature, abhors a vacuum. Her mind and senses could not yet receive comprehensibly the motions of the spirit, but that adoring centre dominated her, and flashes of its great capacity passed through her, revealing if but in flashes, the single world of existence. Otherwise, the senses of her redeemed body were hardly capable yet of fruition; they had to grow and strengthen till, in their perfection, they should give to her and the universe added delight. (DH, p. 207)

This meeting of Lilith and the Virgin and the dissolution of the kingdom of hell that immediately follows ought to be concrete and moving. Instead it begins in an image which is subsequently abandoned for theological/metaphysical abstractions. Pauline is not a woman; she is the love of God. Lilith/Lily is not a demon nor a temptress nor even a disgusting old crone; she is the medieval vice, despair. Moreover, neither of the two is consistent with what Pauline had supposedly felt earlier in her thoughts about poetry or what Lilith/Lily had earlier offered Wentworth. The characters, in short, simply vanish into the theological preoccupations, and the novel is left with neither the absolute grandeur nor the utter ugliness that Williams has tried so hard to create.

This novel, then, like *The Place of the Lion*, ultimately fails because it does not fulfill the requirements of fantasy in setting, tone, and theme. Neither of its worlds is convincing, its tone is largely set by polysyllabic abstractions rather than fully realized characters or descriptions, and its tragic theological themes are at constant odds with its implied comic and ecological patterns.

MANY DIMENSIONS, THE GREATER TRUMPS, AND SHADOWS OF ECSTASY

Many Dimensions and *The Greater Trumps* fall somewhere in between the relative excellence of *War in Heaven* and *All Hallow's Eve* and the relative failure of *The Place of the Lion* and *Descent into Hell.* *Shadows of Ecstasy* seems to me to be so different from Williams's other novels as to lie totally outside the genre of fantasy.

Many Dimensions seems, at first glance, to be quite similar to *War in Heaven*, and the plot outline is indeed similar—a competition between forces of good and evil for possession of a sacred object of immense power. However the similarities end there, for there are no central, unifying themes in *Many Dimensions*. The Crown of Suleiman containing a stone engraved with the Tetragrammaton is the center of all activity, and activity is the central concern of the novel. Reginald Montague, Sir Giles Tumulty, Prince Ali Mirza Khan, Lord Arglay, Chloe Burnett, Angus Sheldrake, and Frank Lindsay all actively seek possession of the stone, while a host of others, including the Mayor of Rich and the British government itself, seek its power for their own specific purposes. Thus the object is not only the motive for the plot in the novel, but it is also the center of a thematic interest which is never fully developed. No major ecological themes are present; in fact no real themes of any kind are present. The half-hearted attempt to present the stone as the end of desire and to suggest thereby the humility and selflessness so important to the Christian tradition falls prey to plots and counterplots more suggestive of a spy thriller than of an ecological, comic, or tragic tradition.

The Greater Trumps, on the other hand, comes much closer to being one of Williams's best novels precisely because the ecological themes are clearly stated throughout. The tarot cards are themselves, in part, representatives of the elements, as Henry indicates when he says, "It's said that the shuffling of the cards is the earth, and the pattering of the cards is the rain, and the beating of the cards is the wind, and the pointing of the cards is the fire."[7] This tie to the elements is further strengthened when Nancy creates the elements from the cards, and it is brought to a dramatic conclusion when Henry calls up and then loses control of the storm. But this tie to the elements does not rest solely on the more obvious plot elements alone, for these elements are ultimately subordinated to the larger idea of the Great Dance. In Williams, as in Lewis, this Great Dance is a statement reminiscent of Dante's *Comedy* and is closely parallel to both the ecological and the comic traditions:

. . . imagine that everything which exists takes part in the movement of a great dance—everything, the electrons, all growing and decaying things, men and beasts, trees and stones, everything that changes, and there is nothing anywhere that does not change. That change—that's what we know of the immortal dance; the law in the nature of things—that's the measure of the dance, why one thing changes swiftly and another slowly, why there is seeming accident and incalculable alteration, why men hate and love and grow hungry, and cities that have stood for centuries fall in a week, why the smallest wheel and the mightiest world revolve, why blood flows and the heart beats and the brain moves, why your body is poised on your ankles and the Himalayas are rooted in the earth—quick or slow, measurable or immeasurable, there is nothing at all anywhere but the dance. (GT, p. 98)

In its insistence upon interdependence rather than isolation, upon system rather than individual, and upon change rather than permanence, the description is ecological in every sense. Moreover, the action in the novel itself centers around this ecological theme, culminating as it does with Nancy and Henry's movement into the center of the figures who represent the whole system of the dance. Thus, nature is at the center of the plot, and the Great Dance is the center of the theme. This kind of structural and thematic integration works to establish a world which is convincingly portrayed and whose fantastic elements meet Tolkien's criterion of being probable within the total context.

The characters in *Many Dimensions* are as shallow and flat as the plot would seem to imply. Lord Arglay is the wise skeptic, Chloe Burnett the true believer, Sir Giles Tumulty the basely evil villain, Angus Sheldrake the greedy industrialist, and Frank Shelton the weak young man. Each character participates in a series of harrowing adventures, but none becomes fully human and none reveals any great complexity. Again, they are more like the characters in a spy thriller or detective novel, each of whom serves a function in the plot but none of whom becomes anything more.

The characters in *The Greater Trumps*, however, are an entirely different matter. Each of them is a richly complex human being in his or her relationship with both the primary and the secondary world. Moreover, each of them acts in a fashion ultimately consistent with the comic, ecological theme. Sybil Coningsby illustrates the central concerns most clearly when she insists that "the present's so entirely satisfactory." (GT, p. 49) She goes on to illustrate that satisfaction as she accepts and accommodates herself to a system that she understands through love. She tells Nancy to "go and live. Go and love." (GT, p. 143) It is the rule she has practiced in her own life, and it has led her to a joy and satisfaction that can reach such diverse people as Joanna and Mr. Coningsby. Likewise, Nancy's success comes, not from domination, but from an accommodation of herself to a system whose demands she only vaguely realizes even as she finds ways to put herself in harmony with it:

It had been she who had pointed the way, the thought of which had been driven from his mind by the catastrophe that had overwhelmed it. It was she who went first, not by his will but by her own—nor could he then guess how much, to Nancy's own heart, her purpose and courage seemed to derive from him. His power was useless till she drew it forth; it worked through her, but it was from him that it still obscurely rose. Though she ruled instead of him in the place of the mist, it was he who had given her that sovereignty, and it seemed to her then that, though all dominions of heaven and earth denied it, she would acknowledge that profound suzerainty while her being had any knowledge of itself at all. (GT, p. 161)

Nancy is not the divinely appointed ruler; she is dependent on Henry, just as Henry is dependent on her and just as all things are dependent on all others in any climax ecosystem. Moreover, Nancy and all the other characters are rich and complex human beings. Nancy may be queen, but she is also the rather silly and headstrong girl who so mocks her father. Mr. Coningsby may be a kind of awkward and foolish stuffed shirt, but he is also a blunderingly loving father and brother. Henry may be a would-be murderer, but he is also a man of strength, compassion, and capacity for repentance. Similar kinds of observations might be made about each of the characters, for all are multidimensional, and they all either illustrate or come to accept the comic perspective of the Great Dance by the conclusion of the novel. And if the Great Dance itself is the emblem of God as it is experienced and understood by the characters, it is tied to their concrete experience, as Nancy indicates in considering the kind of joy it brings: "But the energy that thrilled there was exactly right; its tingling messages announced to her a state of easy health as the throbbing messages of diseased mankind proclaim so often a state of suffering. Joy itself was sensuous; she received its communication through the earth of which she was made." (GT, p. 187)

Setting is as unimportant in *Many Dimensions* as are the characters and theme. Whether in London, on Angus Sheldrake's estate, or in the town of Rich, the setting does nothing more than form a backdrop against which the struggle for possession of the stone occurs. Moreover, it is significant that there are not primary and secondary worlds here. The world of the stone remains a shadowy abstraction, with the most we ever see of it being its capacity to move people through time and space. Thus it appears to be less the creation of a secondary world than a simple demonstration of the laws which affect the primary world. Nor is the primary world any more fully realized. Neither the urban nor the rural setting is important; it just happens to be where another segment of the plot is acted out.

In *The Greater Trumps* setting is important in two ways. First, the actual physical environment of the characters is fully realized and plays a significant role in both characterization and theme. Mr. Coningsby's world as a Warden in Lunacy is briefly characterized, but it is a characterization that effectively suggests the mutual effect that the environment and its inhabitants have upon each other. Henry's grandfather's house on the Downs is even more completely realized, however, because it is here that the majority of the action takes place. It is a world of natural forces conspiring with unnatural forces, with the snow and storm arising directly out of the action of human characters who intend to master and rule nature for their own benefit, just as the tragic character has traditionally done. The result is chaos and destruction, just as it is in any ecosystem when one element is elevated to a position of supreme importance. Of even greater import is that the secondary world of *The Greater Trumps* is realized concretely and fully. Nancy and Henry enter into the dance, and the world there is compellingly true to its own laws. Henry experiences the world as the continually destroyed and rebuilt tower, while Nancy experiences it as a place of suns and moons and golden mists and spectral giants. It is a world to which she accommodates herself in both its pain and its joy, seeking to understand its laws rather than to dominate and rule it for her own ends. And her accommodation does halt the storm as well as defeat the cat, both of which have been unleashed by individuals seeking to fulfill the tragic role. Finally, the two worlds are convincingly joined by Nancy, by Sybil Coningsby, and by a concluding scene that is remarkably similar in tone to that in *War in Heaven*. It is a world that is characterized neither by the tragic suffering of Joanna, the lumbering despair of Mr. Coningsby, nor the godlike aspirations for domination of Henry and his grandfather. Rather it is a world in which joy is possible, in which decay and dissolution are a part of the cycle, and in which experience is clearly more likely to lead to contentment than abstractions of any kind whatsoever.

Shadows of Ecstasy stands outside the pale of Williams's other novels in several ways. First, it is not a fantasy work at all. No attempt is made to create a secondary world; only an attempt is made to suggest one abstraction in the western world being overcome by another abstraction from the African world. The fact that the western abstraction is rationalism and the African abstraction is passion should not lead to the conclusion that *Shadows of Ecstasy* is a romantic novel any more than a fantasy novel (see the discussion of Lewis), for it is much closer to a traditional science fiction or dystopian fiction tale of the invasion of the western world by an alien culture with strange and frightening weapons. And, in a sense, technology lies at its heart, since

CHARLES WILLIAMS / 123

what Nigel Considine seeks is victory over death through human will and learning. Moreover, the novel is tragic in a sense that we do not find in any of Williams's other novels. Consider, for a moment, Nigel's announced goal:

When your manhood's aflame with love you will burn down with it the barriers that separate us from immortality. You waste yourselves, all of you, looking outwards; you give yourselves to the world. But the business of man is to assume the world into himself. He shall draw strength from everything that he may govern everything. But can you do this by doubting and dividing and contemplating? by intellect and official science? It is greater Labour than you need.[8]

This is the creed of the tragic hero from the time of Oedipus: achieve moral superiority over the world and thereby rule it for your own benefit. Marlowe's Faust proclaimed it most succinctly when he proclaimed, "Here Faust! Try thy brains to gain a deity." Nigel is that deity. He represents the ultimate power, though whether that power be for good or ill Williams seems a bit uncertain. The suggestion at the conclusion of the novel is that Nigel might well return: "If now, while the world shouted over the defeat of his allies and subjects, while it drove its terror back into its own unmapped jungles, and subdued its fiercer desires to an alien government of sterile sayings, if now he came once more to threaten and deliver it. If—ah beyond, beyond belief?—but if he returned. . . ." (SE, p. 224) Whether he will return as the risen Christ or the fallen Satan is less clear, though the premise that humans must rule over all things, including death itself, is clear.

Shadows of Ecstasy is also the only one of Williams's novels where his attitude toward his characters is unclear, and correspondingly, where the characters themselves are ultimately contradictory. The two women in the novel play remarkably small parts, particularly when compared with the parts women play in almost every other Williams novel, and it is unclear whether they offer their respective men hope or despair. Roger's quest is almost like that of the disciple who loses himself in the cause of his master, and yet the value of that loss is brought into severe question by Sir Bernard's intellectual skepticism. Inkamasi is either a duped victim or an ennobled martyr, depending on whether Nigel is a god or a demon, and whether Mottreux is a brave assassin or a false Judas is dependent upon the same judgment.

CONCLUSION

Charles Williams's seven novels are certainly the least successful among those of the group of Oxford Christians (Lewis, Tolkien, Williams, and Barfield). Yet they are essential to an understanding of the possibilities and limitations of the fantasy tradition. Perhaps the first and most important limitation is that the creation of a credible secondary world is essential to fantasy. Simply adding some supernatural "mumbo-jumbo" as in *Many Dimensions* or *Shadows of Ecstasy* will not work, for it is not the magic but rather the credibility of the created world and/or the relationship it bears to the primary world that is most important to the reader's acceptance of the novel. Second, the secondary world must be rendered in terms of concrete human experience rather than in vague abstractions or theological symbolism. *War in Heaven*, *All Hallow's Eve*, and *The Greater Trumps* do this and are eminently successful. *The Place of the Lion*, *Descent into Hell*, and *Many Dimensions* do not, and they are markedly unsuccessful. Third, the characters must be fully rounded and complex, and ultimately they must come to affirm and/or prefer experience over abstractions. Lester (AHE) and the Archdeacon (WH) are convincing heroes; Pauline (DH) and Damaris (PL) are not. Finally, the primary and secondary worlds must be rendered in terms of experience rather than in terms of theological or mystical abstractions, for character and setting cannot be subordinated to plot to such an extent that events rather than experiences become the purpose of the novel.

Williams is not a great fantasy novelist, but he is an important one who occasionally created worlds of "arresting strangeness" and compelling reality: Lester's City of the Dead (AHE) or Nancy's world of the Great Dance (GT). And perhaps, even in his failures, he provided a road map by which the later and greater fantasy novelists could avoid potholes and go on to further expand the possibilities of the fantasy novel.

5

FRANK HERBERT

The four novels that make up Frank Herbert's *Dune* series are unique among the works considered in this book for several reasons. The first is that they are, by and large, considered science fiction rather than fantasy, as is evidenced by *Dune*'s having won the Hugo Award and the Nebula Award for Best Science Fiction Novel of the Year. Such consideration, however, seems to result from a lack of care in examining these works particularly and a tendency to generalize from Herbert's other works, which are most certainly science fiction. As I think is shown by the discussion in the remainder of this chapter, *Dune*'s subject matter, theme, and style are all consistent with the romantic novel discussed in Chapter 1 and are more suggestive of Eddison and Tolkien than of H. G. Wells and Robert Heinlein.

The second unique characteristic of this series is that it is perhaps the only fantasy series to take ecology as the central theme from the very beginning. Other novels, as we have seen, present ecological themes implicitly through means of characterization, symbolism, and so forth. The *Dune* series, however, begins with an ecological theme (to transform a planet by managing its climate), introduces a planetary ecologist as the chief author of the events that follow, and includes a discussion of ecological principles as part of the text itself.

The final unique characteristic of the *Dune* series, at least from the perspective outlined in this book, is that, until the last book, so little comedy appears in it. Book I is set largely in the heroic and/or epic tradition, with the principal interest residing in the war between the Atreides and Harkonnens. Books II and III concentrate on the development of the religion, with references to the holy jihad, the development of prescience, and the transformation of the central character into a god. It is only in Book IV that the comedy becomes apparent at all, and even then it is muted by Herbert's obvious preference for the tragic and his inability to follow through in tone and plot the implication of the ecological ethic that comprises the major theme of the work.

The effect of these characteristics is to make the *Dune* series in some ways the most remarkable and the least successful of any of the works considered. It is remarkable in its presentation of the ecological pattern, in its development of characters in Books I and IV, and in its integration of the quotes from the various journals (used as chapter headings) with the narrative itself. It is singularly unsuccessful, however, in its murky and meandering attempts to develop the religious element into a plot which would mesh with the other major themes, in its confusing treatments of time and its pseudophilosophical integration of time with prescience and religion, and in its failure to reconcile an essentially comic theme and an essentially heroic, tragic style.

DUNE

Dune is the first and most successful novel of the series, largely because religion, time, and prescience are treated more delicately and at a more restrained length than in any of the other novels. Yet it is also true that *Dune* is not complete in itself, for the very thematic and ecological patterns that are established are set up precisely so that they can be rejected in the stunning reversal which is logically inevitable but nevertheless aesthetically unexpected in the last three volumes. It is also true that the characters in *Dune*, developed largely in the heroic tradition, become remarkably alive and remarkably human and that the ecological motif in *Dune* is made an integral part of the plot as well as the theme of the novel.

The open statement of its ecological theme is made before the story even begins, for the dedicatory note on the back of the title page reads: "To the people whose labors go beyond ideas into the realm of 'real materials'—to the dry-land ecologists, wherever they may be, in whatever time they work, this effort at prediction is dedicated in humility and admiration."[1] Having set the stage, Herbert introduces Dune, the planet itself, as the major protagonist in the novel. It is true, of course, that the Atreides family's being sent there is part of a trap prepared by the Baron Harkonnen, but it is immediately clear that if the Atreides can accommodate themselves to the harsh conditions of Dune or make the planet accommodate itself to their needs, then defeat of both the Baron Harkonnen and the Padishah Emperor himself is assured. What none of the characters fully understands, however, is that the things that they are saying and doing have implications beyond their limited ability or willingness to understand in this early stage of the novel. Paul, the Duke's son and the principal figure in all the novels, whether in his own or one of his descendants' forms, for example, sets up the whole plot of the series in recounting a conversation with the Reverend Mother, a conversation whose full significance is not apparent until the conclusion of Book IV.

Then she said a good ruler has to learn his world's language, that it's different for every world. And I thought she meant they didn't speak Galach on Arrakis, but she said that wasn't it at all. She said she meant the language of the rocks and growing things, the language you don't hear just with your ears. . . .

. . . She said the mystery of life isn't a problem to solve, but a reality to experience. So I quoted the First Law of Mentat at her: "A process cannot be understood by stopping it. Understanding must move with the flow of the process, must join it and flow with it." (p. 38)

What Paul and his family understand this phrase to mean in the context of their life on the new planet is that they must manage Dune so as to make it more habitable for themselves, must manage the environment for their own ends.

Throughout *Dune*, then, this plan is further developed. Certainly it is in line with the plans of the interplanetary ecologist, Liet Kynes, who secretly plans a series of water traps, plantings, and soil treatments to alter the atmosphere and growing cycles on Dune so as to make water abundant and life both easier and simpler. The expression of Kynes's father's intent, as reported in Appendix I, makes clear the nature of the plan: "To Pardot Kynes, the planet was merely an expression of energy, a machine being driven by its sun. What it needed was reshaping to fit it to man's needs. His mind went directly to the free-moving human population, the Fremen. What a challenge! What a tool they could be! Fremen: an ecological and geological force of almost unlimited potential." (p. 505) The planet is to be transformed using the basic laws of ecology and modern technology so as to make it radically different. The chief of those laws, at least for Dune, is the Law of the Minimum: "Growth is limited by that necessity which is present in the least amount. And, naturally, the least favorable condition controls the growth rate." (p. 146) The purpose of the change is to "have an orderly cycle of water to sustain human life under more favorable conditions." (p. 146) The Fremen are chosen to carry out this grand project because only they have the patience and hardiness to bear the hardships of the desert even while they are transforming it. The fact that the project will take from three to five hundred years requires discipline for even the Fremen to accept, but they can accept it precisely because they are sure that a better life will result.

Appendix I, "The Ecology of Dune," outlines the research that is done to bring about the transformation. Catch basins, windtraps, core samplings, the cycle from little makers to sand plankton, microecology, adaptive zones, and soil transformation constitute the means by which the Fremen will accomplish their goal; and in *Dune*, the goal seems desirable, possible, and even practical. Moreover, it operates to give a true purpose to the Fremen rebellion, for it provides the kind of moral justification that any wholesale change of society requires. It is, in effect, the basis for the hope of heaven, the ultimate abstraction that is necessary in some form or other to ensure that the population will commit itself to suffering and sacrifice over a long period of time. What is most fascinating of all is that the contradiction between the goals of this transformation and the laws of ecology is clearly stated in the appendix, though no one, including Liet Kynes, seems to see the contradiction:

The thing the ecologically illiterate don't realize about an ecosystem . . . is that it's a system. A system! A system maintains a certain fluid stability that can be destroyed by a misstep in just one niche. A system has order, a flowing from point to point. If something dams that flow, order collapses. The untrained might miss that collapse until it was too late. That's why the highest function of ecology is the understanding of consequence. (p. 510)

The immediately apparent contradiction results from the old tragic mistake, the idea that humanity itself is outside of and superior to natural laws rather than a part of them. Here it is clear that the planet must be changed, but what no one seems to consider is that, while the planet is being changed, the people who inhabit that planet will remain the same. In other words, there is a proposal to transform the climate, soil, and life forms of Dune, but there is no recognition that to do so will require a transformation of humans as well.

Structurally, this ecological motif forms the basis for the entire part of *Dune* that centers on the Fremen. The life of the tribe is based on water discipline, from the construction of still-suits to the proscription against the shedding of tears, even for the dead. It is identified with Paul Atreides immediately upon his joining the tribe when he chooses the name Muad'Dib, thereby identifying himself with the small desert mouse that lives so successfully in the harsh environment of Arrakis. It is tied to Jessica, his mother, as she becomes the Sayyadina, the Reverend Mother who presides over the water rites and the religious rituals centered around this central force in the life of the tribe. It is even tied to the tribe's preparations for war, since the storms of the planet and the Makers themselves constitute a major part of that by which the Fremen ultimately overcome the forces of the Baron Harkonnen and the Padishah Emperor.

Besides this obvious structural influence, however, the ecological motif is used also to set up a more complicated structural balance. It is used as perhaps the best illustration of the difference between the value systems of the Atreides and the Harkonnen lines, thereby suggesting a confluence between sound ecological practices and private morality. The attitude of the Harkonnens is clearly illustrated when the Baron instructs his nephew Rabban on how to deal with Arrakis: "Two things from Arrakis, then, Rabban: income and a merciless fist." (p. 248) Combined with his instructions to squeeze the planet for all the spice it can produce, this attitude is clearly that of the exploiter whose only purpose for nature is to use it for whatever benefit it can bring. The benefit on Dune is the spice, and neither the people nor the environment are seen as important in comparison. The attitude of the Atreides is precisely the opposite, as expressed by Jessica on the evening of the Duke's first dinner party: "My Lord, the Duke, and I have other plans for our conservatory, . . . we intend to keep it, certainly, but only to hold it in trust for the people of Arrakis. It is our dream that someday the climate of Arrakis may be changed sufficiently to grow such plants anywhere in the open." (pp. 137–138) This statement, combined with the Duke's concern with saving the men rather than the spice when the spice factory is attacked by the worm, is illustrative of someone who understands the importance of the system and of its individual members and who is unwilling to sacrifice either to an abstraction.

The motif thus begun is carried throughout the remainder of the novel. The Altreides code is constantly contrasted with the Harkonnen code, as Count Fenring notes when he points out that the difference between the promise of Feyd-Rautha and Paul is largely the result of Feyd-Rautha's not having the benefit of the Atreides code. Ultimately, it is even knowledge of this code that determines the battle between the two opposing forces. Paul and the Fremen win the war because they understand that to possess the ability to destroy a thing is to control it, and they possess the ability to destroy the spice. Doing so would destroy them, of course, but they are willing to accept that as a natural consequence. Thus the Padishah Emperor ultimately yields to Paul, not because Paul has won a momentary battle, but because Paul can destroy the spice and thereby make meaningless the system upon which the Emperor depends and for whose control he is fighting. The ecological motif, introduced on the back of the title page, then, continues to determine the novel's basic theme and structure. What must be kept in mind is that the theme is not complete, however, for the fatal contradiction that Dune can be transformed while leaving humans the same is never recognized by any of the characters, though the author indicates clearly enough the fallacies in the appendix and in the laws that he has his characters refer to at various times throughout the novel.

The characters in *Dune* are remarkably well developed for a novel whose bias is so heavily weighted toward the heroic. Virtually all the major characters come alive as realistic, warm, and vulnerable human beings, and even many of the minor characters move beyond the stereotypical roles they serve in the plot.

Paul Muad'Dib is, of course, the central character not only in *Dune* but in the other three books of the series as well, though in the last two it is through his descendants rather than directly that he speaks. Like so many other characters in fantasy, Paul possesses all the characteristics of the heroes of the epic and/or romance. A young man brought to a harsh world, he is wise beyond his years in diplomacy, warfare, and understanding of human behavior. At the same time, he is innocent, for he has never killed a man or made love to a woman. He is marked with special characteristics, as the test with the gom jabbar illustrates specifically, and he knows how to inspire people to follow him in spite of his years. However, he is still a youth who must rely on his mother to remind him of what it really means to kill, and he has the cruelty to take the Princess Irulan in a marriage which can be nothing but torment for her and a strange kind of revenge for himself. Thus the romantic hero becomes human in exactly the same way that Hector and Achilles do in the *Iliad*. Both of them love another human being, and through that love and its attendant sorrow they learn about their own vulnerability. In a similar fashion, Paul loves Chani and the son that is born to them, and through the birth of that son he understands more fully what it means to be not only a man but a prophet and a military leader as well.

Perhaps the most unusual quality of Paul's character as it is developed here is its prophetic abilities. He is the Kwisatz Haderach for whom the Bene Gesserit have been manipulating breeding lines for centuries. This fact, combined with the prescient abilities given him by the spice drug, makes him able to see past, present, and future simultaneously. Nowhere else in fantasy literature, so far as I am aware, is there another character who possesses to the same degree the characteristics of hero, god, and priest. Paul's possession of the special insight usually given to heroes is indicated early in the novel when we learn of his dreams which in turn become predictions for events. That ability to predict allows him to know many of the future events that will occur in Sietch Tabr and to expect many of the people who later become important parts of his life and of the rebellion which he heads. However, those qualities are not heightened beyond the usual mystical aura associated with the hero until after he accepts the religious mantle and changes the poison in the Water of Life. His acceptance of the mantle is at first simply a move of political expediency, one which will allow him to change some of the customs of the tribe, specifically that of having to kill the old leader (Stilgar) to be accepted as the new leader. However, after he transforms the poison in the Water of Life, it becomes a new thing, one which allows him to be in many places at once, those places including the past and future as well as the present. Moreover, it becomes something which takes control of Paul, something through which not only the battle of Arrakis will be fought but the holy jihad will be launched throughout the galaxy. At this point it would be tempting to make the character of Paul totally inaccessible to the ordinary courses of the novel, but Herbert does precisely the opposite. He makes Paul more human here than ever before by using the omniscient author point of view to reveal Paul's own fears, his own uncertainty about the path he is following, and the effect that path will have upon the world which may come to depend on him. We see this clearly as he reflects on the change in Stilgar's attitude and his own increasing isolation from the very people with whom he had sought oneness:

In that instant, Paul saw how Stilgar had been transformed from the Fremen naib to a creature of the Lisan al-Gaib, a receptacle for awe and obedience. It was a lessening of the man, and Paul felt the ghost-wind of the jihad in it.

I have seen a friend become a worshiper, he thought.

In a rush of loneliness, Paul glanced around the room, noting how proper and on-review his guards had become in his presence. He sensed the subtle, prideful competition among them—each hoping for notice from Muad'Dib.

Muad'Dib from whom all blessings flow, he thought, and it was the bitterest thought of his life. *They sense that I must take the throne*, he thought. *But they cannot know I do it to prevent the jihad.* (p. 481)

Paul's role as a prophet is unclear by the conclusion of the novel. The nature of the jihad is uncertain, as is the effect of Paul's prescience beyond its obvious effect in allowing him to defeat the forces of the Baron and the Emperor. What is clear is that the further he moves into prophecy, the further he moves away from those around him and the more he becomes an abstraction. That is another reason for *Dune's* incompleteness. Not only is the action itself incomplete, but the character of Paul Muad'Dib is even more so. The hesitancy and fear illustrated in the quote above is but a beginning, for, as Paul recognizes, it seems to force him into a path whose conclusion is likely to be disastrous. The heading to the last chapter in the novel makes clear that Paul has become something beyond the ordinary:

He was warrior and mystic, ogre and saint, the fox and innocent, chivalrous, ruthless, less than a god, more than a man. There is no measuring Muad'Dib's motives by ordinary standards. In the moment of his triumph, he saw the death prepared for him, yet he accepted the treachery. Can you say he did this out of a sense of justice? Whose justice, then? Remember, we speak now of the Muad'Dib who denied the conventions of his ducal past with a wave of the hand, saying merely: "I am the Kwisatz Haderach. That is reason enough." (p. 477)

And this is the most troublesome aspect of Paul Muad'Dib as a character. He remains, at the end of a five-hundred-page novel, unknown to us, awesomely incomplete. He is the boy frightened by responsibilities beyond his years; he is the father who grieves over his lost child; he is the military leader who sacrifices his Fremen tribesmen in a suicidal frontal assault; he is the prophet who sees in all places and times. Thus he has moved far beyond the usual character of the romance or epic, but he has not become, as Ransom or Frodo or Mor'anh or any of the others have, the hero of a fantasy novel either. He has none of the comic perspective, for Herbert presents him too seriously for us to take him as anything other than a tragic figure, at this point. And what is even more to the point, Herbert presents him as being at the hub of the universe, as being the single cause and/or purpose of the universe, as being in every respect outside of the natural universe and superior to it. However, because the ecological theme has been so clearly stated and so vitally important to the novel's development, the reader cannot help being aware of the conflict between it and the central character, a conflict that will not be resolved until Book IV of the series, and even then resolved in a highly inconclusive and unsatisfactory fashion.

The contradictory elements in Paul result almost entirely from his assumption of the mantle of prophet and from the prescience he possesses. In *Dune*, however, these elements do not become as damaging to the progress of the novel as they do in the second and third books precisely because they do not receive so extensive a treatment. Though Paul has visions throughout the novel, he does not rely on them nor yield to them until after drinking the Water of Life, and the "time twaddle" associated with those visions is given blessedly short shrift. Paramount is the fact that Paul is a complex child, man, father, and ruler and that he must successfully juggle an enormous number of complex variables if he, his Fremen, or the planet itself is to survive. For this reason, his actions are compelling, his feelings convincing, and his role in the ecological theme clear, if equally clearly mistaken. The other characters in the novel are even more convincingly developed, largely because they do not have to bear the burden of ultimate time and purpose.

The Lady Jessica is a Bene Gesserit "witch," but she is also a woman deeply in love and a woman who does not hesitate to use whatever means are necessary to ensure the survival of herself, her son, and the system whose survival is essential to them both. She bears Paul to Duke Leto against the express commands of her Order because, as she tells her accuser, "It meant so much to him." (p. 29) She later uses her sex appeal to outwit the guards sent to destroy her and Paul, and she tricks Stilgar and the Fremen into accepting her and Paul by playing upon the superstition fostered by other Bene Gesserit women: "The revelation shook him, and Jessica thought: *If only he knew* the tricks we use! *She must've been good, that Bene Gesserit of the Missionaria Protectiva. These Fremen are beautifully prepared to believe in us.*" (p. 293) Jessica thus becomes a natural part of the ecological theme, recognizing that she and Paul must adapt to the system rather than expecting it to adapt itself to them: "*Survival is the ability to swim in strange water. . . . Paul and I, we must find the currents and patterns in these strange waters . . . if we're to survive.*" (p. 320) It is Jessica who devises the strategy by which Paul is able to avoid challenging Stilgar, not because she is opposed to killing him, but because his survival is more likely to result in the good of the whole system upon which she has come to depend. Jessica does become Sayyadina and transforms the Water of Life herself, but that is a role she accepts out of necessity, and it never becomes for her the kind of abstraction it does for Paul. She remains to the end committed to survival for herself, for her son, and for the tribe he leads, even giving a word that will render Feyd-Rautha helpless during the battle he and Paul fight at the end of the novel. Paul does not, of course, use the word, for he is the hero of romance or epic at the novel's conclusion; Jessica, however, is consistently one who can appreciate the joy and comedy of life as well as accept its sorrow and tragedy.

The various minor characters are equally compelling and to mention only two is not to suggest that the others are less compelling or important in the establishment of the tone of the novel. However, Harah and Count Fenring are sufficiently opposite types to illustrate my point clearly. Harah, the wife of Jamis, the man whom Paul kills in his battle for initial acceptance by the Fremen, is convincing in her earthiness and in her acceptance of the new conditions of life. A true Fremen, she seeks what is best for the tribe, but she also seeks the things she needs most to exist. When she learns of Jamis's death and of her belonging to a new man, her reaction is not one of vengeance. Rather, she wants Paul to take her completely as his woman, for in that way she can be more certain of her future. When he refuses, she remains undaunted, even recognizing Paul's own youth and inexperience in sexual matters instead of attributing his lack of desire to some mysterious deficiency in herself: "She smiled at him—a knowing woman's smile that he found disquieting. 'I am your servant,' she said, and whirled away in one lithe motion. . . . " (p. 357) Later, when Jessica faces the problem of what to do about the tribe's acceptance of her strange daughter, Alia, it is Harah who provides the answer, for she understands Alia's strangeness and still gives her the love of a woman for a child. Moreover, far from regretting that she is not Paul's woman, Harah joyfully finds and accepts another man to love, acting throughout with the same common sense she shows when she leaves Jessica's quarters before the battle that is so important to both of them: "Your rugs are very dirty in here, . . . So many people tramping through here all the time. You really should have them cleaned more often." (p. 412) Count Fenring stands at the opposite end of the scale from Harah, but he is as convincing in his way as she in hers, and he does as much as do all the minor characters to illustrate and/or advance the ecological theme. The servant of the Padishah Emperor, the Count Fenring is the crippled Kwisatz Haderach, the prophet who didn't quite make it. Unprepossessing of appearance, he nevertheless carries out the Emperor's orders with sufficient force and authority to justify the Baron's description of him as a "killer with the manners of a rabbit— this is the most dangerous kind." (p. 332) Speaking words with double and triple meanings, Fenring is the epitome of the sycophantic, impotent courtier whose major strength lies in the poison of his tongue, but he is also more than this. As he contemplates Lady Fenring's ordered seduction of Feyd-Rautha in order to preserve the blood lines, for example, he acknowledges something of the cost to himself in participating in such actions: "There are some ancient prejudices I overcome, . . . They're quite primordial, you know." (p. 348) It is not until the end of the novel that we see Fenring again, and his actions there clearly indicate both the complexity and the full humanity he possesses. Asked by the Emperor to kill Paul, Fenring knows that he can do so: "*I could kill him*, Fenring thought—and he knew this for a truth. Something in his own secretive depths stayed the Count then, and he glimpsed briefly, inadequately, the advantage he held over Paul—a way of hiding from the youth, a furtiveness of person and motives that no eye could penetrate." (p. 498) Fenring refuses, however, largely out of the brotherhood he shares with Paul, rather than for any abstract reason. Thus, while he may not be tied directly to the ecological theme, by his impotence he illustrates the result of a man trying to force the universe to accommodate itself to him, and by his refusal to kill Paul he illustrates both the strength of the bond between humans of the same type and their ability to alter a course even if they are unable to erase or reverse the effects of their previous actions.

Dune is, then, ultimately successful in spite of its contradictions. The success comes from the strength of characterization, from the blending of the ecological theme with the plot and setting, and from the fact that Herbert concentrates on plot, characterization, and theme rather than on the extended pseudomystical treatments of religion and time. The contradictions lie largely in tone and theme. The tone of the novel is heroic/epic, while the theme is ecological/comic. What complicates this even further, however, is that the "ecological" goal of the Fremen is not ecological at all. Instead, it is a cleverly designed mask for progress and technology, a mask that is fashioned largely from the materials of the tragic ideas of the relationship between humanity and nature. This contradiction leads to the sense of incompleteness at the conclusion of the novel and to dissatisfaction, particularly with the character of Paul Muad'Dib. It is, then, for all these reasons that *Dune* must be continued in further volumes, for the ecological theme must be carried to its completion, and Paul must come to the realization of what the tragic mold imposes. Otherwise, the substantial accomplishments of the novel would be negated by its internal contradictions.

DUNE MESSIAH AND CHILDREN OF DUNE

Dune Messiah and *Children of Dune*, the second and third volumes of the series, are progressively less satisfactory than *Dune* for several reasons. First, they deal increasingly with abstractions, particularly with the abstractions of prescience and religion, with little link to characterization or plot and with a significant lack of internal consistency. Second, the plot becomes increasingly vague, largely because Herbert seems uncertain about how to reconcile the various strands of ecology, jihad, prophecy, imperial intrigue, and time. There are treatments of each, but they never come together, and they are characterized by a vagueness that is starkly at odds with the precision of action and characterization in *Dune*. Finally, the tone becomes increasingly confused, varying between religious ecstasy and soap opera drama, with a consequent loss of credibility for the characters and their actions. What these two volumes do accomplish, however, is to set the stage for the reversal of the ecological pattern that was set in *Dune* so that in the last book of the series the truly ecological pattern can emerge from the muddle.

The ecological theme in *Dune Messiah* is muted curiously, perhaps because of Herbert's attempt to complete the development of Paul Muad'Dib's character. While it is still clear that there is a transformation taking place on Arrakis, it is equally clear that the author's primary interest has turned to what Paul must learn about the laws of ecology in order to transform himself. The first and perhaps most important question turns upon the consequences of his actions. Remembering that in *Dune* Liet Kynes had insisted that the ability to predict consequences was the most important part of an ecologist's job, it is not surprising to note that Paul grows increasingly skeptical of his own ability to make such predictions, even with his prescient abilities: "As the ecological pattern dictated by Muad'Dib remade the planet's landscape, resistance increased. Was it not presumptuous, he wondered, to think he could make over an entire planet—everything growing where and how he told it to grow? Even if he succeeded what of the universe waiting out there? Did it fear similar treatment?"[2] Here, for the first time, the question arises not only of whether the transformation of Arrakis is possible, but of whether it is desirable, of whether the consequences have been examined and understood. Throughout the remainder of the book it is essentially this identical theme that appears. More specifically, Paul comes to realize that in seeking to control Dune, he is making a mistake similar to the mistake he makes concerning the Imperium, on which he has launched the jihad. He learns, for example, that "this planet beneath him which he had commanded be remade from desert into a water-rich paradise, it was alive. It had a pulse as dynamic as that of any human. It fought him, resisted, slipped away from his commands. . . . " (p. 66) Toward the end of the novel he begins to understand the lesson, begins to understand that his mistake has been the mistake of the tragic hero who assumed that he was apart from and superior to nature, who had not only the right but the responsibility to rule over and manage nature. Speaking to Chani out of the sight that has come with his own blindness, he notes, "I think . . . I think I tried to invent life, not realizing it'd already been invented." (p. 225) Then, just before the ghola Duncan Idaho reveals and defeats the compulsion to kill Paul, Paul comes to a last realization about the difference between the religion he has created and the true Fremen "religion": "If you need something to worship, then worship life—all life, every last crawling bit of it! We're all in this beauty together." (p. 232)

At the end of the novel, Paul has walked into the desert, presumably to die there according to Fremen law. In doing so, what he is still seeking is to avoid the responsibility for what he has brought about, to avoid the consequences of the actions he has begun on Arrakis. This does not become clear until the final volume of the series when there is so much discussion of the Golden Path which Paul sought to avoid, though it is a minor theme toward the end of *Children of Dune*. Thus Paul's lesson is still not complete. He has come to know and to understand the laws of ecology both intellectually and emotionally, but he has not come to accept them. The jihad goes on, the transformation of Arrakis continues, and his last action is the action of a tragic hero who is determined to emphasize his own individual nature, his own superiority to the natural system, and his own isolation from even others of his own kind. The ecological theme has been advanced, but only by setting up the conditions of Paul as a tragic figure in such stark terms that, when the necessary reversal takes place in the last volume, the reversal is neither aesthetically nor thematically convincing.

In *Children of Dune*, the ecological theme becomes much more evident, largely because effective characterization and plotting become much rarer. Arrakis has been changed by the great ecological plan. Its new symbols have become greenness and water, but its people have not changed. A conflict becomes increasingly apparent. However, the comments that make it so come, not so much from a single character, as from the commentaries that appear as chapter headings, a fact which emphasizes again the distance between the style and characterization in the novel and the theme toward which Herbert is working. Perhaps the best example is the heading preceding the chapter in which Leto and Ghanima integrate their multiple selves:

A sophisticated human can become primitive. What this really means is that the human's way of life changes. Old values change, become linked to the landscape with its plants and animals. This new existence requires a working knowledge of those multiple and crosslinked events usually referred to as nature. It requires a measure of respect for the inertial power within such natural systems. When a human gains this working knowledge and respect, that is called "being primitive." The converse, of course, is equally true: the primitive can become sophisticated, but not without accepting dreadful psychological damage.[3]

In many ways, this comment is a summation of what the *Dune* series ultimately concerns—the process by which "primitive" people become sophisticated using both the technology and the value systems of the more sophisticated culture to attain their goal. It is equally, however, about the psychological damage that results from such a process. Most important of all, it is about the disaster that both the natural system and the individuals suffer when this process goes on.

To end with such a comment would be to do an injustice to the complexity of the ideas involved in this ecological theme, for there are other considerations as well. Farad'n learns one of them when Tyekanik tells him that "you win back your consciousness of your inner being when you recognize the universe as a coherent whole." (p. 84) This idea is an early statement of Leto's realization late in the novel just before he meets the Preacher, who is, of course, Paul in disguise: "He felt the chord which connected him with all humankind and that profound need for a universe of experiences which made logical sense, a universe of recognizable regularities within its perpetual changes." (p. 338) What the realization is leading to is an awareness of the impossibility of isolating Dune from the rest of the universe, an impossibility which has already become apparent in the political and religious sphere. It is also an almost exact statement of the highest law governing the climax ecosystem, but one with which few are familiar. Most assume that a stable ecosystem is by definition unchanging, but that is certainly not the case. It is in a continual state of change, and it is amazingly similar to the pattern of the Great Dance described by C. S. Lewis.

There is still one more central element to the ecological theme in *Children of Dune*. It lies in the transformation of Leto II and the plan of the Golden Path on which he sets the followers he begins to command. The transformation begins with Leto's assumption of a new skin, one composed of sandtrout, which is part of the essential process by which the spice cycle of Dune is maintained. Couched in the language of both science and mysticism, the transformation becomes part of the ecological theme at the same time as it heightens the mystery of what Leto and Dune itself must become:

He felt the sandtrout becoming thin, covering more and more of his hand. No sandtrout had ever before encountered a hand such as this one, every cell supersaturated with spice. No other human had ever before lived and reasoned in such a condition. Delicately Leto adjusted his enzyme balance, drawing on the illuminated sureness he'd gained in spice trance. The knowledge from those uncounted lifetimes which blended themselves within him provided the certainty through which he chose the precise adjustments, staving off the death from an overdose which would engulf him if he relaxed his watchfulness for only a heartbeat. And at the same time he blended himself with the sandtrout, feeding on it, feeding it, learning it. His trance vision provided the template and he followed it precisely. (p. 329)

Once the transformation is complete, Leto is ready to proceed on the Golden Path which Paul, his father, had sought to escape by his flight into the desert and ultimately by his death before Alia's temple. The exact nature of the Golden Path remains obscure, but its central characteristics are outlined when Leto asks Farad'n to become the surrogate father for his (Leto's) own Atreides line: "It will be the most intensive, the most inclusive training program in all hisitory. We'll be an ecosystem in miniature. You see, whatever system animals choose to survive by must be based on the pattern of interlocking communities, interdependence, working together in the common design which is the system. . . . It is time humans learned once more to live in their instincts." (p. 406) With this statement, the logical progress of the ecological theme is indicated clearly for the last volume. The only problem is that the theme is largely obscured by the vast extent of space devoted in both *Dune Messiah* and *Children of Dune* to what I referred to earlier as the "time twaddle" and by Herbert's still obvious preference for the heroic, epic, tragic tone and style.

Characterization in these middle volumes is significantly less successful than in *Dune*. *Dune Messiah* ought to be successful because it continues to focus on Paul, who was characterized so richly and effectively in *Dune*. It is not successful, however, because Herbert takes what was human and personal in Paul and transforms it into mystical trances and/or visions which can provide neither a convincing motive for action nor a reason for the emotional and psychological turmoil to which Paul becomes victim. The best illustration of this problem and its effects comes early when Paul tries to explain the meaning of his prescience:

How could he express the limits of the inexpressible? Should he speak of frag-mentation, the natural destiny of all power? How could someone who'd never experienced the spice change of prescience conceive an awareness containing no localized spacetime, no personal image-vector nor associated sensory cap-tives?

. . . "The uninitiated try to conceive of prescience as obeying a Natural Law . . . but it'd be just as correct to say it's heaven speaking to us, that being able to read the future is a harmonious act of man's being. In other words, prediction is a natural consequence in the wave of the present. It wears the guise of nature, you see. But such powers cannot be used from an attitude that prestates aims and purposes. Does a chip caught in the wave say where it's going? There's no cause and effect in the oracle. Causes become occasions or convections and confluences, places where the currents meet. Accepting pres-cience, you fill your being with concepts repugnant to the intellect. Your in-tellectual consciousness, therefore, rejects them. In rejecting, intellect be-comes a part of the processes, and is subjugated." (pp. 59–60)

Writers of experimental novels tried to "express the limits of the inex-pressible," and the results were, as in the case of *Finnegan's Wake*, un-mitigated disaster. The same is true here. How can readers accept, empathize with, or understand the actions or emotions of a character who acts and feels for inexpressible reasons out of an experience to which the readers have no reference point? Paul's sadness at the death of Chani is something the readers can understand. His dismay at the manner in which the jihad has progressed is believable and moving. But readers cannot accept the pseudoscientific, pseudomystical expla-nation of a prescience whose only function seems to be to drive Paul to actions that are in themselves inexplicable. Why, for example, does Paul proceed to the house where the betrayal takes place, particularly since he knows that there is betrayal to be found there? Why does he allow himself to be blinded? Why does he allow Chani to die? Why does he allow the religious and political plots to go on? How and/or why is it that those plots are relevant anyway? The answer to all these questions relates to Paul's prescience and to the vision he fears. But this fear is never such that readers can understand or empathize with it. The result is that Paul's actions appear to have little motive or rea-son. He becomes more nearly than anything else a stick figure moved about to illustrate something the author never makes clear.

The same is generally true for the major character in *Children of Dune*. Leto II, Paul's son, is refreshingly, amazingly human in the early parts of the novel, but by its conclusion his actions and motives become almost as inexplicable as those of Paul himself. As he teases Harah, makes judgments about Alia, and even fights for his life against the tigers, he is a child who, because of his experience of the spice, is also a man. He is human, true to both emotional and rational sense, and is convincing in his actions. Even when he and Ghanima dare the trance in which they master the multiple personalities within themselves, the scene is ripe with human emotion deeply felt, and the victory they achieve is consistent with their characters and action. Also consistent is the plan they develop for setting out on the Golden Path. Unfortunately, however, that consistency changes as Leto moves into the latter portions of the novel. His experiences in the desert and his later testing by Gurney Halleck become increasingly muddled parts of an increasingly muddled plot. The relationship of the characters to the various plot lines is not clear, and the reasons for and effects of his testing are even less clear. Once again, the difficulty lies primarily in Herbert's lengthy treatments of prescience, time, and the relationship of these two to the religion founded by Paul. As Leto experiences the spice test ordered by Jessica, he comes, we are led to believe, to successively higher levels of consciousness and understanding, but neither is ever presented in other than abstract, semiscientific, semimystical language:

His awareness flowed on a new, higher level. He felt the past carried in his cells, in his memories, in the archetypes which haunted his assumptions, in the myths which hemmed him, in his languages and their prehistoric detritus. It was all of the shapes out of his human and nonhuman past, all of the lives which he now commanded, all integrated in him at last. And he felt himself as a thing caught up in the ebb and flow of nucleotides. Against the backdrop of infinity he was a protozoan creature in which birth and death were virtually simultaneous, but he was both infinite and protozoan, a creature of molecular memories. (p. 271)

The language is no more intrusive or convincing than the character at this point, for it serves neither to advance plot nor to illustrate theme. And yet it is precisely such language that fills most of the latter portions of the novel. That is perhaps the reason why Leto's predicament at the conclusion of the novel is so unmoving. Ghanima insists that he suffers because he has lost what it means to be human, but neither the humanity nor the reasons for giving it up are clear. Thus there can be little sympathy and little understanding, for the character has become more an abstraction than anything else. That abstraction is doubly troublesome because it does not fit the pattern of the tragic hero which the style and language seem to demand. It seems almost to be caught between a theme that demands a comic perspective and a plot and style that demand a tragic one.

Some of the minor characters in both *Dune Messiah* and *Children of Dune* are successful precisely because they are not put in conflict with the tragic/heroic tone. In *Dune Messiah*, the ghola Duncan Idaho is perhaps the best example. His service to Paul, his love for Alia, and ultimately his struggle to become completely human again are logical developments of both plot and style. His victory over the compulsions placed on him by the Tleilaxu Face Dancers is the ultimate victory which every tragic character is supposed to gain over him or herself, a victory that makes him even more superior to his environment than he has been before. Other successful minor characters include Alia in both her love and lust and Scytale, the Face Dancer who makes such an intriguing villain. In *Children of Dune*, the number of successful minor characters is even higher. The treatments of Alia and Jessica capture both the compexity and the contradictions of those two remarkable women, and the development of Stilgar and Gurney Halleck is accomplished despite the confusion of the plots in which they are engaged. Thus, while neither of the novels is as good as *Dune*, both offer a richness in character insight and a sweep of ecological patterns which cannot be completely overcome by Herbert's seeming confusion about whether he is writing fantasy or science fiction, ecological comedy or modern tragedy.

GOD EMPEROR OF DUNE

God Emperor of Dune, the last volume in the *Dune* series, is both the most and least successful of the four novels. It is successful in its completion of the ecological theme in such a way as to make sense of the laws in the earlier three volumes. It is the least successful in its conclusion, largely because its tragic, martyrlike tone conflicts so sharply with the comic perspective developed for the first time in the series for a central character. This lack of success, however, may be heightened by Herbert's apparent uncertainty about whether he was writing fantasy or the science fiction of his other work.

The ecological theme initiated in *Dune* is brought to completion in this last volume in a logically inevitable fashion. What was once a desert planet has now been transformed into a garden land of green plants, abundant water, mountains, and valleys, with the only remaining desert being that slight bit preserved by Leto. However, that change has brought other changes unexpected by any but Leto himself, or perhaps by Paul in his last visions before giving up the godhead out of fright. The most obvious change, and the most important, is that the Shai-Hulud has died. Poisoned by the water which has become more than the sandtrout can encapsulate and thus wall off, Shai-Hulud has vanished, and with him the spice that was a part of his life cycle. The effects of this are enormous. Leto II is able to maintain control of his empire largely because he controls the distribution of the remaining spice as well as because he himself has become a preworm and is thus the last link to one of the most important processes in the life of the universe. The other obvious change is the change in the people. There are no longer real Fremen on Arrakis; there are only Fremen museums run by dilapidated and decaying people who are themselves suffering from what T. S. Eliot meant when he suggested that the faceless people crossing London Bridge had been undone by death.

The Golden Path first seen by Paul and then accepted as his own by Leto II lies at the heart of this ecological theme, but it is only in *God Emperor of Dune* that it is ever defined. Leto begins that definition when he says: "It (Golden Path) is the survival of humankind, nothing more nor less."[4] In order to bring about the Golden Path, Leto has given the human community 3,000 years of peace. What is remarkable, however, is that he has done so in order to outline for humanity the cost of elevating one aspect of an ecosystem to an abstraction which supersedes all else. In fact, it is precisely to indicate the foolishness of seeing peace as the ultimate good that the Golden Path has been entered upon. The parallel to *Dune* is too apparent to be missed. *Dune* has been transformed by elevating the idea of water to an ultimate good; the result has been the vanishing of Shai-Hulud and the spice. In like manner, the Golden Path has brought peace; the result has been the weakening of humanity, the sublimation of sexual energies, and a distinctly lower quality of life for virtually every human being. This lower quality is evident in the description of the Museum Fremen, in the outline of the foolish rebels, and in the profound difference between the last Duncan Idaho and the first. Thus the Golden Path has been an exercise in teaching humanity, by negative example, of the folly of abstractions, and the clear option suggested by the conclusion of the novel is the same for humanity as it is for Dune. Both must return to a state in which challenge, freedom, joy, and death are inextricably intertwined. For Dune that means a return to the desert state which alone can support Shai-Hulud and create the spice. For humanity, it means giving up the false state of security imposed by the Golden Path for the more perilous ethic and structure of a natural environment in which predator and prey exist in mutual interdependence.

This idea of a predator is the central irony which Leto must bring home to those he rules. He insists that his purpose is to be "the greatest predator even known." (p. 25) Shortly after that, he shocks Moneo by his explanation of himself as predator:

"Predator, Lord?"
"The predator improves the stock."
"How can this be, Lord? You do not hate us."
"You disappoint me, Moneo. The predator does not hate its prey."
"Predators kill, Lord."
"I kill, but I do not hate. Prey assuages hunger. Prey is good." (p. 73)

What is so clearly outlined here is a code of ethics that is frightening and indeed opposed to both the tragic and heroic codes upon which western civilization has been based. Moreover, what Leto has given the people in the Golden Path is the end result of that tragic code, a state that ends in decadence resulting from a lack of appreciation of life due to a failure to recognize death as an inevitable part of the cycle, as something to be struggled against yet simultaneously something that is imperative if the species is to survive at all. As Leto tells Hwi, " . . . it's the survivors who maintain the most light and poignant hold upon the beauties of living. Women know this more than men because birth is the reflection of death. . . . Without readily available violence, men have few ways of testing how they will meet that final experience, . . . Something is missing. The psyche does not grow." (p. 239) When he also affirms the charge that Leto's peace causes humans to wallow in pointless decadence like pigs in their own filth, he completes the idea. As predator, he is forcing humans to think, thereby ensuring their own survival in a way that the passive acceptance of life will not allow. He does so in order to ensure the survival of the system and of his species, and he gains the allegiance of those like Moneo and Hwi because they recognize, though Moneo at least does not understand, that only through Leto is there a chance for survival:

The primate thinks and, by thinking, survives. Beneath his thinking is a thing which came with his cells. It is the current of human concerns for the species. Sometimes, they cover it up, wall it off and hide it behind thick barriers, but I have deliberately sensitized Moneo to these workings of his innermost self. He follows me because he believes I hold the best course for human survival. He knows there is a cellular awareness. It is what I find when I scan the Golden Path. This is humanity and both of us agree: it must endure! (p. 263)

The ecological pattern or theme is completed at the conclusion of *God Emperor of Dune* when Duncan Idaho and Siona kill Leto and Hwi. As Leto's sandtrout skin leaves him to begin anew the cycle whose end result will be the worm and the spice, he gives to his slayers the Golden Path, but not the false one in which he had led them. Rather, he gives them the path both out of and into the past. He points out in his death agony that "only fools prefer the past!" (p. 407) but at the same time he gives them the alternative that might make the past as possible as the future with the new understanding. Leto has, in short, suggested that evolution must continue, but evolution that preserves rather than destroys the system from which it comes:

What am I eliminating? The bourgeois infatuation with peaceful conservation of the past. This is a binding force, a thing which holds humankind into one vulnerable unit in spite of illusionary separations across parsecs of space. If I can find the scattered bits, others can find them. When you are together, you can share a common catastrophe. You can be exterminated together. Thus, I demonstrate the terrible danger of a gliding, passionless mediocrity, a movement without ambitions or aims. I show you that entire civilizations can do this thing. I give you eons of life which slips gently toward death without fuss or stirring, without even asking "Why?" I show you the false happiness and the shadow-catastrophe called Leto, the God Emperor. Now, will you learn the real happiness? (p. 392)

Whether humanity will learn remains unclear at the conclusion of the novel. The excerpt from the summation of the discoveries of Leto's journals reveals that the sandworms have returned to what is now called Rakis instead of Dune, but it also reveals that the Ixians have progressed in their attempts to create a machine civilization and to make spice themselves. Perhaps the most promising element about this conclusion is the last sentence, one that was a central idea of Leto's: "We are the fountain of surprises!" (p. 411) Rebels and sects exist; the arguments for the minority point of view are made by the descendants of Duncan and Siona who have written the secret summation; the struggle to define and encompass happiness goes on unabated. That is the positive view. Equally possible, however, and perhaps even more likely based on the tone of the conclusion, is that the God Emperor has failed, at least in giving his people eternal life. What he may have done is to give his descendants several generations more in which to survive with some measure of happiness and freedom, to provide them the raw data that would make more likely the survival of their species and therefore of themselves. And that, of course, is the ultimate ecological statement. As Meeker suggests, if humans cannot halt their demise, perhaps they can be the first creatures to understand the reasons for it.

Characterization in *God Emperor of Dune* is fascinating because of its contradictory nature. Drawn on the one hand by theme to the ecological comedy implicit in the central characters, Herbert is unwilling to give up the tragic, heroic perspective even when it means violating the basic nature of his characters. Although present in each of the main characters, it is particularly evident in Leto, Duncan Idaho, and Siona.

Leto's character is the most complex and is the one that comes closest to the comic perspective. As Leto seeks the Golden Path, he is keenly aware of his own transformation into a pre-worm and understands through long years of experience as well as prescience the follies and foibles of both his own and others' behavior. Moreover, far from rejecting his ties to the natural world, he has, with his sandtrout skin, become a more intimate part of it than any other, and this experience has made him more rather than less human: "But the closer he came to being a sandworm, the harder he found it to make decisions which others would call inhuman. Once, he had done it with ease. As his humanity slipped away, though, he found himself filled with more and more human concerns." (p. 326) Leto is full of the concerns of the common person. He is, for example, painfully aware of his own incapacity for sexual activity, and yet through the memories of his many ancestors he desires that action greatly. He can grow angry and react violently when Hwi is threatened, but he can also react with tenderness and compassion as well as sternness and strength when Siona is being tested in the desert preserve. He can already alternately encourage, accept, mock, and threaten Moneo, and he can love and support the latest Duncan Idaho even though he knows that doing so will occasion his own death. He can even understand the trap which Hwi is supposed to represent for him and at the same time be amused by both the foolishness of the Ixians and his own favorable responses to what he knows is a trap. And yet above all these things Leto is the God Emperor. He is the religion of countless worlds, and, even though he engages in political actions and thoughts which would make Machiavelli look like a rank amateur, he cannot ultimately go beyond his own godhood. In short, Herbert cannot set aside the tragic perspective. Leto is a tragic hero, and he can never set that condition aside. He must, at the conclusion of the novel, die in agony and pain as a sacrifice for his people, just as he had earlier sacrificed his human body for the idea of the Golden Path.

Now this agony of Leto's is contradictory. Hwi earlier had pointed out that Leto understands the meaning of love, and that that understanding has led him to the basically comic perspective on life: "You have faith in life, . . . I know that the courage of love can reside only in this faith." (p. 383) His faith in life is consistent with his identification of himself as predator, with his insistence on the interconnectedness of life and death, and with his understanding of the importance of experience over abstraction. It is not consistent with his deliberate sacrifice of himself, Hwi, and Moneo at the conclusion of the novel. That Leto is the god who sacrifices himself for the ultimate abstraction of death instead of battling for and manipulating that life which he had earlier praised so highly—that is one reason why the conclusion of the novel is so unsatisfying. The ecological theme emphasizes the transformation back into the sandtrout/worm which will begin the spice cycle all over again, but the description of Leto's agonies in dying is reminiscent of Christ's suffering on the cross or of Beowulf's death before the dragon's lair. The two simply do not mix, and the ambiguity of the last chapter simply complicates the matter further. The question of the popular television show "To Tell the Truth" seems most appropriate here: Will the real Leto please stand up? The problem is that there is no real Leto. Torn apart by the contradictory demands his author has placed upon him, Leto becomes an abstraction unsatisfying as either character or symbol and an apt expression of the confusion that exists throughout the series between theme and style.

Duncan Idaho and Siona suffer from the same difficulty. Both play roles that should ultimately correspond with the ecological theme to make them seek life; in fact, both seek an abstraction which denies their very heritage. Duncan Idaho is the last of a series of Duncans to come from the original. Appointed commander of Leto's Fish Speakers, Duncan is in rebellion against Leto from the very beginning of his life on Dune. He falls in love with Hwi Noree, dismisses as unworthy the ritual of Siaynoq, and ultimately plots to kill Leto. Yet Leto is a composite of all the personalities of the Kwisatz Haderach, and chief among those personalities is that of his father, Paul Muad'Dib, the man whom the original Duncan had served so faithfully and by whom he regained his full self following his Tleilaxian resurrection. So the new Duncan must deny the very loyalty upon which his character is based to kill Leto, the last male of the Atreides line. Moreover, he must do it for, or at least at the urging of Siona, a woman for whom he feels neither love nor devotion. He eventually becomes an impotently weak madman as he kills Nayla out of an ungovernable rage and then yields to Siona's commands and her disgust. Siona summarizes well what Idaho and the Museum Fremen have become when she says of them: "Poor material with which to shape a new universe, she thought, but they would have to serve." (p. 408) Thus she points clearly to the distance the last Duncan Idaho has come from the bravery and courage of the initial Duncan. The point of Duncan's treatment is that he experiences neither for himself nor for the others the kind of love and/or joy which the search for survival ought to bring. He is the tragic hero, but the tragic hero who, like Count Fenring in *Dune*, has a fatal flaw which renders him incapable of fulfilling his role. The problem is that there is need for a comic hero, or at least one who brings the joy of life to the fore. Duncan cannot do so and thus is left without a role of any kind to play.

Siona's role is more complex, but equally flawed. One of the rebels whom Leto tested and supposedly converted, she can never move beyond the role of the tragic heroine. Though she appears to embrace the wisdom of what Leto has shown her in the desert, she places independence above all else, and she revolts against Leto. It is her plot that leads to his death, and it is her willpower that will establish the new universe. She is Lady Macbeth, but without a coherent cause. There appears to be no more valid reason for her killing Leto than for her initial rebellion, and she certainly never appears to value life either for herself or for the other members of her species. She lives by and for an abstraction which can best be described as power. In that she resembles perhaps more than anyone else one of her ancestors, the Baron Harkonnen. Siona is the woman of "grim features" and "low, intense voice." She is never associated with love, sexuality, or life. Dedicated to abstractions at the beginning of the novel she remains dedicated to abstractions at its conclusion, and that would be acceptable, except that it contradicts the role the theme requires her to play. She is the continuance of life and hope and joy, according to the theme of the novel and even according to Leto's words. But nothing exists in her character or actions to suggest that she is capable of fulfilling such a role. Thus she finally contradicts her own role as much as do Leto and Duncan.

God Emperor of Dune, then, remains ultimately unconvincing. The ecological theme is carried to a brilliant completion with the reversal of the processes that began in *Dune* and with the clear indication of the kinds of human and ecological catastrophes which have been brought on by humanity's attempt to place itself in the position of the god who manages nature for its own benefit. The conclusion is not that a return to the past, ecologically speaking, is either desirable or possible. Rather, it is that the process of evolution must occur naturally and that all elements in the system must participate in the change if it is to be successful or if those elements hope to survive. The process is, thus, a fluid one which is governed by precisely the opposite of absolutes:

In all of my universe I have seen no law of nature, unchanging and inexorable. This universe presents only changing relationships which are sometimes seen as laws by short-lived awareness. These fleshly sensoria which we call self are ephemera withering in the blaze of infinity, fleetingly aware of temporary conditions which define our activities and change as our activities change. If you must label the absolute, use its proper name: temporary. (p. 397)

The problem is that there are neither characters nor plot to support this theme. The characters carry out the tragic perspective, and the plot contains all the elements of intrigue and power common to De Casibus tragedies. Moreover, Herbert cannot finally give up the marvelously appealing portrait of a human as the tragic character. Whether it is because he is writing science fiction and is therefore more interested in the mechanics of the Ixian world and the scientific implications of Leto's prescience or because he fears the loss of control that would result from making the characters a part of the animal world, Herbert maintains the high level of abstraction consistent with the tragic view, thereby rendering the novel as fascinatingly incomplete as it is contradictory.

CONCLUSION

Herbert ventured out of the field of science fiction when he wrote the *Dune* series, and his venture resulted in one of the most fascinating failures in the history of the fantasy novel. That failure may have resulted from a confusion on Herbert's part about what he was doing in the series, for if taken as science fiction then the very elements which I have suggested are unsuccessful might be considered both successful and essential. The "time twaddle," prescience, and pseudoscientific mysticism that occupy so much space in the series may easily be traced to the concern of the science fiction writer for predictions of the future, scientific explanations of physical and/or emotional phenomena, and a preoccupation with the relationship between technology and humanity. Likewise, the presentation of the characters as tragic and/or heroic may come from science fiction's preference for the views of the tragic figure and the progress that view heralds as the chief mark of the tragic figure's greatness. It is also possible, however, that the failure may have come from Herbert's overattachment to the stature of the characters he had created; he could not allow them to "sink" back down to the level of the comic after having attained the moral heights of the tragic. Other fantasy writers, notably Tolkien and Lewis, have been fascinated by such a view of their characters but they have managed to let that view pass and, in so doing, to bring their works to both a logically and aesthetically satisfying conclusion. Such is not the case with Herbert.

Herbert has deliberately chosen ecology as the theme of the novel and has deliberately structured the plot so that humans become a part of that ecology, perhaps even a mirror image of its laws in both obedience and rebellion. The problem is that he seems unwilling or unable to accept the consequences of that theme for his characters. Paul Muad'Dib is a noble Atreides; Jessica is a great lady; Leto II is the man become worm become god who must die that his people may have life. Such is the stuff of tragedy, but it is not the substance of comedy nor of ecology. The interdependence of the Fremen and the relationship between the Fremen and their environment in *Dune* is idealized, but it is also rejected by Herbert's insistence that a god must save the people of the galaxy from their own instincts. Let us make no mistake. Herbert has Leto insist that he wants people to return to their instincts, but he then pushes his characters to the point at which they must separate themselves from their environment and rule over it— all for its own good, of course—at any cost, up to and including their own lives. Especially at the conclusion of the series is this curious contradiction between theme and characters present, for there is the Christ-like slaying of Leto II at the same time that there is the projected marriage or at least mating of Duncan and Siona. The first is typical in the tragic; the second is traditional in the comic.

What is most striking, therefore, about this series is that it commits precisely the same mistake that the authors of experimental and/or existential novels have made. That is, its structure contradicts, perhaps even mocks, the theme which has been fashioned for it. The end result is a series which illustrates more clearly than anything else in fantasy literature the indissoluble link between comedy, fantasy, and the ecological perspective which lies at the heart of both. Herbert's work is certainly flawed, but in what it indicates about the limitations and expectations of the fantasy tradition it is, in the words of the poet, "its own excuse for being."

6

JOY CHANT

The evolution of the fantasy novel and the role of ecology in it is perhaps more clearly marked in Joy Chant's two published novels than in the work of any other writer considered in this book. This evolution is specifically illustrated in the subject matter of the two novels. In the first, *Red Moon and Black Mountain*, Chant clearly divides the novel in two parts. One part, that dealing with the Vandarei, is written in the heroic tradition of fantasy most often associated with Eddison and Tolkien. The other part, that dealing with the Khentorei, holds more similarities to Herbert's treatment of the Fremen in the *Dune* series than anything else in fantasy, but with a vastly different tone and a completely different kind of religious element. In her second novel, *The Grey Mane of Morning*, Chant again has taken up the story of the Khentorei, but she has set the story in an earlier time period, one before the Vandarei had come to be. In doing so, she has moved further from the tragic concepts of the heroic tradition and ever closer to the clearly ecological statements of comedy. In commenting upon the development of these two strains in her work, Chant outlines clearly the significance of the direction which her work seems to be taking:

And in the end, the Khentors took most of my heart—I am only sorry that having reached a satisfying mode of life, they have no impetus to do much. They remain the same. It is the more restless, troubled, burdened Harani who produce the stories: and who, being an "I" people produce the individuals while the low-ego nomads, the "We" people, do not so often, unless touched by the Gods. If I try to define the different fascination of each of them for me, the interest of the Harani lies in their burden of responsibility, their separation from others by the power entrusted to them, the difficulty of reconciling destiny with happiness. The Khentor appeal is more atavistic, based on simplicity, harmony with nature, and so on: briefly, for me, they achieve the delight of closeness to the life of nature combined with the richness of the human community.[1]

If solely concerned with the time sequence within the two novels, then a look at *Grey Mane of Morning* would have to come first, since it outlines a time period hundreds of years prior to that dealt with in *Red Moon and Black Mountain*. However, because there is something much more important than the element of time, the books will be considered in the order in which they appeared. This will give a clear scope with which to consider the complex artistic and ecological pattern toward which Chant seems to be moving, a pattern that is typical of the fantasy novel in general and which is also a further affirmation of the romantic strain so central to the development of the fantasy novel in this century.

RED MOON AND BLACK MOUNTAIN

Red Moon and Black Mountain appears at first glance to be a novel in the tragic, chivalric mode because of its apparent focus on the war between the Harani and Fendarl, similar to the war between Aragorn and his followers and Sauron and his. However, such an appearance is misleading, for the novel ultimately lies squarely in the tradition of comedy and squarely in the center of the ecological perspective. The attitude toward nature is one that rejects the oversimplified pastoral, Edenic approach in favor of one emphasizing multiplicity, diversity, and complexity. It insists that humanity affects its environment positively or negatively by its attempt to integrate itself with or to stand superior to a nature which is never seen as a mere symbol of or metaphor for humanity's spiritual state but rather as an actual environment. Finally, *Red Moon and Black Mountain* clearly insists upon a holistic approach to art which emphasizes the existence of a whole system rather than of the individual. Beauty, pain, degradation, and joy are all present, but what is most present is the insistence that life is possible, not because of the abstraction of heaven, but because of the experiences of earth. It is this affirmation of life with its possibilities for joy that sets the stage for Chant's initial blending of the comic and ecological with the traditions of the fantasy novel.

In *Red Moon and Black Mountain*, two seemingly opposed views of nature and humanity's relation to it are at work. One tradition is that represented by the Hurnei (also called Khentorei), the wanderers of the Northern Plains. The other is that represented by the Vandarei (also called Harani), the wielders of the Star Magic.

The Hurnei clearly represent a relationship with nature that differs from the pastoral tradition usually associated with the romantic novel. No happy sheep gambol in the fields while happy shepherds sing plaintive love songs to pure and simple shepherdesses in the warm sunshine. Instead there are hunters whose existence depends on their ability to find game, kill what is needed, and use fruitfully the results of their kill to fortify themselves against environmental conditions that are sometimes harsh and sometimes kind. It is not a simple world in which humans rule over their environment, but an infinitely complex one to which they must adapt if they are to survive. Religion, social structure, and their particular ethical system are based, then, on accommodating themselves to the environment.

This identification of the Hurnei with nature is apparent from the description of the dance which Chant gives shortly after Oliver's appearance in Kedrinh:

And the voices of the men were the dark sea; while the voices of the girls were the flying white foam; or the vast dark plain, and the silver light that ran over it; or the wind-brought rumor of thunder, and the shimmering levin-light. And the drums rumbled and throbbed and passed into the ground; and the sound became the very heartbeats of the Earth herself, beating up through their feet into their feet into their blood, into their brains, into their very bones.[2]

Nature is not, here, a metaphor for humans; rather, humans are a part of the natural world, and not of one aspect only, but of many which are blended to produce a complex whole. Nor is it a world which is simple; rather, it consists of diverse, contradictory elements through which the body as well as the spirit becomes tied to the *things* of the earth in all their light and dark aspects.

Further evidence of the identification with nature can be seen in the relationship between the Hurnei and the animals. The Hurnei are hunters, but they understand fully that wanton destruction is wrong, not because of a moral creed, but because to do so is to destroy the system by which they live. This point is clearly made early in the novel when Hran, one of the tribesmen, is punished for killing animals he does not need:

He had twice killed a doe in fawn, twice animals less than a year old, and had even killed more than he could carry back, and left the others on the plain to rot. The chieftain repeated to him the law of laws of which he had broken: "Accursed be the man who kills without need"—and cried that because of him the whole tribe might have been put under a curse. He had sinned against the tribe; he had sinned against the laws of Mor'anh; he had sinned against Kem'nanh. Had he any excuse? (p. 69)

When Hran can offer no excuse, he is cast out of the tribe in a cere- mony marked by sorrow and grim necessity. As each member of the tribe observes his departure, Chant remarks, "He would not die; but a man who was cast out of the tribe was cast out of life." (p. 70) Oliver, the young man magically transported to Vandarei, suddenly realizes fully the meaning of what had previously been little more than a game to him:

Alone, he thought; outcast. He looked at the spearheads glowing red in the fire. In this vast land what was one man? Where was he without his tribe about him?
He felt like a child who has played long in the sunlight at a cave's mouth, and suddenly hears from within it a bear's snarling. I never saw the harsh side before, he thought. Now the game is over. Now they have done with treating me gently. (p. 70)

Two other minor but important points reinforce this identification that the Hurnei feel between themselves and their environment. First, the tribe wanders, not at its own whim, but at the urgings of Dhalev, the King. That would not be unusual save that Dhalev is not a human king at all but rather the mighty stallion who rules the horse herd of the Hurnei, and his moves are based on the weather and the availa- bility of grass and water rather than on abstractions of either culture or convenience. Second, the social structure of the Hurnei is based on the demands made by the environment. As Oliver notes several times, the girls are "tomboyish hoydens," but seemingly at a moment's notice they can become women who pack the home, move with the caravan, and keep the young out of harm's way: "To a nomadic peo- ple on the move the women were no more than baggage, completely dependent on the men. He understood how the girls who were at the moment riding their ponies with the men could turn almost overnight from the wild, headstrong tomboys they were to the silent unobtrusive women—as soon as they were tied to a wagon." (pp. 67–68) Thus the Hurnei accommodate their life style and social structure, not to an abstract creed or dogma, but to the exigencies of an environment that is complex, beautiful, harsh, and demanding by turns.

Perhaps the most important factor of all in demonstrating the relation between humanity and nature that Chant portrays in the novel is that of the Hurnei religion. (It is also one of the factors which undergoes most development in *Grey Mane of Morning*). Now religion is not usually a part of any comic treatment (unless it be satiric), even in serious comedy, for comedy eschews abstractions, and religion is perhaps the greatest of abstractions. Nor is it traditionally associated with ecology, which is more concerned with processes than with theology. It is, however, an integral part of the system in this novel, much as Dante portrays it to be in the "Paradiso." Although there are references made to a kind of supreme deity who rules over the world of Vandarei, that is not the god with which the Hurnei are concerned. Marenkalion may shield Oliver after his defeat of Fendarl, but it is Vir'Vachal, the author of the earth magic, who is worshipped and whose demands must be met both by Oliver and the tribe. Chant describes her as she first appears to Nicholas:

She too was sturdily built, square and strong, with a broad, rather sullen, peasant face and weather-beaten skin. . . . Her eyes passed over the travellers, and Nicholas shuddered. He could not see their colour, but he [sic] felt their fierceness. A slow, deep savagery moved in them, and as she rode heat rippled from her. Not warmth-heat. She was coarse, she was primitive, she was frightening—and yet she was beautiful. She was beautiful in a way he had never dreamed of, did not understand, yet seemed to remember. And looking at her, everything that he had ever called beautiful faded, paled, seemed but husks beside her, and the very thought "beauty" reshaped in the mind until it fitted her; for it had been made of her, and for her, and now all at once it seemed a richer, brighter, more terrible thing. (pp. 131–132)

All elements of the primitive earth goddess are here, but Vir'Vichal goes beyond that traditional stereotype. Her appeal is instinctual and passionate, and she becomes the force that must be accommodated if the Hurnei are to continue their existence or if Oliver is to complete his task and return to his world. Thus she becomes a symbol of nature itself, nature which abhors the unnecessary death of humans or animals. Drawn by the scent of blood to the battlefield, she brings the life of flowering, growing plants to cover the dead, but as Chant notes, "it was not for the slain that she mourned; but for the injured earth itself." (p. 230) When Kiron, the King of Vandarei, draws his lip back in disdain, the Earth Priestess angrily points out his folly:

Oh, you northerners, you lords of men, with your talk of right and wrong! You put on scorn like a robe and curl your lip because in our worship blood is shed. Yet in one night you will spill more blood than we in a thousand years, and no god has demanded this offering! Yes, Vir'Vachal is drawn by the scent of death, and you do not like it. But where she found death, she had left life; and you—what did you do, King Kiron? (p. 231)

This statement carries far beyond Vir'Vachal and the world of *Red Moon and Black Mountain*; it is a clear rejection of the tragic, heroic code represented by the Star Warriors of Vandarei; it is even a rejection of the battle that has just been fought and an indication of the total futility of that battle. It is a negative statement about the kinds of abstractions for which battles are usually fought in contrast to the positive affirmation of life which is the goal of comedy and ecology. It is this latter affirmation of life the Priestess is making here, and it is to that goal which Oliver is led in the dramatic conclusion of the Vir'Vachal segment.

Following the battle and Oliver's return to the Northern Plains, he finds that he has become a spiritual outcast. And even worse, he must find his own way home, a way that is tied to the dark passion of Vir'Vachal, who must be bound, who must live under the earth rather than over it if people or animals are to live and be sane. Blood is all that will bind her, and, to save the life of many of his fellows, Oliver offers himself. Three things are significant here. First, Oliver is not the tragic hero falling because of a conflict with forces to which he must ultimately prove himself morally superior. If hero at all, he is the culture hero who understands that the survival of the system is more important than the survival of the individual within it. Second, in binding Vir'Vachal, Oliver and the Hurnei do not defeat nature nor assume mastery over it. Rather, they accommodate themselves to the needs of a system which possesses a complex balance in which Vir'Vachal provides life and growth rather than the unbridled sexual passion which, undisturbed, would destroy both man and animal. What they are doing, then, is not conquering, reforming, or changing their world; they are simple restoring the norm that abstractions have disturbed, and that is precisely the process followed in literary comedy as well as in climax ecosystems. Finally, Oliver's choice is not made to attain a moral superiority for himself, nor is it one he makes with joy. Rather, he makes it to save the lives of the young men, particularly Mnorh, who are his friends, and also because he sees in it the way home which the gods have told him he must find for himself. An outcast in Vandarei, he must return to and become a part of the system of his own world, for it is clear that the outcast cannot survive with even a minimal amount of freedom and happiness.

Even with these sound reasons, however, Oliver still greatly fears the choice he has to make. With the instinctual fear of any animal of its own death, Oliver first hopes his offer will not be accepted, then exists, as Chant describes him, at times "dizzy with fear." And yet it is worth noting that during the five days preceding the offering Oliver again felt at one with the tribe. He was no longer an outcast, for, as Chant says, "It was that someone had to go, and he could not stay." (p. 252) Thus the offering is finally made out of a sense of responsibility to the tribe, out of logic which pointed out that ultimately there was no loss to the tribe since he could not stay under any circumstances, and out of the practical necessity of taking the only way home that he could find. Oliver is, then, not the tragic hero at all, for what he affirms is life rather than abstractions. As Oliver thinks to himself, "But 'life' was such a huge word. It meant everything," (p. 254) he is perfectly in the line of the comic tradition as well as of the ecological, and it is perfectly appropriate that Oliver finds a god who fits what he has learned and demonstrated: "He was filled with delight and wonder at this strange new form of Godhead, a divinity undreamed of, a god without majesty, a god of harmony without law, with such vitality." (p. 267) It is equally important that Oliver gains from the god a renewed appreciation of life and that he recognizes that innocence has been replaced by an experience that he cannot or will not put aside.

Oliver's story and that of the Hurnei is, however, only half of the novel's plot. The other half—the one which suggests that the novel is part of the tragic, chivalric, epic tradition—relates Nicholas and Penny's adventures with the wielders of the Star Magic. However, even in that telling, it is clear that the Star Warriors are not a natural part of their world, that their battles are necessary precisely because they have set up an abstraction against which one has revolted, and that their stay is likely to be short-lived when compared to those forces that integrate rather than divorce themselves from nature.

The Star Warriors, children of a god, possess all the traditional characteristics of the heroes of the tragic, chivalric, epic tradition. Immediately upon the appearance of the first person they see in the new world to which they have been brought so abruptly, Nicholas and Penny recognize a Princess: "A Princess led them. So tall she was, so beautiful, proud, and gay, she could have been nothing else. Her hair was very long and black as jet, blowing out behind her; her face was pearl-pale, and her lovely laughing mouth the color of amber. They saw no jewels, only a plain cloak wrapped her; but her royalty needed no trappings." (p. 12) Later we learn that the High Lords chose the Star Warriors "to guide and to rule them [men] and to bear the brunt of the battle that was to be waged. . . . " (pp. 142–143) Kiron has a "stern and royal face," "the face of a king carved in alabaster: handsome, dignified, and still," and eyes that were "clear green, reserved and even a little sad, with the loneliness of kings." (p. 166)

Thus they are the traditional stereotypes, but stereotypes with one difference: their rule and power are limited. They are limited first by the fact that they cannot participate in the common elements of humanity. As Princess In'serinna tells Penny about feeling cold: "You see, feeling cold is a matter of contrast, of being warm within and cold without, of being accustomed to warmth. But everything has its price; and the price of Star Magic is this, that we forsake warmth forever. All warmth." (p. 53) Their second limitation is indicated by the fact that their battle against Fendarl, even if it be won, is at best a temporary victory. As Kiron tells Oliver, "And there lies our sorrow. It is certain grief if we lose; but not certain joy if we win. For if Fendarl has the victory we are lost; but if he falls we do but live to fight again." (p. 190) When this "temporary" victory is seen in light of the fact that, as has already been pointed out, the Star Warriors cannot bring life to be, as Vir'Vachal can, the transitory effect of this tradition is clearly highlighted.

The result of these limitations is that the Star Magic and the Star Warriors will pass away, leaving nothing permanently changed. The lasting effects will be wrought by Princess In'serinna, who gives up the

Magic for warmth, for love, and for life, and by the Iranani, who will endure past all others in the Great Council: "We of the Iranani, we have no magic and no strength of arms to offer, but we are his enemies. And if it comforts you I think he may find our power, the power of life and laughter, the hardest in the end to overthrow; too quick to catch, too frail to bind. We cannot destroy him, if you fail; but we can outlive him." (p. 175)

In short, the Star Warriors and Fendarl are abstractions. They divorce themselves from and set themselves up as superior to nature with a predictable effect, the destruction of each other and the environment. The pollution of nature comes from both sides, the good as well as the evil, for if Kunil-Bannoth has brought about the bleakness of stone and weather on the Black Mountain, Kiron and his forces are equally responsible for the deaths which only Vir'Vachal can mend. Significantly, however, no such pollution is associated with the Hurnei or their god for reasons we have already seen and will see further outlined in Chant's other novel, *The Grey Mane of Morning*.

In similar fashion, all real hope in the novel springs from those elements that reflect the comic sense of multiplicity, accommodation, and diversity. From the forest wanderer who troubled Nicholas because he "looked fiercely mortal—even earthy" (p. 106) to the ageless forests of Nelimhon which were not for men because " . . . this is the shadow, not the substance. . . . you are a man, and men are not timeless," (p. 117) it is clear that tragic abstractions are to be avoided, regardless of how attractive they may be. Humans must acknowledge their ties to the animal world and follow the instincts that come from that heritage. Oliver does so with regard to the battle, and it is only by doing so that he is able to kill Fendarl and thus to himself survive. Even at that, however, he acknowledges that there is no real victory: "But he could remember only the death wail of a man in great terror, a man whom he had killed in the end not out of justice or necessity, but in the rage and hatred of his heart." (p. 225) The intraspecific ethic against killing one's own kind thus clearly operates to indicate the extent to which abstractions bring humans to harmful actions—destruction of the physical environment, the slaughter of other creatures needlessly, and a harmful separation from the system of which one must be a part. Even Oliver recognizes this as he notes the difference between the Star Warriors and the Khentorei:

He stood stricken with the truth of it. At last he understood. This was what had been oppressing him. This was the loss for which he mourned. This was the thing which divided him from the Khentorei. This was the unadorned fact in all its cruelty. There was blood on his hands.

He thought of the Khentorei, whose hands were not stained by the blood they shed, with infinite regret but no bitterness. He did not even try to believe that what was true for them need therefore be true for him. He recognized that just as for all their violence they remained truly the gentle people, so in some way the savagery of war left their innocence unassailed. And even so, for killing as he had killed, consciously and deliberately, there could among the tribes be only one penalty: outcasting. (pp. 238–239)

In this fashion, then, the two halves of this novel are brought together. Oliver must be returned, along with Penny and Nicholas, to the world from which he has come, for there is no longer a place for him among the Khentorei. The Star Warriors will continue for a while, but they will ultimately be cast aside just as Oliver has been, for they cannot endure in a world in which their existence brings death rather than life. Blood, passion, warmth, sexuality, and an appreciation of their place as parts of rather than rulers of the natural order are the things which the Star Warriors do not possess. Thus the god to whom Oliver has come as a result of binding Vir'Vachal and thereby identifying finally with life rather than abstractions does not give him eternal life; instead the god gives him "new life, and heart to enjoy it." (p. 266) With that new life comes a new maturity, an acceptance of the things he has lost, and a knowledge that even that loss is part of the reality which he now knows. Oliver does not drink from the cup offered by the god, even though he knows it will save him pain: "He saw again the fire in the evening, the leaping dance, Yorn's tiger-lily hair. He remembered Derna's growl, and the silver voice of Mnorh raised in song, Silinoi's face, Mneri's eyes. He thought of H'ara Tunij, and Kiron. He remembered Dur'chai. All things have their price. He [the god] held out the goblet. 'I thank you,' he said, 'but I will not drink.' " (p. 267)

Oliver returns to his own world with the knowledge that the pain and joy he experienced in Vandarei are inextricably mixed, and he accepts rather than denies that mixture because in so doing he accepts life itself. Perhaps this is the reason why, when Chant returns to the enchanted world of Vandarei, she returns to a tale of the wanderers.

THE GREY MANE OF MORNING

Grey Mane of Morning is unique among contemporary fantasy novels, for perhaps more than any other it rejects completely the trappings of romantic heroism and almost completely the epic and/or mythologic qualities so evident in Tolkien, Lewis, and most of the other fantasy authors at whom we have looked. Or, perhaps more accurately defined, it rejects the pretensions of royalty in a way that is an implicit rejection of the tragic ideal in favor of what Chant herself has called "the delight of closeness to the life of nature combined with the closeness of the human community."

Far more complex than the limited scope afforded for character development of the Khentorei in *Red Moon and Black Mountain*, the characters in *Grey Mane of Morning* suggest the kind of complex interrelationship with the natural system that is evident in the "Paradiso" segment of Dante's *Comedy*. As a result, they create a mood that is comic in the highest sense of the term, for it involves wonder before the processes of nature, reliance upon those processes for survival, and a rejection of those abstractions which would make survival difficult if not impossible. At the same time, there is a clear movement toward reliance upon emotions and instinct in preference to reason and an implicit determination to experience life immediately with as much joy and freedom as possible. By looking at the ways in which the central characters are developed, the nature of the religion practiced, the relationship between these two things, and their effect upon the overall pattern of life, we can easily see that Chant's work constitutes a significant enlargement upon the fantasy novel and a strong argument for it as part of the fantasy novel's continuing enlargement of the concept of formal realism which formed so much of the basis for the original development of the novel.

The characterizations in *Grey Mane of Morning* are almost frightening in their depth, their vividness, and the allegiance to the world of the novel as well as of the romance. Often cast in the mold of the epic hero, they call to mind echoes of Beowulf, of Cassandra, of Sigurd, and of the more complex and tragic of the gods of Greek and Norse mythology (e.g., Dionysus and Odin). At the same time, however, they carry with them a note of the innocence and sincerity of children. This is perhaps one reason for the increase in the richness of characterization between this novel and Chant's first. In the first she uses children as central characters; here she combines the essential element of the child—a humility before the world in which he or she is living—with the emotional complexity of the adult. The second reason for the increasing richness and complexity of the characters lies in the fact that Chant has realized them as fully alive men and women who have all the contradictory characteristics of Dostoyevsky's Ivan, Flaubert's Emma, or Hardy's Jude. Finally, she integrates each character with his or her environment in such a way as to suggest a total pattern from which it is impossible to isolate the individual without destroying the whole.

Mor'anh, "Spear of the Sky," is the most fully realized of any of the characters. The son of the Tribe's leader, the nineteen-year-old man is also the tribe's priest. Yet despite these trappings of the traditional romantic hero, Mor'anh is marvelously human. Full of human doubts, failings, and longings, he is the vessel through which Kem'nanh reveals himself to his chosen people. From the first of the novel, Mor'anh's uniqueness is clearly indicated:

There was nothing about Mor'anh which did not set him apart from other men. Had he not begun by killing a leopard unaided before he had even reached manhood? Did he not wear his hair cut short, as no other man had ever done? Best of wrestlers, greatest of hunters: he had never failed in anything he attempted. Even his appearance singled him out. Other men might be good to look on—Hran was one. But Mor'anh was to them as the sun to the stars, surpassing them in this as in all else. Beauty lay on him like sunlight on the Plain, beyond the reach of age or injury.

Right from the womb it seemed the Gods had marked him: for at his birth his mother, who had been a priestess with much deep knowledge, had given him a strange and ominous name. For whereas men usually bore names taken from the animals—Ilna the Grey Wolf, Hran the eagle—Mor'anh was named for the lightningbolt, which sweeps the Plain with fire.[3]

Throughout the novel these qualities are enhanced and developed, and new ones are added. There is, for example, Mor'anh's quality of thoughtfulness. He questions such things as the path of the river, the relationship between the tribe and the Golden Men, and the age-old prohibition against wandering beyond the Plains without the tribe. In these things he becomes very much like the tragic hero and very much unlike the hero of comedy. When to these qualities are added those of the supreme warrior and military strategist, it would seem that Chant were creating another Lancelot or Perceval.

However, Chant never lets us forget that this "hero" is also very much a man, with all of the potentials for joy and for stupidity, nor will she allow us to forget that Mor'anh does as he does for the tribe, for himself, and for Nai rather than for some abstract concept. This humanity is particularly well shown in Mor'anh's sexual appetites. We are never allowed to forget that Mor'anh has slept with many women and that he finds sexuality a kind of natural appetite which is pleasant to fulfill within the framework of customs set by the tribe. His desire for Runi is largely a sexual passion, and, when unable to fulfill it, he turns to Manui: "The lampflame lit tall and shaking, quivering into black smoke, casting over her rich light and swaying shadow; and suddenly he wanted her, not as before, but fiercely and possessively." (p. 61) Moreover, many of his understandings are cast into sexual terms. When, for example, the Old One talks of disliking old age, Mor'anh cannot understand why until he points out that he is now too old for a woman: " . . . Mor'anh's wry smile turned to a grimace and a shudder. The old man smiled grimly. 'Ah, that touches you, does it? I have heard about you. Well, if you are ever as old as I am, you will not please the women so much. You will not find them so willing then!' " (p. 71) Nor are all of Mor'anh's sexual passions idle pleasures or symptoms of a noble love. In the very moment of his savage rejection of Runi for her treatment of Marat, he desires to possess her, to hurt her, and to humiliate her:

There was sweetness in humbling her. Anger had not killed his body's longing; her beauty shook him as never before. Her fear was a goad, stinging him with thoughts of holding and hurting her, of punishing her with his desire. He longed furiously to force her, enjoy her submission, possess her at last. This hating lust, that sought pleasure in pain, was new and dreadful to him but it rose as fast as his anger. (p. 169)

And so Mor'anh becomes sexually the kind of character who is only hinted at in *Red Moon and Black Mountain*: he is Oliver grown up and made human. He makes love, he desires passionately, he experiences the kind of desire that is so rare among heroes of any kind, and he rejoices in the son born of his union with Manui. The effect of all this is not to diminish Mor'anh's importance as a hero, but rather to tie him more closely to the natural environment of the tribe and to make him unique among characters of fantasy, for the sexuality here is not romanticized nor made noble or grand, as it is in Lewis, for example. Mor'anh is priest and warrior and leader of the tribe, but he is also the sexual animal who responds to natural desire in those ways appropriate to the continuation of the tribe and to the enhancement of his own and his partner's mutual enjoyment. Finally, it renders him more a character in the ecological comedy than anything else could possibly have done.

Because Mor'anh is a participant in an ecological comedy, he acts out of experience rather than out of abstraction. After the Golden Men have captured Nai, for example, Mor'anh desires to rescue her and to destroy the Golden Men, but he restrains his desire, for he does not know what to do or how to do it. It is not until after his encounter with Kem'nanh, who assures him of what he must do and leads him to believe that he (Kem'nanh) will provide a way for accomplishing it, that Mor'anh comes directly into conflict with his enemies, and even then he does not wildly or foolishly commit the tribe to war for revenge, either for Nai or for the death of Ilna, his father. Instead he first prepares the tribe for war by insisting upon their daily practice with such weapons as they have. Then, when it becomes apparent to him that such weapons will only lead to their defeat, he determines to take the awesome step of leaving the tribe to seek a city where the weapons can be obtained. As he tells Hran: "What do we need before we meet the Kalnat again? Think, Hran! If they choose to fight us, we have our spears, but after that, hunting knives. While they have their long spears, their knives, the long knives I have not seen, which killed Ilna—all of metal. I will not let the Alnei follow me to their deaths. We need weapons, Hran." (p. 122) He knows that he can find the City because a traveler has told him about it and shown him a map of the route, and, when he returns, it is experience, not his hatred, that assures him that there will be war: " 'And yet you plan to fight the Kalnat.' 'Not plan. Not unless we must. Not if they will let us go without it. But they will not. They are a people who have no fear of killing!' " (p. 266) Finally, it is significant that, at the conclusion of the novel, Mor'anh again rejects abstraction, this time the abstraction of owning, of conquering and being master of the town he has won. Instead of claiming the town, setting up a capital, and becoming lord of a new set of abstractions, Mor'anh returns to the people and experience he has always known: "Mor'anh's back was to the Kalnat lands. He was cantering back to his people, and the soft night

wind blew in his face, sweet and wild with the scents of the Plain."
(p. 332)

The depth of characterization seen in Mor'anh is seen also in the three most important female characters of the novel. Nai, the priestess of the tribe and Mor'anh's sister, prays for the good of the tribe, but she is human enough to pray for herself as well: " 'Let the danger be only to me, O Mother, let the Tribe be safe!' So she prayed from her heart; but tears pricked at her eyes, and after a moment she whispered, 'Great Nadiv, have mercy on me!' " (p. 9) Nor does this trace of utter humanity end when she becomes the captive of the Golden Men. She remains sullen and does nothing to provoke her own death, preferring instead to live in the certain knowledge that freedom will come to her. Equally broadly based are the characters of Runi and Manui. Runi's beauty and independence are balanced by fear and heartless pride, and yet all are understandable in terms of what she has seen and understood of her mother's death: "—to always bend my will to a man's, never to be thought of, and to bear children year after year until I am no longer light, and at the last to die as my mother died, too worn to bear her last child. I saw her—so much blood—I will not! No!" (pp. 48–49) Her brutal treatment of Marat, her attempts to insult Manui and to bring Mor'anh under her thumb, and her death in battle all suggest the unhappy condition of a creature caught in an environment to which it cannot or will not adjust. Like the Lady of Gondor in Tolkien, Runi seeks death. Unlike that lady, however, she finds it, for she is unwilling to bend her spirit to the needs of the Tribe. And yet, even so, there is a loss, a loss noted by Mor'anh as he weeps over her: "Then he had taken her in his arms and laid her head on his shoulder and stroked her streaming hair and wept, for all that was gone, and all that had never been." (p. 328) Manui is also treated in full perspective. The gentle woman who finally becomes Mor'anh's wife, her portrait offers more opportunity for stereotyping than any of the others, but that stereotyping never occurs. She is truly gentle and kind, but she is also full of passion, fear, strength, and will. She desires Mor'anh as much as he desires her even at the beginning of the novel when she knows that his love is given to Runi. Yet she is angry at herself for that desire and ashamed of the weakness her own love reveals: "She was shocked to discover the depth of her own bitterness. . . . She swallowed, anger crumbling into misery, fighting the wish to cast her arms around him and sob: 'help me, help me, make me forgive you; if I do not love you I am nothing.' " (p. 65) Her knowledge of herself, however, continues throughout the novel and is simply confirmed when Mor'anh brings her the mirror as a present from the City. As she looks into it, she realizes its double focus, to tell her of the beauty of her hair and her "ordinary, pleasant face." Even more significant, however, is her understanding of what it tells her of Mor'anh and of her confusion in the truth she faces directly: "And she did not know whether her painful laughter was blessing him for not knowing, or reproaching him for making her know." (p. 293) Thus each of the women, although different in character, is fully realized in a way which is rare indeed in a genre where the temptation is to make women into stereotypes.

Minor characters in the novel are sketched with the same care as are the major ones. Kariniol, the one among the Golden Men who seems capable of understanding the strength and potential power of the Alnei (the tribe of the Khentorei led by Ilna and Mor'anh), betrays the oath he has made to Mor'anh, not alone out of treachery or shame at his own defeat, but out of a bewildering array of motives including loyalty to his own people, a desire for power and respect among them, and the basic denial of the bastardy which he at once rejected and embraced. Marat, the girl who saves Mor'anh and is subsequently blinded by the Golden Men and savagely abused by Runi, has the courage to aid Nai and Mor'anh and the strength to escape to the tribe, but she cannot face the truth of her own ugliness or the fact of her impending death. Even the people of the City, who come closer to being stereotypes than any of the other characters in the novel, have touches of this depth. Yo-Pheril, the prince, is a young man of great beauty but of no responsibility; Jatherol, the princess, is a woman of charm and beauty but even she is conditioned at first to reject Mor'anh as a barbarian who can bring little to the city; Pheruthal, the beautiful wife of a lord of the City, is also a woman who lusts after Mor'anh's strangeness and masculinity. The Old One of the Tribe, who desires death when he can no longer have a woman; Ilna, the father of a son whom he so desperately loves and can so ill understand or accept; Hran, the friend who follows Mor'anh's leadership though he can neither understand nor accept what that leadership will ultimately demand of him—all of these characters become more than the stereotypes which Chant created among the Star Warriors in *Red Moon and*

Black Mountain; they become full participants in a world in which magic and religion play a part but in which they are ultimately responsible for their own joy or sorrow and for the survival of themselves and of the Tribe to which they belong.

The religion of the Khentorei is in concert with that outlined in *Red Moon and Black Mountain*, with some notable exceptions. Kem'nanh is the god who chooses the Dha'lev, the "king" of the magnificent horned horses who leads the tribe in its wanderings. He is also the Ruler of the Wind and Lord of the Herds. The only other gods mentioned are Ir'nanh, the God of the River and the Lord of Life, and Nadiv, the goddess served by the women of the Tribe. Conspicuously absent is Vir'Vachal, the primitive earth goddess who demands the blood sacrifice in *Red Moon and Black Mountain*. That absence is, however, perfectly in accord with the absence of the Star Warriors and of Fendarl, the abstractions for good and evil that dominate the action in the earlier novel, for in *Grey Mane of Morning* there are no such abstractions. There are good and evil, but they exist in the form of what the characters say and what effect those sayings and doings have upon the world of which they are a part. The religion is, therefore, simpler, more direct, and more closely tied to experience than to doctrine or creed, and the priests and priestesses of that religion experience their gods personally and directly. Finally, obedience to the gods' commands is natural for the people, for the commands are all based on common sense and upon the necessity to accommodate themselves to the environment of which they are a part.

Although both Ir'nanh and Nadiv are referred to in the novel, Kem'nanh is the only god who plays a major role, for it is Kem'nanh who directs the destiny of the tribe and whom Mor'anh serves. It is significant that there is neither holy text nor strict dogma for the worship of Kem'nanh. There is some slight ceremony, and a tent is set aside for the priest and priestess, but other than that the god's effect on people's lives is outlined only in the practical matter of following where the Dha'lev leads, of obeying the laws of hunting, and of caring for the environment. All three of these matters are, of course, matters of common sense as well. The Dha'lev leads the herd to good grass and water, a matter of necessity for a people who are herdsmen who neither own nor seek to own any land or fields. The hunting laws, as discussed earlier in the section on *Red Moon and Black Mountain*, are necessary to preserve the animal species upon whom the tribe depends for much of its food and clothing. The reverence for the environment is essential to the way of life the people of the Tribe lead. Thus religion becomes more a statement of reverence for the conditions of life in which the Tribe lives and a determination to preserve those conditions and, by extension, the Tribe's existence with all the joy and freedom which is possible.

Kem'nanh's claiming of Mor'anh constitutes a significant part of the novel, particularly since Mor'anh thereafter acts to fulfill the god's will. The kind of claiming is a traditional one for any religion:

What had the God put on him? A garland, or a halter? He was ready as he had always been, to give whatever was asked him, his love, his loyalty, his trust and utter obedience; but not till now had it occurred to him that maybe the God wanted more. What if the chief part of his life were not enough, but Kem'nanh demanded it all, so that there was none left for living to please himself? Maybe Kem'nanh wanted not simply his worship and obedience, but all his will, all his self: wanted him. (pp. 149–150)

Likewise, the possession that comes upon him is traditional, composed of power, strength, and a kind of madness. During those moments of possession, Mor'anh learns that he is the son of the God, that the God has chosen the Alnei to bear the particular burden of his laws, and that the Tribe is no longer to obey the Golden Men. What is truly remarkable is that the God defines humanity's role in the world in terms that are remarkably in accord with the philosophical stance appropriate to ecology and comedy rather than that appropriate to tragedy:

Man has gone awry and given his will to wrong. The world was made to be whole: we, Gods whose natures can be known, to link you to Kuvorei; you, with thinking souls in mortal bodies, to be a bond between us and the animals. But man has forgotten this, and that which should have joined now divides. Man, made Lord of the mortal earth, has abused this trust and tried to make himself its master. . . . Each man feels in his heart the break in creation, and tries many ways to close it. Not all is forgotten. Some men remember their duty to the earth they tread. (pp. 206–207)

What the God commands is life and order. Echoes of C. S. Lewis's Great Dance sound unmistakably here, but equally unmistakable are the comic insistence on the integrity of the system and the ecological requirements for maximum diversity within any climax ecosystem. If the Alnei are to free themselves from the Golden Men, it is because they cannot continue their obedience and still find the degree of happiness and freedom consistent with the world's potential. And yet it is clear that they cannot simply replace the Golden Men as rulers, for to do so would be to tie themselves to the abstraction of place that would make them susceptible to destruction and static in a world which demands accommodation to the continuing changes of the environment. As Kem'nanh tells Mor'anh, "Never forget that I am Lord of the Wind and that you are a wandering people. Follow my Dha'lev, and cling to nothing that pickets your hearts. If you build yourself walls I shall not follow you within them. When you put your faith in them, your trust in me is gone." (p. 208)

For all of these reasons, the religion that permeates *Grey Mane of Morning* is in a line similar to that in every other one of the contemporary fantasy novels at which we have looked. It is traditional and demanding in ways as typical of tragic Christianity as Mor'anh implies when he says:

I do not think the Gods are always thinking of our peace and happiness when they guide us. I think they have their own reasons. It is their right. But what obedience brings us may not please us at all. Jatherol, I once said to you that I must obey Kem'nanh because only then do I have quiet. I was answering lightly. A man should not obey his God because this will bring strength, or happiness, or peace. He should obey because it is his God, and for no other reason. (pp. 266–267)

What could, out of context, be taken as a statement of the kind of commitment to an absolute which is inimical to comedy and ecology becomes quite another thing here. What Kem'nanh commands is what the heart and instinct of Mor'anh and the Tribe know is sound. It guarantees, as much as anything can, that the Tribe will continue with the maximum degree of joy and freedom possible; it asserts the complexity of the entire system of which humanity is a part; and it leads to a way of life that is physically, spiritually, and ecologically sound. The accuracy of these observations should become apparent from looking briefly at what life is really like for the Khentorei, at their attitude toward death, and at their reactions to both the idea and the fact of killing others of their own species.

Life for the Khentorei is one based almost completely upon the exigencies of their physical environment, and it is a life with all the qualities of existence, both good and evil:

To me too our life seems very good: but is is not easy. The summer is one thing; but I think if these people knew what winter can mean they would envy us less. To be close to earth—it is like being close to a tiger: it may not be pleasant. Yo-pheril, there are two of your friends who say this, Ya-Thoron and Yu-Bareth. To them I would not say it because it seems to insult them; but had they been born on the Plain, they would not have lived to be men. . . . It is not all cruel. There is summer; the tiger is beautiful; it is a good life. And we have the Tribe. That is best of all. (pp. 260–261)

Such a description as this is far from the pastoral ideal or the romantically simplified nature that is so often associated with the "simple, natural life." It is harsh, demanding, and relatively unforgiving, but it is also passionately desirable. Death is a part of it, but so is life, sexuality, and joy, and all of them are experienced rather than talked about or abstracted. Death, for example, is an eminently practical response to a natural condition: "For the Horse People, there was no slow decline towards death; it came as an ambush, the sudden call of the Horn that could not be defied. The Gods, on giving them their span of years, had been sternly practical; they lived long enough to rear their children." (pp. 25–26) But along with death is also a love of life which is always present in its most appealing form: "The girls danced close together, arms twining shoulders, with quick delicate steps; swaying, rippling, showing the grass how to grow thickly, deep and rustling. The men shouted and leapt, higher each time, urging it to grow tall. Life giver, do not fail us, prayed the dance: live, live and feed us, be strong, grow green, stand tall. Life, cried the music, life, life." (p. 80) Thus, while all eleven of a woman's children may die at birth and while men may be killed or injured in the hunt, there are the compensations of the feasts, the dancing, the sexuality, and the full participation in an emotional life more complex and rewarding than is experienced even by the wise and comparatively joyless men of the City.

The time for the Khentorei is ever the present, for their concern is with daily existence rather than with long-range plans, and they are an inseparable part of nature rather than master or ruler of it. When, for example, the drum is beaten to welcome the dawn, "for a magic confused space it was hard to tell which had called, and which obeyed the summons." (p. 6) With this attitude goes an acceptance of the natural world and its events. Mor'anh tells his father, "What is coming will come," (p. 69) and the Old One reiterates this acceptance when he insists, "A year that begins badly may easily grow better. But if it does not, it is only one year. There will be more." (p. 71) Such acceptance ensures a pragmatic response both to natural conditions and to abstractions. When faced with the question of whether or not the Tribe fears wolves, Mor'anh points out, "this is not winter. There is food for them in plenty. The wolf is nothing to fear." (p. 113) There is here no suggestion that wolves are not to be feared, only that they are to be feared under the proper conditions, and that under those conditions humans will take the extra precautions necessary. In a similar fashion, Mor'anh notes the difference between how humans and the Gods see time: "This is how the Gods must see Time, and the lives of men; not as something which passes and is gone, but which is all there, always. While we, moving with the water, see the trees on the bank pass and think they are gone for ever." (pp. 234–235) However, having noted the difference, Mor'anh makes no attempt to change his own view, nor does he suggest that the Tribe's view ought to change. It is enough to note it, just as it is enough to note the life of the inhabitants of the City. The differences are important to the extent that they may influence the Tribe's reactions or enhance the potential for dealing with the Gods and/or the conditions they create. Otherwise, they are of no value.

This life style is reflected in the Khentorei's attitude toward death. Never does death become a frightening specter for them, but never is it a welcome guest either, for the Khentorei each desire life to the fullest extent. Mor'anh reacts predictably when he thinks that Marat has come to kill him or to allow him to kill himself to avoid the shame and pain inflicted by the Golden Men: "Have you come to kill me? . . . Because if you have, even if it is in mercy, I will not let you. I will suffer any torment they have for me, but I will not let go of my life one heart-beat before I must." (p. 136) He elaborates on this attitude later when he rejects Jatherol's explanation of suicide: "Let me be taken by surprise! Death is the great enemy, and who would go willingly to him, holding out his hand? No, let Horn-blower choose my time." (pp. 272–273) What is particularly noteworthy here is the fact that there is no code, heroic or otherwise, which demands that the Khentorei sacrifice their lives. That humans die is inevitable, but that they seek to die is not. The Gods do not demand it, and life is too full of the possibility of freedom and joy to make the Khentorei seek it.

With these attitudes, it is not surprising to note that the Khentorei see themselves as participants in rather than as rulers of their environment. When Yo-Pheril explains that the people of the City are people of stone and the Kalnats people of metal, he asks Mor'anh what he and his people are composed of:

"Of, of the beasts, our sharers of the earth. We love and know them."
"Yet you hurt them," said Yo-Pheril.
"How else would we live? But we understand them, we live among them and suffer their fears. We know them as they are, and love them for that, not for the use we can make of them. That is why it is a thing we punish, to harm them without need. The Gods have put them in our keeping . . . to protect them, and guide them. We share the earth; but only we were given wisdom." (pp. 259–260)

The word "sharers" is of importance here, as are the verbs "to protect" and "to guide." Nowhere is there reference to ruling, dominating, or using. The animals are necessary for the Tribe to live, so the Tribe kills what it needs, but to kill more would be wasteful. Moreover, the killing is never done wantonly, but with respect for the hunted as well as the hunter, a respect which is heightened by the fact that the ethical codes of the tribe closely reflect those of the natural world. There is, for example, the powerful prohibition against killing a member of one's own species. We are made aware of this when the Tribe responds first with disbelief and then with passionate anger to Marat's story that Nai's baby has been killed, and it is made more explicit when Chant catalogues the reactions of the Khentorei to killing the Golden Men.

When Hran kills Deram, neither he nor the Tribe rejoices in the victory. Rather, Hran must be purified, for he has killed another human, and though the purification may be able to remove the guilt, it can never remove the knowledge that others have of his deed. Even more frightening is the knowledge that to some the deed appears brave and noble, an idea that Mor'anh and Hran both reject, for they understand that the dangers to the Tribe are far greater from that abstraction than from any other thing. Shortly after, when Mor'anh kills one of the Golden Men who have come to capture Hran, his imme-diate reaction is one of fear and disgust: "Loathing and panic filled him. Then with ghastly abruptness the spear came free and the man rolled back. Dropping the spear Mor'anh doubled over and was sick." (p. 108) Moreover, the night after the killing, Mor'anh seeks the comfort of Manui for the first time in a long while, and the cause of the seeking is the knowledge that he has killed and that such killing was a violation of the very law by which he and other members of the Tribe lived: "But he had sought her that night for comfort as much as for pleasure—because what he had done appalled him, because, she knew, he could not spend a night alone with the thought of the man he had killed." (p. 121)

Now it might be argued that Mor'anh is able to overcome these scruples easily since he goes to the City to seek weapons with which to fight the Golden Men. However, that argument ignores the fact that there he acknowledges receipt for the weapons with a statement of his own fear:

Sometimes when I see where I am leading my people, I grow afraid. After I had killed the Golden Man, I felt such horror. . . . I had never guessed how easily it can be done; and now I cannot forget. Whenever I am angry with a man, the knowledge will be there: I could kill him. Will the terror of it al-ways always hold my arm? The Golden Ones do not feel it, and I think your people do not. . . . Maybe this sounds foolish to you. But there is a name my people have for themselves; ker'ivh meni, the gentle people. I do not want to take that name away from them. (p. 265)

When Yu-Thurek notes that the "gentle people" are nevertheless planning to fight the Kalnat, Mor'anh's response is predictable: "Not plan; not unless we must. Not if they will let us go without it." (p. 266) And his reasoning goes a step further toward the ecological ethic when he indicates that the reason for his fear lies in his own under-standing of death: "And killing is death, only showing a different face. Each time I have killed, I have smelled the bitterness I must drink one day. And so I say, Lord, I fear the spear in my own hand as much as the spear in my enemy's hand." (p. 266) Thus, though Mor'anh is willing to prepare his people for war and killing, he will not seek it. He will go so far as to avoid it, even though doing so means that Nai will never return, but only if that avoidance still guarantees a life where the possibility of joy and freedom continues.

When avoidance is made impossible by the continued demands of the Golden Men and their refusal to allow the Tribe to continue in peace, the Alnei go to battle, but battle with a difference. During the battle itself, they are possessed with a kind of blood lust, "a horrible happiness," (p. 317) but immediately following there is a different sensation, particularly for Mor'anh. There is sorrow for the friends and companions who have been lost, but more than that there is sorrow for the law of nature which has been violated and for the terrible burden of guilt that must be borne:

Now he bowed his shoulders and wept again, deep shaking sobs that released his knotted grief, stretching and easing his soul. After a while he wept not only for Runi, but for Yaln; for Ralki, beating her own grief under her feet as she led the dance to welcome Nai; for Kariniol. He wept for the end of striving, for relief, for gratitude. He wept to empty his heart of turmoil. He wept for guilt, and pity, and weariness. (p. 328)

Moreover, there is the knowledge of the aftereffects of the killing, of the women and children who may starve, of the abandoned town, and of the fact that "This was never what I [Mor'anh] sought." (p. 332) Thus there is the final knowledge that, while such killing may have been necessary in this case, it was not and could never be justifiable by any abstraction, and that even here the end result will be suffering and pain beyond that which anyone can envision. As Oliver notes in *Red Moon and Black Mountain*, the Alnei remain a gentle people, but, as Chant makes clear here, they pay for breaking the prohibition, and they remain gentle only because of their still-instinctive reactions against killing one of their own kind.[4]

CONCLUSION

Joy Chant, then, presents a kind of fantasy which grows out of the ideas of the romantic novel in Chapter 1 and in the discussion of Lewis in Chapter 3. More than that, however, it is a kind of fantasy that enhances the concept of nature and the natural world, not by a return to a simplified, Edenic, pastoral world, but by portrayal of a life in which humans are a part of the system and from which they draw their codes of behavior. It is a world which Chant believes to be realistic, in the same sense which has been used throughout this book:

What I wish to say really is that I do not consider fantasy a light form, one which evades the vicissitudes of reality. It uses strangeness and glamour, but if that is a lack of seriousness I share it with Homer, Malory, Milton, Blake—although obviously no comparison is intended. I deny that reality is defined by drabness. Indeed, fantasy is "unrealistic" only in externals: it is within ourselves; and it is in our relationships with others that we live. These are reality. I may bring different tensions to bear on my characters, but I hope that only serves to underline their basic reality, and the humanity which is the perpetual concern of the writer.[5]

That her reality is consistent with an ecological ethic and model should not be surprising to anyone who has followed the course of fantasy in this century. Neither should the direction of Chant's work be surprising. While it is different from the heroic fantasy of Tolkien and Lewis, particularly in *Grey Mane of Morning*, it is not different in the kind of affirmation it is making. Rejecting a simplistic acceptance of unbridled romantic optimism, heroic pessimism, or existential despair, Chant presents a picture of a complex world in which humans acknowledge their participation in the processes of nature, not as rulers, but as "fellow-travelers." She draws on the traditions of fantasy to demonstrate more clearly the "wholeness" of the earth and all its creatures, the joys to be drawn from that wholeness, and the penalties of that joy. As Mor'anh's son is born, he acknowledges enchantment first, then fear, for he sees clearly the inextricable link between the various elements of existence:

Mor'anh was enchanted, and then suddenly overwhelmed with fear. He cradled Ravalsh in the crook of his arm, and looking down into those hazy eyes he knew for the first time all that fear could be. He had been afraid before, but the danger past has been forgotten. Now he must feel it always, the dread that is the penalty of love, the aching to protect what cannot always be protected. He had put the life of his heart into another's keeping, and he was invulnerable no more. (p. 325)

And that is, thus far, Chant's principal contribution to the fantasy novel. She has shown the incredible joy and the incredible sorrow which are the indissolubly linked halves of humanity's experience with the world as it is, and by stripping away the veil of familiarity, she has suggested the continuation of life based upon that kind of recognition and that kind of complex interrelationship between humanity and its world which alone makes life either possible or worthwhile.

7

CONCLUSION

Western humanity's propensity toward the tragic ideal for the last three thousand years has brought it aesthetically, philosophically, and ecologically to the point where Yeats insists the falcon has come when it can no longer hear the falconer. That is part of what this book has been about—showing what happens when humanity violates the basic ecological principles that govern humanity's external world as well as its art. What happens, I think, is that neither humanity nor its art has what Bateson termed a "snowball's chance in hell" when that violation is combined with an advanced technology. But it is precisely that snowball's chance that was the occasion of this book's being written, for there is presently and always has been an alternative world view which has refused to be dismissed. The comic view has insisted that "environment" includes social, political, economic, and physical perspectives as well as the traditional geographic and climatic ones. It has offered multiplicity and interdependence as the norm, adaptability and survival as the virtues, spiritual and emotional self-aggrandizement as the vices, and the pursuit of abstractions as the ultimate folly. With these insistences it has, perhaps, opened a window by which humanity's self-created hell can be cooled and the snowball's chances, if not guaranteed, at least greatly improved.

Nor should it be surprising to note that it is within the last hundred years that the fantasy novel has developed to the point at which it may well move into the mainstream of twentieth-century literary development. Certainly fantasy itself has existed in various forms since humans first began telling stories, but the fantasy novel itself had to await the development of the romantic critical tradition and the exhaustion of the tradition of formal realism. Early fantasy writers like William Morris, Lord Dunsany, and E. R. Eddison—all writing more from an implicit rather than an explicit critical stance—outlined the possibilities of the fantasy tradition, but it remained for J. R. R. Tolkien, C. S. Lewis, and Charles Williams to develop formally the critical theory that would tie the fantasy novel so closely to the basic ecological patterns of comedy and to outline clearly in their works the limits of the genre. Borrowing the concepts of "arresting strangeness," "escape," and "the consolation of the happy ending" directly from the romantics, Tolkien combined them with the extended concept of reality to which modern science had been forced to grant credibility. The result was the affirmation of the "reality" of a created world which was true to its own laws and which acknowledged the fact of humanity's inevitable defeat in time. Lewis, with his insistence on the Platonic concept of myth and his application of that concept directly to novelistic form, tied fantasy and comedy directly in with a sense of Christian values which had previously seemed directly antithetical to anything but the tragic view. Williams, in his seven novels, eschewed critical theory, but he practically indicated, both by his successes and his failures, the essential limits to which the fantasy novel must be confined. Frank Herbert and Joy Chant, then, continued the expansion and definition of the limits of the fantasy novel as they became representative of both the degree of excellence which the fantasy novel has attained presently and its increasingly explicit ties to the comic, ecological tradition.

From our examination of the precepts of tragedy, comedy, and ecology and from our analysis of the five fantasy novelists, there are some increasingly apparent conclusions that can be made with regard to the basic critical/theoretical bases of the fantasy novel as well as its structural and thematic demands.

The basic critical perspective of the fantasy novel is romantic, but romantic with some important distinctions from the traditional romanticism of Coleridge, Kant, and Keats. Taking as its starting point the "willing suspension of disbelief" of which Coleridge made so much, the fantasy novel goes on to embrace Kant's basic acceptance of a priori knowledge and Keats's concept of "negative capability." It also takes the basically Platonic concept of an enlarged reality, but it ties that concept to the comic tradition of experience to produce a complex system which accepts the validity and truth of the emotional and/or spiritual experience as well as the primacy of the physical universe. In essence, it simply ignores the mind/body, spiritual/physical dichotomy imposed by Cartesian rationalism, scientific empiricism, and the traditional tragic/Christian tradition. Artistic truth thereby becomes dependent on an enormously complex, interrelated system whose existence is more important than its philosophical justification. Applying these ideas directly to the novelistic tradition, it replaces the idea of formal realism as described by Ian Watt and others with the idea of the novel's being a mirror image of humanity as described by Henry James. It also rejects the traditional ideas of romance as they had been applied to the novel by Hawthorne, Scott, the Brontes, Dumas, and others, preferring instead the development of a prose form which emphasizes the development of a parallel world whose reality is drawn from its own internal consistency and its conformity to the laws of experience. Ultimately, therefore, there comes to be a striking similarity between the critical precepts of the fantasy novel and those of the picaresque. Tolkien's "Beowulf: The Monsters and the Critics" and "On Fairy Stories" and Lewis's *Experiment in Criticism*, *Allegory of Love*, and *Letters* are the best sources for further investigation of these ideas.

The most important structural demand of the fantasy novel seems to lie in the nature of the setting. Proceeding in part from the enlargement of Watts's idea of formal realism, the fantasy novel succeeds best when it constructs a secondary world (to borrow from the terms of both Coleridge and Tolkien) that is complete in and of itself and true to the laws which govern it. That world may be connected with the primary world, but the connection is usually minimal, no more than a device for moving into and out of the novel, and the tale itself is focused on the secondary world rather than on any allegorical or symbolic representations of the primary. We see the importance of this consideration when looking at the works of Williams in particular, for several of his novels fail precisely because they do not create the secondary world in any believable sense. In like fashion, Lewis's least successful fantasy novel is *That Hideous Strength*, which tries only partially successfully to apply the general laws and conditions of Malacandra and Perelandra to Earth. That the application is successful at all arises from two factors. First, the general laws most frequently applied are the laws of ecological comedy emphasizing diversity, interdependence, and a recognition of a hierarchical structure that emphasizes function rather than position. Second, the secondary world is enlarged to include Merlin and the myth of Logres, thereby enhancing the consistency of the laws which govern the combined primary and secondary worlds.

A second and closely related structural feature of the fantasy novel lies in its requirements for consistency in plot and tone. The fantasy novel tells a straightforward tale, usually in chronological sequence, of a series of events which are treated explicitly whether they are comic or tragic in tone. However, it is not the tale itself that is of paramount importance. Rather, it is the combination of the characters and the tale interacting to reveal something about the nature of the world which they inhabit that is of prime interest. Thus the plot alone cannot assume all importance, as it does in a detective novel. Williams tries this in *Many Dimensions*, and the result is failure. Neither, however, can character subsume the importance of action and setting, for when that occurs a psychological novel unfolds that makes nearly impossible the credible rendering of any secondary world at all. *Shadows of Ecstasy* suffers from precisely this difficulty, and the result is that neither the African invasion plot nor the characterization of the Messiah and his followers assumes any reality for the reader. Finally in this regard, the fantasy novel must present both characters and plot seriously. By seriously I do not mean tragically. I simply mean that it must regard its tale as worth telling. It cannot become allegoric, satiric, or mocking, for to do so would be to deny the validity of the form itself, and that self-destructive characteristic of most modern novels is not shared by the fantasy novel. This is, after all, one of the principal reasons for the success of Tolkien's work. His world is real and important, just as are Chant's, Herbert's, Lewis's, and Williams's (at his best).

With this kind of critical and structural perspective, it is no surprise to note the profound divergence of the thematic concerns of the fantasy novel from most other forms of the modern novel. Those concerns begin from the perspective Henry James noted when he insisted that the novel itself would exist only so long as humans considered themselves worth looking at. As indicated above, the fantasy novel always regards its subject as worth telling about, and its subject is always the same: humanity, in its relation to a world of which it is an integral but not superior part. There are, however, several significant points to be made about this treatment of theme in addition to those already mentioned.

First, the successful fantasy novel is almost invariably a contest and/or quest between good and evil. However, the nature of that conflict or quest is always modified by a central character or characters who refuse to fulfill the time-honored role of tragic hero. Such a character— such as Tolkien's Sam, Herbert's Leto, or Chant's Oliver—absolutely refuses to become a martyr. Instead, he or she seeks life individually and communally. When pressed, the character will fight, but he or she does so unwillingly and only when it becomes evident that to do otherwise would be to risk destruction of the system and thereby the loss of life. At the same time, this central character is usually surrounded by other characters who, acting in the completely tragic mold, seek personal death in order to fulfill a higher moral commitment. Sam and Frodo are surrounded by Aragorn and Gandalf; Nancy and Sybil are surrounded by Henry and his grandfather; Orual is surrounded by Fox and Ungit. The result of this strange combination of characters is that the tragic characters pass away, either immediately or imminently. The central character, who can accurately be termed comic, endures, and with her or his endurance guarantees the survival of the system precisely because it has the ability to adapt. That is one of the principal reasons for the fantasy novel's growth in popularity: it sees the need for both literature and life to adapt to the exigencies of a constantly changing world. In short, then, the fantasy novel suggests in theme as well as in structure a continually changing world which requires the evolution of all forms. It sees death and destruction as an inevitable part of that cycle, but it also sees the renewal of life and the continuance of an ever-dynamic system as at least possible.

Now it may be objected that fantasy writers seem to be continually turning to the past and that they uphold the glory of the tragic tradition. Such has, unfortunately, been the central implicit or explicit idea in most critical commentary. However, those critics have confused affection for the tragic tradition and sorrow at its passing with commitment to its ideals. That the fantasy writer finds the tragic ideal attractive should not be surprising, for western humanity has found it to be so for over three thousand years. Tolkien builds much of his story around tragic characters as do Chant and Lewis and Williams and Herbert. But it is interesting to note that each writer succeeds to the extent that he or she is able ultimately to let the tragic grandeur pass away for the more homely virtue of survival with as much freedom and happiness as possible in a distinctly imperfect world. Conversely, failure to let go of the tragic ideal marks more clearly than anything else the reasons for the failure of Herbert to hit the mark in *God Emperor of Dune*, resulting in the abruptly contradictory and painfully unsatisfactory conclusion to one of the most ecological of all fantasy novels. Moreover, affection for the past does not mean, necessarily, a dependence on the tragic tradition. As Meeker shows in his discussion of the comedy in Dante's *Comedy*, the medieval world held a view which in many ways substituted a much more comic, ecological view of humanity's participation in a complex system for the more absolute models of the tragic. Thus it should not be surprising that many fantasy writers project the general attitude of that time period regardless of where their own work is set.

A second major aspect of the fantasy novel's treatment of theme lies in its insistence upon the primacy of experience over abstractions. Clearly going beyond the picaresque in this regard—the picaresque is the other genre of the novel to hold most promise for its future—the fantasy novel understands experience to include emotional and spiritual experiences as well as physical ones. Thus Lewis's Ransom understands the necessity for fighting Weston/Un-man, not in a theological debate, but rather in a physical battle in Perelandra, while Chant's Mor'anh experiences the possession of Kem'nanh in a way that transcends but does not deny the physical world. Magic and/or supernatural events are accepted, not because of an abstract dogma or creed which demands such acceptance, but rather because they are manifested in the kind of emotional/physical/spiritual terms found in Williams's *All Hallow's Eve* or in Herbert's *Dune*. Moreover, magic, prophecy, and other "supernatural" powers are not, strictly speaking, supernatural in the world in which they occur. Elves and orcs are creatures consistent with Tolkien's world, just as Vir'Vachal and the Iranani are in Chant's; and the powers of Herbert's Leto, Lewis's Green Lady and Chant's Mor'anh are drawn from, not imposed upon, the natural laws of the worlds of which they are a part. Abstractions are offered in the worlds of fantasy novels just as they are in the primary world, but they are subsequently dismissed. What is more amazing, is that clearly a much greater connection exists between those who hold abstractions, even though they be representative of the opposing forces, than between those members of the same side who hold to the opposing views of abstractions and experience. There is, for example, a clear link between Sauron, Saruman, Aragorn, and Gandalf which is much closer than that between the hobbits and any of these tragic heroes.

Nor is it surprising to note the difference between the fate of the two groups. Those who hold to abstractions die or pass away regardless of whether they have represented "evil" or "good"; those who hold to experience live and offer promise of the continuation of the system of which they are a part precisely because they accommodate themselves to it rather than insisting that it conform to their wishes and conceptions. It is, in effect, the victory of humility over pride, not because the former is a nobler virtue, but because it is a more practical way of responding to a system whose continuation is essential to their own survival.

What I am suggesting, then, is that the fantasy novel insists upon life as a virtue to be actively pursued. Its pursuit requires cunning, adaptability, and hardiness as well as humility, and it understands and accepts death, decay, and change as essential parts of a system which also contains satisfaction, joy, and freedom. It means that those who pursue it are less noble and less important than western humanity has been wont to consider itself and that it sees itself as part of a system in which compromise and change are far more important than victory or defeat and absolutes. Lewis's Orual dies because she does not learn this fact until too late; Herbert ends the *Dune* series with Leto's murder because he (Herbert) cannot bear to accept the consequences of allowing his man-god to become the man-animal which his ecological theme demands.

At this point, however, it is important to note a central feature of all of the fantasy novels discussed in this book and one I have found to be true of fantasy novels in general. It is that they usually involve a religion as a significant part of theme and/or setting. In some, like Tolkien, such involvement is implicit; in others, like Lewis, Chant, Herbert, and Williams, it is explicit. The reasons for this are many, but the most important are two. First, religion provides a sense of ritual which well accommodates plot elements of magic and sorcery. Second, and most important, the hierarchical pattern inherent in religious worship of any kind is similar to the basic laws of both ecology and comedy. Indeed, I suspect that it might be very persuasively argued that the patterns of the climax ecosystem are the prototypes of most hierarchical patterns of religious worship. Certainly the Great Dance portrayed so effectively by Lewis and suggested by each of the other novelists is reminiscent of that pattern. Whatever the case, it is imperative to note what religion is *not*, at least for the fantasy novelist. It is not a series of abstractions, for when it becomes so the novel falls apart under its own weight—Williams's *Descent into Hell* is a good example. Neither is it a separation of humanity from its environment, as Chant illustrates so beautifully in her two very different novels. Vir'Vachal is an earth goddess whose bloody rites serve to bring life as well as death and who must be bound, not defeated or made subservient. Mor'anh serves as the priest possessed by a god who is himself part of the elements and who never lets his "Spear of the Sky" forget that earthly spears are needed for defense or that the killing of one's own kind is fraught with all the dangers of self-destruction for both the individual and the species. What religion actually accomplishes, then, is to enlarge the boundaries of formal realism to include the emotional and/or spiritual elements which have always been a part of humanity's experience but which the false myths of scientism and rationalism have taught it to distrust and disregard.

The development of the fantasy novel, then, is not surprising, though its importance cannot be overstated. Literary forms, like other parts of a climax ecosystem, must adapt if they are to survive. If only because the survival of the novel is so closely tied to the survival of humanity, it is imperative to note what the fantasy novel is doing. It is affirming that humanity is worth looking at. It is suggesting an adaptive rather than a maladaptive posture in the struggle for a survival whose likelihood seems increasingly slim. It is offering a way of understanding something more of the relationship between the laws of nature and art. Finally, it is showing both art and its principal subject, humanity, a way out of their self-destructive narcissism. That the mainstream novelistic tradition is changing to admit the fantasy novel as a major part of its tradition is, I think, unquestionable. Whether humanity can similarly adapt is still open to question, though the very existence of this book suggests at least the possibility of a future in which humans, though they may step in dung heaps and be more remarkable for their pratfalls than their tragic grandeur, may live with compassion and joy because they understand that they are stewards rather than masters of their environment.

NOTES

CHAPTER 1

1. Joseph Meeker, *The Comedy of Survival: Studies in Literary Ecology* (New York: Charles Scribner's Sons, 1974), p. 4. All further references to *The Comedy of Survival* are to this edition and are noted by page number in parentheses in the text.

2. Lynn White, "The Historical Roots of Our Ecological Crisis," in *Western Man and Environmental Ethics*, ed. Ian Barbour (Reading, Mass.: Addison-Wesley Publishing Co., 1973), p. 25.

3. White, pp. 29–30.

4. Gregory Bateson, *Steps to an Ecology of Mind* (New York: Ballantine Books, 1972), p. 462.

5. Rene Dubos, *A God Within* (New York: Charles Scribner's Sons, 1972), p. 92.

6. Paul Shepard, *The Tender Carnivore and the Sacred Game* (New York: Charles Scribner's Sons, 1973), p. 29.

7. Shepard, p. 90.

8. Shepard, pp. 277–278.

9. Bateson, pp. 484–485.

10. Harold Schilling, "The Whole Earth Is the Land's," in *Earth Might Be Fair*, ed. Ian Barbour (Englewood Cliffs, N.J.: Prentice-Hall, 1972), p. 109.

11. Lewis Moncrief, "The Cultural Basis of Our Environmental Crisis," in *Western Man and Environmental Ethics*, ed. Ian Barbour (Reading, Mass.: Addison-Wesley Publishing Co., 1973), p. 37.

12. Ian Barbour, "Attitudes toward Nature and Technology," in *Earth Might Be Fair*, ed. Ian Barbour (Englewood Cliffs, N.J.: Prentice-Hall, 1972), p. 151.

13. Bateson, p. 437.

14. Walter Kerr, *Tragedy and Comedy* (New York: Simon and Schuster, 1967), p. 35.

15. Karl Jaspers, "Awareness of the Tragic," from *Tragic Is Not Enough*, in *Tragedy: Modern Essays in Criticism*, ed. Laurence Michel and Richard B. Sewall (Englewood Cliffs, N.J.: Prentice-Hall, 1963), p. 8.

16. Gilbert Murray, *The Classical Tradition in Poetry* (Cambridge: Harvard University Press, 1927), p. 55.

17. Joseph Wood Krutch, "The Tragic Fallacy," in *A Krutch Omnibus: Forty Years of Social and Literary Criticism* (New York: William Morrow and Co., 1970), pp. 23–24.

18. Jaspers, p. 15.

19. Kerr, p. 56.

20. Dorothea Krook, *Elements of Tragedy* (New Haven: Yale University Press, 1969), pp. 14–15.

21. George Steiner, *The Death of Tragedy* (New York: Hill and Wang, 1963), pp. 9–10.

22. Alexander Pope, "Essay on Man—Epistle Two," in *Alexander Pope: Selected Poetry and Prose*, ed. William K. Wimsatt (New York: Holt, Rinehart and Winston, 1967), p. 138.

23. Suzanne Langer, *Feeling and Form* (New York: Charles Scribner's Sons, 1953), p. 327.

24. Wylie Sypher, "The Ancient Rites of Comedy," in *Comedy*, ed. Wylie Sypher (1956; reprint ed., Baltimore: Johns Hopkins University Press, 1980), p. 220.

25. Kerr, p. 152.

26. Cyrus Hoy, *The Hyacinth Room: An Investigation into the Nature of Comedy, Tragedy, and Tragicomedy* (New York: Alfred A. Knopf, 1964), p. 18.

27. Kerr, pp. 199–200.

28. Langer, p. 328.

29. Langer, p. 349.

30. Kerr, pp. 78–79.

31. James Feibleman, *In Praise of Comedy: A Study in Theory and Practice* (New York: Russell and Russell, 1962), p. 273.

32. Ian Watt, *The Rise of the Novel* (Berkeley: University of California Press, 1959), p. 11.

33. Watt, p. 32.

34. Austin Warren, "Nature and Modes of Narrative Fiction," in *Approaches to the Novel*, ed. Robert Scholes (San Francisco: Chandler Publishing Co., 1961), p. 196.

35. Northrop Frye, "Fictional Modes," in *Approaches to the Novel*, ed. Robert Scholes (San Francisco: Chandler Publishing Co., 1961), pp. 31–32.

36. Wilbur L. Cross, *The Development of the English Novel* (New York: Macmillan Co., 1899), p. xv.

37. Arnold Kettle, *An Introduction to the English Novel* (New York: Harper and Brothers, 1960), p. 31.

38. Francis Stoddard, *The Evolution of the English Novel* (London: Macmillan and Co., 1900), pp. 41–42.

39. Paul Weiss, *Within the Gates of Science and Beyond: Science in the Cultural Commitment* (New York: Hafner Publishing Co., 1971), pp. 197–198.

40. Paul Shepard and Daniel McKinley, *The Subversive Science: Essays Toward an Ecology of Man* (Boston: Houghton Mifflin Co., 1969), p. vii.

41. Bateson, p. 492.

42. Joy Chant, *Red Moon and Black Mountain* (New York: Ballantine Books, 1971), p. 175.

CHAPTER 2

1. For a more complete discussion of Tolkien's concept of the imagination as it relates to romantic critical theory see: Don Elgin, "The Romantic Imagination: A Study of Romantic Thought in the Critical Writings of J. R. R. Tolkien" (M.A. thesis, Texas Tech University, 1967).

2. J. R. R. Tolkien, "Beowulf: The Monsters and the Critics," in *Proceedings of the British Academy* (London: Oxford University Press, 1936), p. 257. All further references to this essay are noted by page number in parentheses in the text.

3. J. R. R. Tolkien, "On Fairy Stories," in "Tree and Leaf" in *The Tolkien Reader* (New York: Ballantine Books, 1966), p. 10. All further references to this essay are noted by page number in parentheses in the text.

4. J. R. R. Tolkien, *The Lord of the Rings* (New York: Ballantine Books, 1965), I, p. 19. All further references to *The Lord of the Rings* are noted by volume (Volume I, *The Fellowship of the Ring*; Volume II, *The Two Towers*; Volume III, *The Return of the King*) and page number in parentheses in the text.

5. Joseph Meeker, *The Comedy of Survival* (New York: Charles Scribner's Sons, 1974), p. 85.

6. Hugh Keenan, "The Appeal of *The Lord of the Rings*: A Struggle for Life," in *Tolkien and the Critics: Essays on J. R. R. Tolkien's The Lord of the Rings*, ed. Neil Isaacs and Rose Zimbardo (South Bend, Ind.: University of Notre Dame Press, 1968), p. 62.

7. Gregory Bateson, *Steps to an Ecology of Mind* (New York: Ballantine Books, 1972), pp. 484–485.

CHAPTER 3

1. Helen Fowler, "C. S. Lewis: Sputnik or Dinosaur," *Approach: A Literary Quarterly* 32 (Summer 1959): 10.

2. C. S. Lewis, "De Descriptione Temporum," in *Selected Literary Essays*, ed. Walter Hooper (Cambridge: Cambridge University Press, 1969), p. 21.

3. Dabney Adams Hart, "C. S. Lewis' Defense of Poesie" (Ph.D. Diss., University of Wisconsin, 1959), p. 21.

4. Hart, p. 78.

5. C. S. Lewis, *Letters of C. S. Lewis*, ed. W. H. Lewis (London: Geoffrey Bles, 1966), p. 271.

6. C. S. Lewis, "The Funeral of a Great Myth," cited from Peter Kreeft, *C. S. Lewis* (Grand Rapids, Mich.: William B. Eerdmans Publishing Co., 1969), p. 14.

7. C. S. Lewis, *Experiment in Criticism* (Cambridge: Cambridge University Press, 1961), p. 8.

8. C. S. Lewis, *Letters*, pp. 266–267.

9. C. S. Lewis, *Letters*, p. 260.

10. C. S. Lewis, "On Science Fiction," cited from Peter Kreeft, *C. S. Lewis* (Grand Rapids, Mich.: William B. Eerdmans Publishing Co., 1969), p. 38.

11. C. S. Lewis, *Out of the Silent Planet* (New York: Macmillan Co., 1965), p. 23. All further references to *Out of the Silent Planet* are to this edition and are noted by page number in parentheses in the text.

12. C. S. Lewis, *Perelandra* (New York: Macmillan Co., 1965), pp. 42–43. All further references to *Perelandra* are to this edition and are noted by page number in parentheses in the text.

13. C. S. Lewis, *That Hideous Strength* (New York: Macmillan Co., 1965), p. 374. All further references to *That Hideous Strength* are to this edition and are noted by page number in parentheses in the text.

14. John Phelan, "Men and Morals in Space," *America* 113 (October 9, 1965): 406.

15. C. S. Lewis, *Till We Have Faces* (Grand Rapids, Mich.: William B. Eerdmans Publishing Co., 1964), p. 28. All further references to *Till We Have Faces* are noted by page number in parentheses in the text.

16. C. S. Lewis, "A Reply to Professor Haldane," in *Of Other Worlds: Essays and Stories* (New York: Harcourt, Brace and World, 1966), pp. 76–77.

17. Victor Hamm, "Mr. Lewis in Perelandra," *Thought* 20 (June 1945): 286.

18. Joseph Meeker, *The Comedy of Survival*, paperback ed. (Los Angeles: Guild of Tutors Press, 1980), p. 137.

19. Chad Walsh, "C. S. Lewis: The Man and the Mystery," in *Shadows of Imagination*, ed. Mark R. Hillegas (Carbondale: Southern Illinois University Press, 1969), p. 14.

CHAPTER 4

1. T. S. Eliot, Introduction to *All Hallow's Eve*, Charles Williams (New York: Avon Books, 1969), p. ix.

2. Charles Williams, *War in Heaven* (Grand Rapids, Mich.: William B. Eerdmans Publishing Co., 1968), p. 118. All further references to *War in Heaven* are to this edition and are noted by abbreviation (WH) and page number in parentheses in the text.

3. Saul Bellow, *Herzog* (New York: Fawcett Crest, 1965), p. 414.

4. Charles Williams, *All Hallow's Eve*, Bard ed. (New York: Avon Books, 1969), pp. 124–125. All further references to *All Hallow's Eve* are to this edition and are noted by abbreviation (AHE) and page number in parentheses in the text.

5. Charles Williams, *The Place of the Lion* (Grand Rapids, Mich.: William B. Eerdmans Publishing Co., 1969), p. 190. All further references to *The Place of the Lion* are to this edition and are noted by abbreviation (PL) and page number in parentheses in the text.

6. Charles Williams, *Descent into Hell* (Grand Rapids, Mich.: William B. Eerdmans Publishing Co., 1949), p. 99. All further references to *Descent into Hell* are to this edition and are noted by abbreviation (DH) and page number in parentheses in the text.

7. Charles Williams, *The Greater Trumps*, Bard ed. (New York: Avon Books, 1969), p. 32. All further references to *The Greater Trumps* are to this edition and are noted by abbreviation (GT) and page number in parentheses in the text.

8. Charles Williams, *Shadows of Ecstasy* (Grand Rapids, Mich.: William B. Eerdmans Publishing Co., 1965), p. 72. All further references to *Shadows of Ecstasy* are to this edition and are noted by abbreviation (SE) and page number in parentheses in the text.

CHAPTER 5

1. Frank Herbert, *Dune* (New York: Ace Books, 1965), n.p. All further references to *Dune* are to this edition and are noted by page number in parentheses in the text.

2. Frank Herbert, *Dune Messiah*, Berkeley Medallion ed. (New York: Berkeley Publishing Corp., 1970), p. 41. All further references to *Dune Messiah* are to this edition and are noted by page number in parentheses in the text.

3. Frank Herbert, *Children of Dune*, Berkeley Medallion ed. (New York: Berkeley Publishing Corp., 1977), p. 69. All further references to *Children of Dune* are to this edition and are noted by page number in parentheses in the text.

4. Frank Herbert, *God Emperor of Dune* (New York: G. P. Putnam's Sons, 1981), p. 23. All further references to *God Emperor of Dune* are to this edition and are noted by page number in parentheses in the text.

CHAPTER 6

1. Joy Chant, About the Author in *The Grey Mane of Morning* (New York: Bantam Books, 1980), n.p.

2. Joy Chant, *Red Moon and Black Mountain* (New York: Ballantine Books, 1971), p. 28. All further references to *Red Moon and Black Mountain* are to this edition and are noted by page number in parentheses in the text.

3. Joy Chant, *The Grey Mane of Morning* (New York: Bantam Books, 1980), p. 17. All further references to *The Grey Mane of Morning* are to this edition and are noted by page number in parentheses in the text.

4. For a lengthy but excellent discussion of this prohibition and its treatment in literature, see "Hamlet and the Animals," chapter in Joseph Meeker's *The Comedy of Survival*.

5. Joy Chant, About the Author in *The Grey Mane of Morning*.

WORKS CONSULTED

Barbour, Ian, ed. *Earth Might Be Fair*. Englewood Cliffs, N.J.: Prentice-Hall, 1972.

Barbour, Ian, ed. *Western Man and Environmental Ethics*. Reading, Mass.: Addison-Wesley Publishing Co., 1973.

Bateson, Gregory. *Steps to an Ecology of Mind*. New York: Ballantine Books, 1972.

Bellow, Saul. *Herzog*. New York: Fawcett Crest, 1965.

Chant, Joy. *The Grey Mane of Morning*. New York: Bantam Books, 1980.

Chant, Joy. *Red Moon and Black Mountain*. New York: Ballantine Books, 1971.

Cross, Wilbur L. *The Development of the English Novel*. New York: Macmillan Co., 1899.

Dubos, Rene. *A God Within*. New York: Charles Scribner's Sons, 1972.

Elgin, Don. "The Romantic Imagination: A Study of Romantic Thought in the Critical Writings of J. R. R. Tolkien." M.A. thesis, Texas Tech University, 1967.

Eliot, T. S. Introduction to *All Hallow's Eve*, Charles Williams. Bard ed. New York: Avon Books, 1969.

Feibleman, James. *In Praise of Comedy: A Study in Theory and Practice*. New York: Russell and Russell, 1962.

Fowler, Helen. "C. S. Lewis: Sputnik or Dinosaur." *Approach: A Literary Quarterly* 32 (Summer 1959): 8–14.

Hamm, Victor. "Mr. Lewis in Perelandra." *Thought* 20 (June 1945): 286.

Hart, Dabney Adams. "C. S. Lewis' Defense of Poesie." Ph.D. diss., University of Wisconsin, 1959.

Herbert, Frank. *Children of Dune*. Berkeley Medallion ed. New York: Berkeley Publishing Corp., 1977.

Herbert, Frank. *Dune*. New York: Ace Books, 1965.

Herbert, Frank. *Dune Messiah*. Berkeley Medallion ed. New York: Berkeley Publishing Corp., 1970.

Herbert, Frank. *God Emperor of Dune*. New York: G.P. Putnam's Sons, 1981.

Hillegas, Mark R., ed. *Shadows of Imagination*. Carbondale: Southern Illinois University Press, 1969.

Hoy, Cyrus. *The Hyacinth Room: An Investigation into the Nature of Comedy, Tragedy, and Tragicomedy*. New York: Alfred A. Knopf, 1964.

Isaacs, Neil, and Rose Zimbardo, eds. *Essays on J. R. R. Tolkien's The Lord of the Rings*. South Bend, Ind.: University of Notre Dame Press, 1968.

Kerr, Walter. *Tragedy and Comedy*. New York: Simon and Schuster, 1967.

Kettle, Arnold. *An Introduction to the English Novel*. New York: Harper and Brothers, 1960.

Kreeft, Peter. *C. S. Lewis*. Grand Rapids, Mich.: William B. Eerdmans Publishing Co., 1969.

Krook, Dorothea. *Elements of Tragedy*. New Haven: Yale University Press, 1969.

Krutch, Joseph Wood. *A Krutch Omnibus: Forty Years of Social and Literary Criticism*. New York: William Morrow and Co., 1970.

Langer, Suzanne. *Feeling and Form*. New York: Charles Scribner's Sons, 1953.

Lewis, C. S. *Experiment in Criticism*. Cambridge: Cambridge University Press, 1961.

Lewis, C. S. *Letters of C. S. Lewis*. Edited by W.H. Lewis. London: Geoffrey Bles, 1966.

Lewis, C. S. *Of Other Worlds: Essays and Stories*. New York: Harcourt, Brace and World, 1966.

Lewis, C. S. *Out of the Silent Planet*. New York: Macmillan Co., 1965.

Lewis, C. S. *Perelandra*. New York: Macmillan Co., 1965.

Lewis, C. S. *Selected Literary Essays*. Edited by Walter Hooper. Cambridge: Cambridge University Press, 1969.

Lewis, C. S. *That Hideous Strength*. New York: Macmillan Co., 1965.

Lewis, C. S. *Till We Have Faces*. Grand Rapids, Mich.: William B. Eerdmans Publishing Co., 1964.

Meeker, Joseph. *The Comedy of Survival: Studies in Literary Ecology*. New York: Charles Scribner's Sons, 1974.

Michel, Laurence and Richard B. Sewall, eds. *Tragedy: Modern Essays in Criticism*. Englewood Cliffs, N.J.: Prentice-Hall, 1963.

Murray, Gilbert. *The Classical Tradition in Poetry*. Cambridge: Harvard University Press, 1927.

Phelan, John. "Men and Morals in Space." *America* 113 (October 9, 1965): 405–407.

Pope, Alexander. *Alexander Pope: Selected Poetry and Prose*. Edited by William K. Wimsatt. New York: Rinehart and Winston, 1967.

Scholes, Robert, ed. *Approaches to the Novel*. San Francisco: Chandler Publishing Co., 1961.

Shepard, Paul. *The Tender Carnivore and the Sacred Game*. New York: Charles Scribner's Sons, 1973.

Shepard, Paul, and Daniel McKinley, eds. *The Subversive Science: Essays Toward an Ecology of Man.* Boston: Houghton Mifflin Co., 1969.

Steiner, George. *The Death of Tragedy.* New York: Hill and Wang, 1963.

Stoddard, Francis. *The Evolution of the English Novel.* London: Macmillan and Co., 1900.

Sypher, Wylie, ed. *Comedy.* 1956; reprint ed., Baltimore: Johns Hopkins University Press, 1980.

Tolkien, J. R. R. "Beowulf: The Monsters and the Critics." In *Proceedings of the British Academy.* London: Oxford University Press, 1936.

Tolkien, J. R. R. *The Lord of the Rings.* 3 vols. New York: Ballantine Books, 1965.

Tolkien, J. R. R. "On Fairy Stories." In "Tree and Leaf" in *The Tolkien Reader.* New York: Ballantine Books, 1966.

Watt, Ian. *The Rise of the Novel.* Berkeley: University of California Press, 1959.

Weiss, Paul. *Within the Gates of Science and Beyond: Science in the Cultural Commitment.* New York: Hafner Publishing Co., 1971.

Williams, Charles. *All Hallow's Eve.* Bard ed. New York: Avon Books, 1969.

Williams, Charles. *Descent Into Hell.* Grand Rapids, Mich.: William B. Eerdmans Publishing Co., 1949.

Williams, Charles. *The Greater Trumps.* Bard ed. New York: Avon Books, 1969.

Williams, Charles. *The Place of the Lion.* Grand Rapids, Mich.: William B. Eerdmans Publishing Co., 1969.

Williams, Charles. *Shadows of Ecstasy.* Grand Rapids, Mich.: William B. Eerdmans Publishing Co., 1965.

Williams, Charles. *War in Heaven.* Grand Rapids, Mich.: William B. Eerdmans Publishing Co., 1968.

INDEX

Hamm, Victor, 88
Happy endings, 36
Hart, Dabney Adams, 61-62
Hell: Lewis's view of, 86; Mordor as, 45; Williams's view of, 115
Herbert, Frank, 26, 97, 109, 125-52, 179
Heroes: comic, 182; tragic, 149-50
Heroic themes, of *Dune* series, 125-26, 131
Heroic tradition, *Lord of the Rings* in, 48-49
Heroism, and survival, 57
Herzog (Bellow), 103
Hierarchical patterns of religious worship, 184
Hierarchy of values, 88
Historical destiny, 6
Historical periods, defined by Lewis, 61
Holistic approach to art, 154
Hoy, Cyrus, 17-18
Human action, effect on nature, 43-47
Humanity: beliefs of, 29-30; as center of universe, 4-5, 7-8, 85, 93, 133; comic view of, 16, 17-21, 23; continued existence of, 15-16, 24, 30, 36, 105, 144-45; dominance of nature, 9-12, 15, 45-47, 55-56, 150; relations to environment, 1, 154-57, 177, 181, 185; superiority to natural laws, 49, 84-87, 128-29, 137-38; tragic view of, 10-11
Human morality, tragic view of, 12-13
Hunter-gatherer culture, 5-7, 27, 69; portrayed in *Red Moon and Black Mountain*, 155-57

Idealization of nature, 37-38
Imagination, and myth, 62

Individual: survival of, 58; tragic view of, 13-15
Individualism, tragic, 49
Industrial pollution, symbolized by Tolkien, 44, 46-47
Industrial Revolution, 8-9
Interdependence, 8, 28, 93, 178; ecological, 27; of Great Dance, 89-91
Interdependence theme: in Chant's novels, 177; *Descent Into Hell*, 113-14; *Dune* series, 139, 140; *The Greater Trumps*, 119-20, 121; *Lord of the Rings*, 54

James, Henry, 180, 181
Jaspers, Karl, 11, 12

Kant, Immanuel, 32, 179
Keats, John, 179
Keenan, Hugh, 58
Kerr, Walter, 10, 13; on comedy, 17, 18, 20
Kettle, Arnold, 22
Killing: and abstractions, 161-62; attitudes to, 174-76
Krook, Dorothea, 13
Krutch, Joseph Wood, 12

Langer, Suzanne, 16
Language: of *Descent Into Hell*, 117-18; of *Dune* series, 142-43. *See also* Rhetoric
Lewis, C. S., 25-26, 31, 60-96, 102, 179; secondary world of, 180-81
Life, comic affirmation of, 16; in *Lord of the Rings*, 58
Life force, elemental, 39
Life style, natural, 173
Literary dinosaur, Lewis as, 60-61
Literature, 1-2; and ecology, 27; function of, 3-4; Lewis's theory of, 63; tragedy, 10-16

About the Author

DON D. ELGIN is Associate Professor of Humanities at the University of Houston. His numerous articles on the literature of the fantastic have been published in various literary magazines.